Antiques

Antiques

Plantagenet Somerset Fry

CHANCELLOR
PRESS

Photographic acknowledgments

The author and publisher wish to thank the staff of the Bridgeman Art Library, London for supplying the following photographs:

American Museum, Claverton Manor, Bath 46, 47, 68, 110 top; Ashmolean Museum, Oxford 87 left, 247; Asprey and Company, London 178 top right; Trustees of the Will of the 8th Earl of Berkeley Deceased 242; Birmingham City Museum and Art Gallery 266-267; N. Bloom and Sons, London 187 top, 192 bottom; W. & F. C. Bonham and Sons, Auctioneers, London 29 top left, 29 bottom, 228, 238, 282, 284, 285, 298, 299; Harriet Bridgeman and Elizabeth Drury 295; Bristol Museum and Art Gallery 96; British Museum, London 85, 164, 165, 167 right, 172, 173 bottom, 200, 217, 220 top, 244; Brown Military Collection, Providence, Rhode Island 216; Borough of Bury St. Edmunds 180 top; The Button Queen, London 277 bottom; Camden Antiques, London 281 bottom; Cameo Corner Collection, London 190, 195; Chateau of Versailles, France 28; Christie's, London 21, 26, 27, 30, 33 top right, 35 left, 52 top, 55, 62, 65, 67, 71, 81, 104, 105, 106, 107 right, 109 bottom, 149, 153, 155, 169, 170 left, 181, 187 bottom, 189 bottom, 229 bottom, 231 centre and bottom, 232, 236, 269, 279, 280 top; City Museum, Sheffield 129; Clandon Park, Guildford 50; Corning Museum of Glass, New York 94 top; Cotehele House, Cornwall 34, 112; County Museum, Truro, Cornwall 59, 77; Delomosne and Son, London 88, 89, 91 right, 92; Richard Dennis, London 101; H. F. Du Pont Museum, Winterthur, USA 124; Fenton House, London 249, 253; Greenfield Village and Henry Ford Museum, Dearborn, Michigan 69; Guildhall Library, City of London 198-199 top, 204 top, 207, 208 bottom, 221 top; Hakin and Sons, London 283 bottom; Hanley Museum and Art Gallery, Staffordshire 78 top; Cecil Higgins Art Gallery, Bedford 94 bottom; Jellineck and Sampson, London 141; John Judkyn Memorial, Bath 82-83; Kingston Antiques, London 178 bottom; Knole, Kent 11, 12-13; Lady Lever Art Gallery, Port Sunlight 17; London Transport Museum 213; Louvre, Paris 31, 33 centre; Charles Lumb and Sons Ltd., London 35 right; Thomas Lumley, London 108, 118; Mallett and Son (Antiques) Ltd., London 15, 16, 19, 20, 29 top right, 33, 36 bottom, 38, 40, 133, 135, 167 left, 259 bottom, 275 top, 289; The Map House, London 220 bottom, 222, 223, 227; Munich, Deutches Jagdmuseum 156-157; Musée de Sèvres 52 bottom; Museo Nazionale (Bargello), Florence 131; Museo Vetrario, Murano 99, 100; Museum of London 263; National Army Museum, London 214-215; National Maritime Museum, London 230 right; Duke of Northumberland Collection, Alnwick Castle 226; Nostel Priory, Yorkshire 23; Park Antiques, London 278 top; Frank Partridge and Sons, London 130; Pattern Room Collection, RSAF, Enfield Lock 159 top; S. J. Phillips Ltd., London 112, 121, 188, 189 top, 191, 193, 229 top, 230 left, 233, 234, 235, 239, 240, 241, 260, 276 bottom, 286-287; Pilkington Glass Museum, St. Helens 84, 98; Pinto Collection 258; Private Collections 24, 33, 39, 40 bottom, 41 top, 42, 43, 54, 57, 58 bottom, 61, 62, 64, 78 bottom, 90, 91 top, 93, 110 bottom, 111 bottom, 132, 138, 139, 140 top, 142, 143, 146 top, 157 top, 158-159 centre, 159 bottom, 160, 161 top, 166, 168, 170 right, 174, 176, 178 top left, 182 top, 205, 237, 259 top, 265, 270, 271, 273 left, 274, 275 bottom, 276 top, 277, 278 bottom, 281 top, 290, 291 top, 292, 293, 294; Redburn Antiques, London 171; Royal College of Music, Museum of Instruments, London 243; Royal Horticultural Society, London 211; Royal Pavilion, Brighton 37; St. Paul's Cathedral, London 136; S. J. Shrubsole Ltd., London 111 top; Smithsonian Institution, Washington D.C. 273 right; Sotheby's Belgravia, London 36 top, 107 left, 120, 129, 296; Sotheby Parke Bernet, New York 44, 45; Stourbridge Glass Museum, Worcestershire 102; STRIKE ONE, London 177; Sturbridge Museum, Massachusetts 179; Syon House, London 32; Tower of London Armouries 163; The Toy Museum, Sonnenberg, W. Germany 268; E. J. Tyler Collection 182 top; Ulster Museum, Belfast 185 top; Victoria and Albert Museum, London 9, 10, 12 left, 14, 22, 40 top, 41 bottom, 51, 53 bottom, 56, 58 top, 60, 66, 70, 72, 74, 75, 76, 79, 80, 87, 95, 97, 103, 109 top, 114, 115, 117 top, 134, 137 top, 140 bottom, 144, 162, 173 top, 185 bottom, 192 top, 194, 208 top, 210, 212, 245, 246, 250, 251 both, 252, 254, 257, 272; Weinreb and Dowma, London 219; Wolverhampton Art Gallery and Museums: Bantock House 291 bottom, 297; Worshipful Company of Clockmakers, Guildhall, London 175, 180 bottom; Harriet Wynter Arts and Sciences, London 231 top; Wynyards Antiques, London 261, 262, 263 top, 264

Other Sources

Angelo Hornak, London 103, 182 bottom, 183 (J. Gersham Parkington Memorial Collection, Bury St. Edmunds); The Mansell Collection, London 197, 198, 201, 202, 203, 204 bottom, 206, 209, 218, 224, 225; Jeremy Pembrey, Cambridge 116, 117 bottom, 119, 122, 148, 150-151, 152, 154, 156, 280 bottom, 283 top; Picturepoint, London 300

Front cover: Silver tea-urn by Paul Storr, 1809 (The Bridgeman Art Library/Courtesy of Christie's, London)
Back cover: Georgian bowfront mahogany tallboy, c. 1800; George II mahogany occasional table with Rococo-style gallery; alabaster urn set with 'blue john'; bronze and ormolu candelabrum, c. 1810 (Table, candelabrum, urn and box courtesy of Shield and Allen, London; location and tallboy courtesy of Rocco D'Alessandro, London)
Frontispiece: (Top) German 18th century gold-mounted agate scent bottle; (Centre and bottom) group of 18th century boxes, mostly French (The Bridgeman Art Library/Courtesy of Christie's, London)

First published in 1984 by
The Hamlyn Publishing Group Limited
part of Reed International Books

This 1992 edition published by
Chancellor Press
Michelin House
81 Fulham Road
London SW3 6RB

Contents

Introduction

Antiques are very big business. Not only have more and more people come to regard them as a useful hedge against the shifting value of money. The great variety of television and radio programmes devoted to the subject, pioneered to a large extent by that remarkable personality Arthur Negus, have brought what was once a rarified preserve confined to a small sector to a huge and appreciative public who are avid visitors to the proliferating series of antiques fairs held up and down the country, or to the growing number of antique shops in the high streets and back lanes of Britain's cities and towns. To meet this expanding industry – for that is what it is – there is a valuable and regular turnover in informative books on antiques, specialist works based on considerable research on particular fields, and more general works on collecting, pricing and restoring antiques.

This book is for the new collector, particularly the person of more modest means who wants to add to the decorative and functional environment of his or her home, something that combines elegance with usefulness, and which also can appreciate in value.

The antiques discussed and illustrated were made before about 1850, with a few exceptions. At the end of the 1950s a number of antique dealers, who were only a minority of all those claiming to be 'in the trade', agreed that anything labelled as antique but manufactured later than 1830 was unacceptable as an antique. This was an attempt to stem the tendency to market good, early Victorian (or outside Britain, contemporary with Victorian) pieces and call them antiques. The rule still holds in most quarters, only the cut-off date has been advanced to 1851, the year of the Great Exhibition in the Crystal Palace, then in Hyde Park. This is not at all to say that many post-1851 artefacts are not elegant, indeed beautiful, or that the craftsmanship in many cases was any less high than in earlier generations. By the end of the present century there will be a whole corpus of artefacts that will be classed as antiques, many of which will stand comparison with what has gone before.

It is unrealistic to imagine that any one person can be an incontestable authority on any one field of antiques, much less on a range of fields, and I make no such claim. I am immensely grateful to many people of superior knowledge and experience for much help and guidance, among whom I should single out Gerald Gifford (musical instruments), Michael Horner (arms and armour) and Raymond Lister (metalwork). Above all, I owe a huge debt to Thane Meldrum (furniture, prints and maps, clocks) whose material contributions, undertaken with such swiftness and skill, have been indispensable. For any errors that remain, I am alone responsible. I want also to thank Faith Perkins for so swiftly and skilfully handling the picture research for the book.

Plantagenet Somerset Fry

Furniture

Furniture is by far the most popular category of antiques. For every dealer who specializes in china, there must be ten who sell furniture, and for every book on silver or glass, there are five or six on furniture styles. And yet it cannot be collected in the same way as the other articles looked at in this book. No one would really think of accumulating breakfront bookcases or Knole sofas, and only a very few people of immense wealth can afford to collect 18th-century French commodes.

Thus, perhaps the best way to indulge a taste for fine furniture – which does not always have to be outlandishly expensive – is to set out to furnish your home with it. Apart from a soft bed, you should find every piece you need amongst 18th- and 19th-century furniture, and inexpensive pieces are still obtainable at dealers and in salerooms – indeed, prices have dropped in some styles over the past three years. However, great care should be taken before signing a cheque for a well-polished sofa-table marked 'circa 1810', which may in fact have been made in 1970 out of old wood and fittings, or a set of six Sheraton chairs priced in four figures (Sheraton never made any furniture at all as far as we know, and the label only refers to the style).

Furniture is always functional in some degree, but it is not always elegant. As it is a necessity of life, it has been made by every country in nearly every age in civilized history: there is a chair in the Cairo Museum on which Pharaoh Tutankhamun sat, about 3,500 years ago. More than forty individual styles have emerged from Europe and the Near East between the fall of the Roman Empire in AD 476 and the

English oak chest, of c. 1600, with arcaded front, decorated with carved 'knulling' on the rails.

1830s. But this chapter deals principally with the sort of furniture you are likely to encounter – or read about someone else buying – in Britain or America, that is, chiefly English, Welsh, American and some French.

Very little English furniture survives from the Medieval period (that is, from before about 1500) and those pieces which have come down to us are mostly well-documented and in museums or known private collections. However, the market abounds with specimens of 'Gothic' oak, which should be viewed with the utmost suspicion, especially by the new collector. Since the early 19th century there has been a thriving cottage industry supplying an almost insatiable demand for early oak curiosities, ranging from extravagant Victorian fantasies of carving, culled from every known style, to the more subtle fakes of more recent years. These clever copies often incorporate fragments of old carving, oak floorboards and pieces of otherwise unsaleable furniture (known in the trade as 'breakers') which retain their aged surface.

The age of oak

The period from the Middle Ages until the end of the 17th century has rightly been called 'the age of oak'. Oak was the main timber used for furniture, housebuilding, ships and a host of utilitarian objects that had to be durable. Records tell us that other woods used included beech, chestnut, deal, elm, ash and fruitwood, but most must have perished through worm and rot, to which they were more susceptible than the hardwearing oak. On the Continent there was a greater use of walnut, particularly in France and Italy. The Mediterranean countries lacked the dense forests of good oak common further north, so we find more furniture made of olive wood, cypress and cedar in those areas.

Early-16th-century English oak coffer, the top comprising one large framed panel, with linenfold panelling, unusually set horizontally (instead of vertically).

The ideas of the Renaissance did not begin to affect the art and architecture of England until the 16th century. Furniture then began to be decorated with Italianate or classical motifs, such as strapwork carving, arcades, the 'Romayne head' profile carved on panels, and various classical architectural features, but the methods of construction remained more or less unchanged until the last decades of the 17th century. A framework, joined together with mortise and tenon joints and secured by square pins hammered through them, enclosed panelling plain or carved. This was the Gothic tradition, universal in Europe until

A late 16th-century oak draw leaf table on vase form legs surmounted by Ionic capitals, and (at right) two 'joyned' stools of the same period. Victoria & Albert Museum.

the new ideas dictated new technical solutions. A small linenfold carved chest of the late 15th century was similar, apart from its surface decoration, to the late 17th-century chests so often seen in antique shops (which can still be bought for modest prices).

In the last quarter of the 16th century, the great dining-table tops were frequently placed on framed bases with plain turned or carved legs, instead of the loose, purely utilitarian trestles of earlier times. The Italian fashion for inlay work started to find favour, and the fronts of chests or the friezes of tables were decorated with geometric or floral designs in bog oak, holly or box.

Some Elizabethan furniture can still be found today, the most common pieces being the large draw-leaf table with bulbous 'cup-and-cover' supports, the court cupboard, also with carved bulbous supports at the front, and the rectangular 'joined stool', upon which all but the grandest gentry sat as a matter of course. Beds – the greatest status symbols amongst household objects – have survived in some numbers, but many that appear to be genuine are in fact made up from old panelling, chest fronts and table legs. This practice was more common in the last century, when the constituent items for such fakes were themselves more numerous and thus much cheaper.

There are great collections of late 16th-century furniture at such places as Hardwick Hall and Hatfield House, and the new collector would do well to study these to acquaint himself with the look of true age and patina, that elusive quality of furniture that can best be described as a surface produced by age and contributed to by generations of polishing and use.

Early in the 17th century there was an important development, the insertion of drawers into cabinets. At first these tended to be just two at the base of the usual lidded chest, but by the 1650s many beautiful chests of drawers were being made with interesting arrangements of deep and shallow drawers, decorated with geometric mouldings and raised panels. These early drawers were often crudely made with large dovetails, or only nailed together (the latter a practice continued through the 18th century in Dutch and Flemish furniture). The drawers were hung on runners that moved in rebates in their sides.

The exuberant decoration associated with the Catholic courts of

Elizabethan (or perhaps early Jacobean) tester with decorated panelled back.

11

Europe had been somewhat muted by the Puritan element in English society, and the accession of James I did nothing to alter this conservative taste in interior decoration. In fact, the amount of carving on furniture decreased – the sculptured 'cup-and-cover' supports of Elizabeth I's time gave way to plain turning.

Chairs, however, which had previously been the prerogative of the higher ranks of society, were becoming more common. The joined stool acquired a back, and thus the back stool or farthingale chair was born, so called because it was once thought that these chairs were designed to display the huge hooped farthingale dresses to their best

This is a bobbin-turned chair in walnut, made in Shropshire in the late 17th century.

The Spangle Bedroom at Knole, Sevenoaks, Kent c. 1610-20. Hangings and coverlet are of red satin with silver tissue appliqué. This magnificent bed is part of a rare set including stools and chairs.

effect. They are rarer than the great panel-back armchairs that were made in some quantity until the last quarter of the 17th century.

Upholstery, previously unknown in England, started to appear during James I's reign (1603–1625), the most famous surviving examples being the chairs at Knole Park in Kent, some still covered with their original red velvet. Understandably it is unusual to find even 18th-century chairs and settees covered in their original upholstery.

The furnishings of the more humble home continued in a more restrained manner right through the Commonwealth of Cromwell to the Restoration of Charles II (1660). Despite the fairly large amount of

oak that survives, the average home was sparsely filled by modern standards. Inventories mention stools, chests, cupboards and bedsteads, as well as tables and chairs. The beds were mostly of the panelled head-and-footboard type, sometimes known as 'yeomans beds' to distinguish them from the grander fourposter. Although single chairs of the panel-back variety are found quite often, a set is extremely rare, and auction prices running into thousands for a set of six reflect this.

It is worth saying here that if you are starting to collect, it is always best to go for the finest pieces you can afford, since quality furniture always has a market and holds its value despite the vagaries of fashion. Early oak furniture hit peak prices in the mid to late 1970s, and although this has been levelling or even falling since, the really fine pieces have held their prices. Quality does not always mean the finest workmanship, though this is a consideration, but is measured by several other factors such as beauty of colour, originality of surface, absence of restoration, and a general sense of good proportion throughout. Fine colouring can in some specialists' eyes elevate the simplest joined box above the level of the better-made chest, and this may explain apparent discrepancies frequently encountered by new collectors in the field.

Ideas from abroad

The Restoration of Charles II marked the beginning of the end of the solid oak furniture which relied for its effect on carved decoration, some simple inlay and turned rails. The king's connections with the European courts during his exile had given him an enthusiasm for the latest in both art and science, and during his reign, French and Dutch ideas came over to England with craftsmen from those countries, who brought with them techniques already well tested abroad. There was a revolution in the construction of cabinet work, the old framed types being replaced with carcases made of planks glued together and dovetailed at the corners, on which veneers of more valuable wood were glued. Sometimes many veneers were cut together in floral patterns or geometric shapes. Formerly these designs had been actually inlaid into rebates in the solid rail or panel. As veneering became more common, pine took the place of oak as a base wood, because it was found that this was not only a better timber to glue veneers to, but it was also cheaper as a result of increased imports from the Baltic countries.

By the end of the century the veneered fronts of drawers were almost invariably made of pine in England, though in France and Holland oak was favoured. The sides, bottoms and backs of drawers were of oak on the best pieces, though pine and other available woods were used in country pieces. Drawers which had previously been side-hung were now made with thinner sides with runners underneath resting on dust boards or strips let into the sides of the chest (the latter method was used in Holland).

Veneers were of every exotic imported or home-grown timber from lignum vitae, kingwood and snakewood to laburnum and yew. But by far the most common veneer used was walnut, and it is this wood that has given its imprint to the period roughly between 1680 and 1725. It is a period that represents one of the high points of English furniture design. The outline of cabinets became simpler and effect was gained by well-chosen veneers, with strips of ebony or boxwood inlay earlier, to be superseded by the well-known 'feather' and cross-bandings after 1690. It was the Dutch who gave us the 'barley-twist' (or 'barley-sugar') leg, and this was used in the supports for tables as well as chests and cabinets on stands. Today, there are very few of these stands with original walnut legs, as they were often top-heavy, and worm quickly took its toll, if mishandling did not. Some of the little single-drawer

Top: *A fine walnut* secrétaire, *with feather banding, the fall-front enclosing pigeon-hole drawers and centre cupboard; made in about 1700.*

Above: *Late-17th-century walnut writing desk, with arabesque and seaweed marquetry decoration in boxwood and hollywood, perhaps of c. 1690.*

Right: *William and Mary walnut half-circular card table, of c. 1690, on six legs (including two rear gatelegs) united by stretchers, and with turned feet.*

side-tables with shaped stretchers have their twist supports in ash, which was obviously an attempt to lengthen their useful life by using a more resilient timber.

The typical chair of the Charles II/James II period is well known, having a cane seat and back panels, with both carved rails and twist turning on legs, stretchers and back uprights. The carving often incorporated a royal crown held by two cherubs (or 'boyes' as they were called). As the century drew on, the backs of these chairs became higher (which makes them unwieldy and fragile) but in the author's opinion they are, compared with most other furniture of the time, very undervalued today. Late models of this sort of chair began to be made with the new hoof-footed cabriole leg – a development championed by the royal cabinet maker from Holland, Daniel Marot (1663–1712).

The full expression of the cabriole leg came in the early years of the 18th century. The short period of Queen Anne's reign (1702–14) was indeed a highpoint of English furniture design, and it has probably given rise to more reproduction in this century than any other style. It is certainly no exaggeration to say that the 'Queen Anne' chair, with its sinuous curves, represents an almost perfect blend of aesthetics and practicality.

Since trade with the Far East increased from the 1660s, lacquer work became increasingly popular as a surface decoration for woodwork in England, France and Holland. The best examples are imports from China, but sometimes European woodwork was sent out to the Far East to be lacquered in the correct manner and returned. In 1688, two Englishmen, John Stalker and George Parker, published *A Treatise of Japanning and Varnishing*, giving detailed instructions on the art. This led to a craze for 'Japan work' amongst amateurs, and a fair amount of this poor-quality home produced stuff has survived. Even in the best examples, Western lacquer is usually not as hard and smooth as the Oriental, and the trained observer will note the distinctly European faces and costume of the figures depicted. By far the commonest lacquer to be found today is that with a black background; red or crimson comes second, and green, brown, blue and white are increasingly rare. Lacquer is an acquired taste – some would say they never could acquire it – and authentic period pieces are often damaged or covered in layers of varnish, which makes them costly to restore.

Left: *Late-17th-century English cabinet in red, black and gold lacquer decoration, on a contemporary gilt wood stand, c. 1690.*

Opposite page: *Queen Anne period walnut fall-front bureau with well, on bun feet, perhaps of about 1705.*

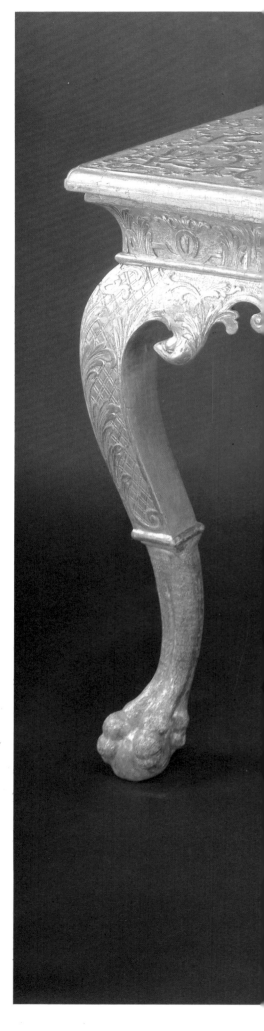

English carved gesso gilt side-table of about 1720.

New types and designs

The rise of the prosperous middle class in the early 18th century meant a great increase in the number of homes that needed to be furnished. There was a growing demand for bookcases and bureaux – for the pursuit of culture – and tea- and card-tables – for social pleasures. The long sideboard with turned legs was superseded in fashionable houses by the cabriole leg side-table, sometimes with a marble top in the manner of William Kent. The big refectory dining tables were relegated to the country farmhouses, along with many more examples of fine oak, and the habit of eating in groups at smaller gateleg tables was popular. This may explain why there are so few large dining tables in the early 18th-century style, and it was not until the later years that the big mahogany pedestal tables made their appearance. The gateleg table developed from an early 17th-century type of half-round table with a fold-over top and one pull-out gate (these are sometimes erroneously called credence tables). By the end of the century the design we know today was becoming common and, judging by the number still existing, was made everywhere in a variety of native timbers and with turned legs of baluster, bobbin or gun-barrel profile. Contrary to the rule with most antique furniture, the value of these tables rises dramatically with size.

The English bureau was fully developed by the time of Queen Anne's death, and the success of its design is shown today by the demand for these pieces from dealers all over the world. The first bureaux in Charles II's time had been simply writing boxes with sloping fall-fronts set upon stands (these are extremely rare today). Later, this box was supported by a chest-of-drawers) which was accessible only from the inside of the desk section. This well tended to disappear after about 1715. The chest-on-stand, so popular in Charles II's and William and Mary's reigns, had faded from fashion in all but the remotest areas by the 1730s. In its final form it stood upon graceful cabriole legs, but the chest-on-chest, or tallboy – an altogether more useful space-filler – was gaining ascendancy.

It is easy today to overlook the luxurious nature of many of these objects. A good case in point is that of mirrors. When the Duke of Buckingham established the now-famous glass works at Vauxhall in 1665 it was not easy to make large sheets, and so most mirrors of the last quarter of the century were small and usually square, or if bigger, were made up of more than one piece. They were also extremely expensive, the glass costing much more than even the most highly carved surround. The early frames most often seen today are the so-called 'cushion frames', which are simply side convex mouldings of oyster or cross-grained veneer. Originally most had crestings in the Italian manner, and the very finest were decorated with marquetry or perhaps lacquer. Early in the next century gilt gesso frames carved with shells, acanthus and egg-and-dart patterns were produced. Another type made right through the mahogany period was of a basically rectangular shape with a moulding and gilt strip round the plate and shaped veneered boards at top and bottom.

Left: *A lovely William and Mary period marquetry decorated cushion-framed mirror, with fine fretwork and marquetry cresting.*

Opposite page: *An unusual walnut bureau with many small drawers, on bun feet. English, c. 1710.*

Mahogany began to be imported into the British Isles in noticeable quantities in the 1720s, although small amounts of it had been used even as early as Charles II's reign. This San Domingo or 'Jamaica wood', as it was sometimes called, was very hard and heavy and, after years of polishing with oil, tended to become almost black in colour. In the mid century Cuban mahogany took precedence, and this, though still heavy, retains its reddish-golden tone and displays a lovely sweeping figure. Finally, later in the 18th century and after, the timber from Honduras was most common. This is a far lighter, more open-grained wood than the others, and though capable of exciting effects of 'fiddleback', 'plumpudding', or 'blister' figuring, responds less well to friction polishing and does not wear so well.

Two features of mahogany which immediately became apparent to the craftsman were its suitability for crisp carving (in comparison with the softer walnut) and its availability in wider planks than our native species of trees. Furniture design did not change very quickly, however, and the favourite pieces like the three-drawer lowboy, the bureau and the tallboy, continued to be made in mahogany in just the same styles as before. By the 1740s, carving appeared on the legs and backs of chairs in greater profusion, the motifs being grotesques or lion masks on the knees of cabriole legs, acanthus work, paw feet, and elaborate architectural entablatures on important cabinets.

The designs for Plate 16 in Thomas Chippendale's the Gentleman and Cabinet-Maker's Director, *the 3rd edition (1762), showing six styles of chair back.*

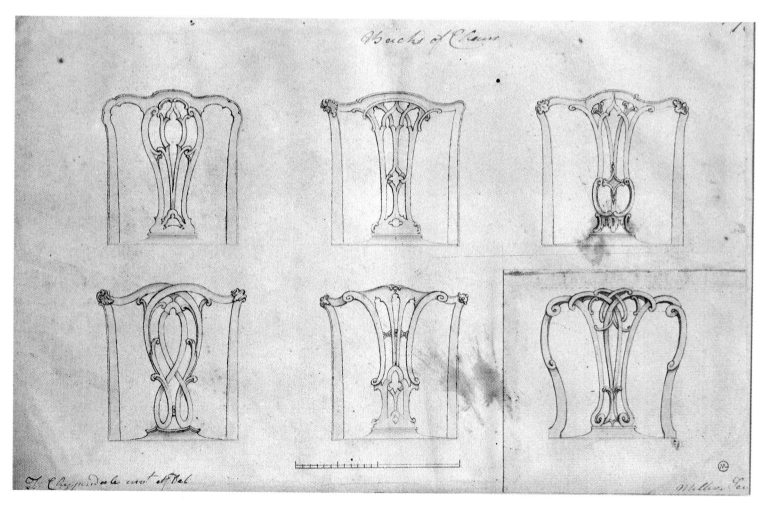

The splendid mahogany library table made and supplied by Thomas Chippendale to Nostell Priory, West Yorkshire, in 1767. The cost was £72.10s.

Whilst the court of Louis XIV had brought France to the fore in European art and culture, its influence was less strong in England. Italian, German, Austrian and even Dutch furniture of this time follows the French pattern of bulbous bombé commodes (chests-of-drawers), with parquetry or marquetry of exotic woods, many of them tropical, and with ormolu mounts.

In 1754, Thomas Chippendale's great book, the *Gentleman and Cabinet-Maker's Director* appeared. In it there were 161 engravings of different articles of furniture in the styles that were then at the height of fashion, a fashion Chippendale himself had done much to establish. These styles included the 'Chinese', the 'Gothick' and the French, although many of the illustrations show the influence of all three together. The methods of decoration were principally of two kinds – carving and fretwork. The chairs and commodes in the French taste were carved with scroll feet and acanthus foliage, but they differ from their European cousins in that they are mostly in solid mahogany rather than having ormolu mounts and exotic veneer patterns (one of the exceptions is Chippendale's fine marquetry and ormolu desk in Harewood House).

Chinese or 'Gothick' furniture, with fretwork applied to it, was much more widely copied by smaller workshops than the French designs, and this may in part be put down to the anti-French feeling in England for much of the 18th century. At the same time, the English were looking for a national style, which in the event turned out to be Gothic – at least according to Horace Walpole, whose house at Strawberry Hill became a showpiece of this style. Once begun, the Gothic revival was to continue until the end of the 19th century, although there is a world of difference between the fantastical confections of the mid 18th century and the almost obsessive purism of A. W. N. Pugin in the mid 19th century. The pointed arch motif can be seen in many of the glazing bar patterns of bookcases, but the more common astragal form owes its origins to the Chinese example. In November 1983, a set of twelve Gothic-style dining chairs of about 1760 were sold in an East Anglian saleroom for the record price of £85,000. It could be said that the Gothic revival is still not over!

Small mahogany chest-of-drawers of about 1790, surmounted by a mahogany book press.

French furniture

Opposite page: *A Louis XV marquetry* table à écrire *(writing table), attributed to Bernard van Risenburgh, who often stamped his pieces with the initials B.V.R.B.*

As mention has been made of English furniture in the French taste, it would be helpful to look briefly at the furniture made by the French in the late 17th and the 18th centuries. Although France was to lead Europe in most matters of taste in those years to an extent we in Britain can hardly comprehend, before about 1660 the French had been relatively backward in the field of furniture design and construction, and had relied upon Italian styles, employing largely Italian craftsmen. In 1661, Cardinal Mazarin, who had managed the affairs of France during the minority of Louis XIV, died, and the young King, now twenty-three, assumed control of his kingdom. Within a few years he had taken practical steps to make Paris the intellectual and artistic centre of Europe. He appointed Jean-Baptiste Colbert, one of Mazarin's ablest assistants, as controller-general of finances, with an instruction (among other things) to provide enough inducement for the best available craftsmen in Europe to come and work in Paris. The King and his minister set up a state organization, La Manufacture Royale des Meubles de la Couronne, with premises at Gobelins, on the city outskirts, where for some years workshops had been producing tapestries. New workshops were built for gold and silver work and for furniture-making, and the organization was put under the charge of Charles Le Brun (1619–90), one of the leading painters and decorative designers of the day. It was commissioned to produce furnishings and decorations for the royal residences of the Tuileries, St Germain and the new palace that the King wanted to graft on to his father Louis XIII's hunting lodge at Versailles. Le Brun personally supervised the work of the organization, providing many of the designs, and the workshops soon acquired the highest reputation. The craftsmen were better paid than those anywhere else, and French workers mixed well with the large intake of foreign craftsmen who settled in Paris.

The years between about 1670 and 1790 represent the zenith of French – indeed of world – furniture craftsmanship, and this is certainly reflected in the prices paid for pieces that come on the market today. In December 1983 nearly £1m was paid for a Louis XVI cabinet at Sotheby's – the highest price ever paid for any item of furniture. The period is generally divided into the Louis XIV style (*c.* 1670–1710), Régence (*c.* 1710–35), Louis XV (*c.* 1735–60), Transitional (*c.* 1760–70) and Louis XVI (*c.* 1770–95). Naturally the periods overlap to some extent, as do all arbitrary artistic periods.

A Louix XIV period ormolu mounted Boulle-work decorated commode à vantaux, *the marquetry being ebony, brass and tortoiseshell.* A commode à vantaux *had large drawers enclosed with two doors in front.*

The first period was dominated by the craftsman André-Charles Boulle (1642–1732), famous for pieces enriched by tortoiseshell and brass inlay work, such as armoires (wardrobes), cabinets and desks. This tortoiseshell and brass was imitated widely in the 19th century in some European countries and in England. It was often known as Buhl furniture, and pieces can still be bought for a few hundred pounds. If any name can be given to the style of this period, it might be said to be Baroque, that is, classical in background but richly decorative, with much foliage, rounded contours and symmetrical volutes, with concentration on dramatic effects of light and shade.

The Régence period was marked by a flight from heavy Baroque forms to lighter, gayer, more irresponsible shapes, emphasized by asymmetry, in which the principal motif was an almost limitless variety of shells. This is the Rococo style (from *rocaille*, French for shell), characterized by the cabriole leg, the serpentine-fronted drawer, and the amply curved backs and sides to chairs. By the time this period arrived, craftsmen had split up into practitioners of different skills, each with their own guilds, like *menuisiers* (solid-furniture makers), *ébénistes* (cabinet makers specializing in marquetry surfaces), *fondeurs-ciseleurs* (who cast and roughly chased bronze and brass mounts that surrounded table edges or commode corners and fronts) and *ciseleurs-doreurs* (who produced finely finished mounts and gilded them).

Above: *Perhaps the most famous piece of furniture in the world, the Bureau du Roi, a roll-top desk made for Louis XV of France by Jean-François Oeben and completed after his death by Jean-Henri Riesener. The desk was worked on by several other craftsmen and took nearly ten years (c. 1760-69). It is at Versailles.*

Right: *One of a pair of Louis XIV-style cabinets, possibly 18th-century, decorated with Boulle work and ormolu bas reliefs and mounts, with marble top.*

A 19th-century side-table, decorated with Boulle-type brass and tortoiseshell marquetry.

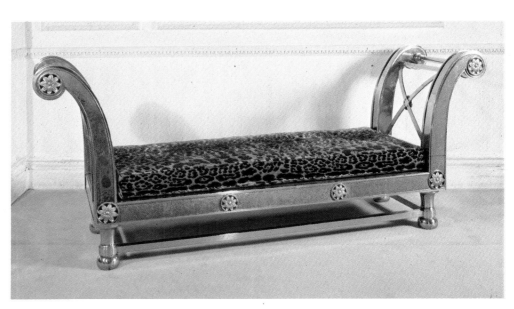

French Empire-style hall bench, decorated with simulated lapis inlay.

Chief among the craftsmen of the Regence were Charles Cressent (1685–1768) and Antoine Gaudreaux, both of whom continued to work well into the Louis XV period. This is typified by what might be described as Rococo gone over the top – bronze decoration so ornate that it concealed rather than heightened the lines of wooden parts, new pieces devised for pleasure-seeking noble families, with complex mechanical locking and moving devices, armchairs and sofas, daybeds and bergère chairs finely upholstered in rich, light silks, or more simply caned, and marvellously framed in carved wood.

The Transitional period represented a return to the classical merging with the Rococo, and though it was short it was very rich. More sparing use of bronze, greater skills in marquetry, less pronounced curves, use of decorative porcelain plaques and panels, notably from the Sèvres workshops, an even greater range of exotic foreign timbers, all featured in a range of pieces that are among the best of all 18th-century French furniture. This age was dominated by Jean-François

Left: *A mid-18th-century French secrétaire en pente (lean-to-desk) decorated in black and gold lacquer with ormolu mounts, stamped 1 DUBOIS (Jacques Dubois).*

Above: *A fine bureau-plat (writing table) in kingwood and tulipwood veneer, with ormolu mounts, by Charles Cressent, one of the greatest of the 18th-century Paris ébénistes. Made in c. 1725-30, it is now in the Louvre, Paris.*

Oeben (*c.* 1715–63) and Jean-Henri Riesener (1734–1806), two peers whose skills reach their apogee in the greatest article of furniture of all time, the *Bureau du Roi*, now at Versailles, produced over a period of about nine years (1760–69), and bearing contributions from several other craftsmen.

The Transitional bridged the gap between Louis XV and Louis XVI furniture styles, the latter demonstrating the final triumph of the classical over the Rococo, with a return to architectural principles, a decline in the sumptuous decorative bronze and gilt as the money supplies were tightened, and a wider use of solid woods such as mahogany and kingwood, without veneers.

All these styles were imitated in the 19th century in France in great numbers, from the time of Louis Philippe (1830–48) to the end of the century, and some of these imitations were so good that only a few specialists can tell the difference. They were also copied in other countries, including England, and some items, such as armchairs, marble-top occasional tables and so forth, can still be picked up for a few hundred pounds.

Gilt decorated Neo-classical-style card table inlaid and veneered with harewood and satinwood, of about 1770. Attributed to P. Langlois, an emigrant French craftsman working in London.

The 18th century in England

Meanwhile, in England, as the 18th century progressed the diversity of styles began to mirror the new Romantic movement's love of the exotic and the ancient. The well-tried classical forms became lighter – more Greek – and Chinese and Gothic details were used in a quite arbitrary manner.

A large quantity of 18th-century mahogany furniture from more humble origins survives, and can be purchased in antique shops surprisingly cheaply today. Consider, for example, the thousands of rectangular drop-leaf tables and 'country Chippendale' chairs with their square appearance and chamfered straight legs. Such pieces are nearly always of good proportion and reliable craftsmanship, and in the case of the chairs can be acquired individually to make up 'harlequin' sets for less than the cost of modern reproductions. Many plain but useful chests-of-drawers, bureaux, clothes presses and tripod tables can also be bought within the average household income.

British furniture in the second half of the 18th century was to be greatly influenced by the ideas and designs of the Scottish architect Robert Adam (1728–92), after whom a whole period of architecture and interior design has been named.

Robert Adam was the son of William Adam, a well-known Scottish architect, and he was inspired by the new interest in the ancient world through archeology rather than by the ideas of the classical past as interpreted by the artists of the Italian Renaissance. In the late 1750s Adam began to get commissions for remodelling large house interiors, and it is this work, rather than his actual furniture designs, that influenced other cabinet-makers. The straight fluted leg, the honeysuckle pattern or the frieze of Vitruvian scrolls were adapted for less grand households by such men as Hepplewhite, Linnell and Gillow. Many new kinds of furniture were appearing towards the end of the 18th century, partly as a result of changing social habits and pastimes. The ladies' small secrétaire (or *bonheur du jour*) was a more delicate form than the bureau. It had a small writing area and various arrangements of little drawers and pigeon-holes which were sometimes visible, but more often lay within the newly fashionable *tambour a cylindre*, a rising and falling shutter. Work-boxes, on slender tapering supports, often splayed near the feet, have survived in some quantity.

Painted furniture, especially chairs, was being made, and there was a return to the cane seat (typical of the Charles II and James II high-back chairs of the previous century. There is great delicacy about much of this painted work, the treatments usually being floral or with classical motifs.

The Eating Room (now called the Dining Room) at Osterley Park, Isleworth, Middlesex. Osterley was remodelled by the great architect and designer, Robert Adam (1728-92). This room has typical Adam mantlepiece, ceiling and wall panels, all in Neo-classical style. Some of the furniture items were also made to Adam designs.

Right: *The secrétaire bookcase differs from the bureau bookcase by having the writing desk part incorporated in a drawer whose front falls to make a flat writing surface, behind which are pigeon-holes and drawers. Beneath is a cupboard with shelves, or long drawers. The upper stage is a bookcase with glazed doors and the top often consists of a shaped pediment. This example is in satinwood, and was made probably in the 1780s.*

A black and gold lacquer decorated bombé commode, in the French style; English, mid-18th century.

Top right: *A George III break-front bookcase with pierced scroll pediment and dentil cornice above the two central glazed cupboard doors.*

Above: *English mahogany serpentine-fronted four-drawer commode, with carved canted corners and brushing slide, c. 1760. On top is a swing-frame oval dressing mirror on a bow-fronted boxwood inlaid base, of about 1780.*

33

In the dining room, bow-front sideboards of three drawers in line took the place of the heavy serving table with its carved front legs. The Cuban and San Domingo mahoganies had been used solid, but the Honduras mahogany of which these later products were made was used as a veneer. This change in method led to a revival of inlay and marquetry work, ranging from the simple boxwood line edging to the exquisite flowers and trophies of a commode in the French taste.

The latter part of the 18th century is dominated in English furniture by the names of Hepplewhite and Sheraton. These two designer-draughtsmen, (there is no authenticated piece by either of them) produced books of designs that were obviously used by other cabinet-makers. George Hepplewhite (d. 1786) is famous in the popular imagination for his shield-back chairs, either with a wheat-ear spray or Prince of Wales' feathers at the top. Little is known about his life. He had a workshop in Cripplegate in the City of London but does not seem to have been recognized among the designers fashionable in his day. The *Cabinet Maker and Upholsters' Guide*, a book of his drawings and patterns, was not published until two years after he died in 1786, and it was issued by his widow, but it made his name famous. The account books of great houses such as Carlton House, which was being re-furbished by the Prince Regent at the time, record the names of men like Robert Campbell and Thomas Scott who, ironically, are not now remembered despite their skills.

Thomas Sheraton's *Cabinet-Maker and Upholsterers' Drawing Book*, produced in sections between 1791 and 1794, shows many of the same objects as earlier works had done, but there is now less emphasis on carving, and much more evidence of the new vogue for painted furniture. The outlines of furniture also became lighter, even fragile. The slender tapering leg and an increased use of satinwood are among the key features of the last decade of the 18th and the first years of the 19th century. The great dining tables with their many leaves, turned supports and splay legs continue to be made of solid mahogany and are not often decorated with stringing or crossbanding (despite the fashion for so doing in modern reproductions).

Opposite page: *A Georgian inlaid mahogany shaped-front sideboard, on square tapering legs, of about 1790.*

Below left: *A late-18th-century English armchair made in the 'French' manner, characterized by the cabriole front legs.*

Below: *A late-18th-century mahogany cylinder desk with tambour shutter, surmounted by a bookcase with glazed doors. Tambour shutters were made from rows of narrow reeded mouldings glued side by side on canvas, the ends fitting into grooves to enable sliding movement.*

Another kind of table that reached the zenith of its popularity in the last quarter of the century was the Pembroke table, which Chippendale called a breakfast table, but which is supposedly named after the Countess of Pembroke who was one of the first to order one to be made. Both Hepplewhite and Sheraton suggested designs for it. These useful little tables, with a drawer at one end and a flap along each long side, found employment in many rooms of the house, and still today act as writing, small dining or side-tables. They consistently appear in sale rooms, and can sometimes be bought for less than £300, though you would not get an unadulterated 18th-century article for so little.

The slightly later sofa-table has its flaps at the ends and is commonly

Adam-style card table, made in the 19th century, decorated with painted motifs, on square tapering legs. The half-round top lifts up and back to form a round table, the flap being supported on the tops of the two rearmost legs, which open backwards.

Below: *A Regency sofa-table of rosewood, with ebonized lion masks on X-frame supports on paw feet.*

An interesting couch in the form of an ancient Egyptian river boat, in green-painted and gilded wood, of about 1806-10, in the Royal Pavilion in Brighton.

raised on two standards, perhaps of lyre shape, united by a longitudinal stretcher. Because of its size and practicability this kind of table is much in demand today, and so prices are high. Good examples seldom fetch less than £1000, which does seem a lot for a relatively simple piece of furniture. As a result, many fakes have been made, by taking low-value two-drawer tables, removing the legs, adding flaps, and fitting supports from an old cheval mirror attached beneath.

Many beautiful copies of this period of furniture were made in the late Victorian era, and eighty to a hundred years of age have given them a look almost of the original.

The 19th century

The Regency period is personified in the eccentric figure of the Prince Regent himself, and the furnishings of the Royal Pavilion at Brighton represent his exotic tastes at their least restrained. But, in the country as a whole the first twenty years of the 19th century are characterized by the increased use of dark lustrous woods such as rosewood, calamander and zebra wood, with brass stringing and inlay, alongside a

Above: *Two single painted Regency chairs on sabre legs, one with arms.*

Right: *A pair of Regency oak hall chairs in the Gothic style.*

renewed fashion for gilded console tables and pier glasses. Whilst most of the 18th-century styles continued to be popular, there were new additions to the range, amongst which were sabre-legged chairs, revolving bookcases and nests of tables. The last-named always seem to attract high prices today – a nest of four early 19th-century tables frequently costs over £1000, which seems unnecessarily expensive. Many of these were influenced in their design by the architect and furniture designer Thomas Hope.

The basic outline of Regency furniture continued until the end of the 1820s, and then it became considerably coarsened and appeared more and more heavy during the reign of William IV (1830–37). The large furniture manufacturers who established themselves at about this time made full use of new mechanical aids emerging from the Industrial Revolution, even to the point of employing machine carving. Though

Left: *Pair of painted Regency period English armchairs, c. 1810, with cane seats and loose cushions (of later date).*

Below: *A Regency rosewood three-tier* étagère, *on elbowed feet, with brass galleries and a Regency kingwood table in the Egyptian taste.*

some early Victorian furniture has merit, it took the inspired ideas of William Morris, Philip Webb, Colcutt and the other members of the Arts and Crafts Movement to rekindle the traditional skills of the English wood craftsmen.

'Country' furniture

Throughout the centuries and from the earliest times the country artisan in the British Isles has produced countless unremarkable items of everyday household furniture, most of which have perished. There is good reason to believe that the construction of such objects changed little from the Middle Ages to the present century, despite the changes in fashion in more urban centres. The simplest form of chair or stool, with three or four legs hammered into holes bored into a solid seat, and perhaps a few spindles for a back, was being made in both the 15th (and probably earlier) and the 19th centuries, especially in Wales and Ireland. From these primitive country forms were developed the stick-back chair and the Windsor chairs of the 18th century, and a revived interest in all countryside things has given the best examples of these, made in yew wood, a value not dreamt of twenty years ago. The Windsor chair as we know it is not recorded much before the 1720s. There is little doubt that the early examples were probably painted (usually black or green) and used as garden chairs. Sometimes chairs can be found still with this original paintwork, and in the author's opinion they have more value as antiques if left unstripped, which is borne out in saleroom prices.

The Windsor chairmakers developed their craft into a sizeable industry, their products competing well with more sophisticated designs. Long before the end of the 19th century this manufacture was centred on the beech woods of the Chiltern hills in Buckinghamshire, where the timber was cut, turned in its unseasoned state and, sometime later, carted to the workshops to be assembled by the framer. These chairs can now be found almost everywhere in the British Isles, with slight regional variations.

Right: *An 18th-century ashwood Windsor chair with hoop back and elmwood seat, with turned arm supports and legs.*

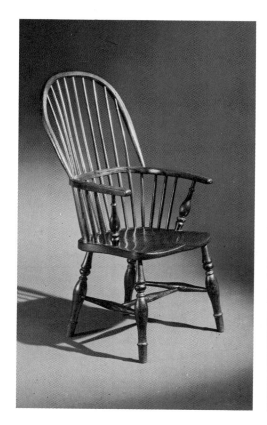

A room wallpapered and furnished in William Morris styles, laid out in the Victoria & Albert Museum. The wallpaper is his pomegranate pattern, c. 1864; the carpet, his lily pattern produced by Wilton, c. 1870. Among the furnishings are two Sussex rush seat chairs, an adjustable armchair designed by Philip Webb, and (at left) a cabinet decorated by Morris himself.

Far left: *Octagonal-top walnut table, inlaid in Gothic style, perhaps designed by A. W. N. Pugin and made by Crace & Sons, in about 1847. Note the ogee arch motifs in the table supports.*

Left: *An interesting armchair, one of a set of six, made of beech and stained dark, with rush seat. The set was made in the 1880s by Morris, Marshall, Faulkner & Co., the firm started by William Morris.*

Other popular types of so-called 'country' chair are the ladder and spindle backs, with rush seats. These are generally associated with the north (Lancashire, Cheshire and Yorkshire) and, although often thought to be of rural origin, are generally the result of a well-organized urban industry in the latter part of the 18th century.

Oak continued to be used in all provincial areas well into the early 19th century. Some pieces are straight copies of walnut and mahogany furniture made in the solid even where the originals may have been veneered. Others are quite distinct regional styles of which the Welsh is perhaps the best known.

Many people automatically attach the word Welsh when talking of dressers. The high dresser with enclosed base of drawers and cupboards and the low, open type with pot board beneath, were both made extensively in the western half of England as well as on the other side of the Welsh border for several generations. The English favoured the low dresser without pot board. In the 1730s this piece often had cabriole legs at the front, thus making it more like the conventional side tables. These dressers were, on the whole, never meant to have plate racks above, and it was later fashions that caused many to be so fitted.

A truly Welsh item of furniture is the *cwpwrdd tridarn*, a kind of high dresser with integral cupboards and racks on three levels. This is evidently a development of the earlier English court cupboard, but in the 18th century when most of these cupboards were made it was not heavily carved. Usually beautifully joinered, these solid pieces relied for effect on the choice of good timber, and the decorative appearance of fielded panels of differing shapes and sizes.

Large cupboards and dressers were often an integral part of the house for which they were made, a sign of the permanence of taste in the rural areas. If a Westmorland livery cupboard, for instance, comes on to the market without a back or with one side plain and unpolished, it is probably because it had always stood in the corner of a room as part of the architectural structure.

Above: *Ladder-back armchair with rush seat, late 18th century. This type of chair was made in quantity in country districts, generally in sets of eight, ten, twelve or fourteen, some sets having two armchairs and the remainder without arms.*

Opposite page: *A simple English pinewood dresser, of the mid-19th century.*

The Victorian period

The introduction of mechanized furniture production led to a flood of cheap mahogany furniture during the Victorian period. The firms producing it presumably regarded it as a good way of making a big profit by convincing the poorer classes that they were now able to refine their homes with more fashionable modern styles (an attitude that is not unknown today). As a result, the sturdy pieces of earlier times were replaced with these shoddy wares, which were so often of poor quality veneer laid upon even worse quality and very flimsy pine carcases. In the kitchen or servants' quarters, pinewood furniture – sometimes painted and lined – was the order of the day, the descendant of the plain oak pieces made in the 18th century. Today, stripped and waxed, it has become very fashionable, and is given pride of place in numerous dining rooms. The fact that most of this furniture was not intended to be stripped can be seen from the amount of filler and the variety and quality of the timber used in its construction.

In the 1880s there was a craze for everything Japanese, and it had a marked impact on furniture styles. E. E. Godwin (1833–86) was one of the first enthusiasts, and his designs have the balanced composition of true Japanese art (there is a fine black and lacquer cabinet of his in the Victoria and Albert Museum, London).

American mid-18th-century carved mahogany armchair in the Chippendale manner.

This is a late-18th-century American lowboy in walnut, made in Philadelphia, in the Chippendale manner.

American furniture

American antique furniture is rich and vigorous, and much of it is original in design. Naturally, many of the styles resembled British and, after the War of Independence, European styles, but even these adaptations had peculiarly native characteristics. Moreover, American furniture was, on the whole, extremely well made. It is a splendid field for collecting, although an expensive one, and to start presents a formidable challenge to the ingenuity of collectors in Britain and elsewhere, since few good pieces are found in shops or the ordinary salerooms.

American craftsmen made more or less the same sort of pieces as the British, but they also developed their own ideas. Many adaptations of British styles are regarded now by an increasing number of experts as better in quality than the models they derive from. When these adaptations followed styles prevalent in Britain, there was a gap of about a generation. American Queen Anne furniture, for example, lasted well into the middle of the 18th century, and in some instances the newer developments of the earlier Georgian period in Britain were incorporated into pieces made by American craftsmen. A splendid example of American Queen Anne furniture is the high chest-of-drawers on a stand, sometimes called a highboy. It was first made in Boston in the decade 1740–50.

In the 1760s Chippendale designs, already dominating British furniture, reached America and were an immediate success. But American craftsmen did not copy them slavishly: they elaborated freely on the basic ideas. The term 'Chippendale' furniture has a much wider application in American furniture than it has in English. Much of it is not in line with British contemporary work: for example, smaller chests-of-drawers in the Chippendale style differed from typical British ones in such features as heavy shell decoration across the top or the bottom drawers. The chests often had block fronts, a very American conception, where the middle of the chest recedes in a kind of flattened arc and ends protrude in a bulge of the same geometric shape as the middle part. Such a chest, in cherrywood, could be expensive, but might cost less if it was a country piece with less refinement of detail and finish.

A very good example of American mid-18th century highboy, in mahogany, made in Philadelphia, probably about 1765-75. It is about 7 ft. 6in. (2.29 m.) tall.

American Hepplewhite styles were fashionable from about 1790 into the 19th century, and were followed by American Sheraton, along with American Directoire and Empire ideas from France. Typical Hepplewhite features were thin legs on chairs and small tables, and fine and subtle decoration of the flat surfaces, using inlay or carefully graded grain. The tambour door was adapted in a number of pieces as a most elegant feature, in such pieces as washstands, desks and cupboards.

The American Hepplewhite, Sheraton and French styles were sometimes mingled, and a 'school' of furniture of this kind prevailed in the early years of the 19th century. This is sometimes – though not very accurately – called the 'Federal Style'. One of the cabinet-makers who specialized in it was Duncan Phyfe (1768–1834), a Scottish emigrant who set up a business in New York and made some of the finest American furniture of the period. He made sofas, chairs in the Hepplewhite and Sheraton manner, sideboards, pier tables, and secrétaire-bookcases, among other pieces, and his work is in great demand. How many he himself had a hand in we shall never know, but it is said that about a hundred craftsmen at one time worked for him. There are consequently a number of pieces available, but at a high price, even for a simple card-table.

Looking back a little, some original American pieces of the 17th century are of great interest. The first immigrants who arrived in the *Mayflower* were relatively poor, and they had little but the clothes they stood in. They brought few pieces of furniture, probably only those which were strictly functional, such as chairs. Much furniture therefore had to be made by themselves, and at first it was crude, like the country furniture made in Britain. But it appears to have been well constructed, for it had to last for a long time.

The colonists made the usual pieces, such as gatelegged tables, press cupboards, chests and chairs, with and without arms. A particularly interesting type of chair was the 'Dutch' armchair with turned posts and spindles. There were two kinds, the Brewster and the Carver. The Brewster had two rows of four spindles in the back between horizontal rails, and another row under a horizontal arm on each side. The Carver differed in having three spindles between the horizontal rails. Both chairs were generally made of ash or maple, and they had rush seating. The Brewster was named after one of the immigrants in the *Mayflower* who, it is said, brought such a chair with him from England, while the Carver was named after John Carver (1576–1621), the first governor of the colony set up by the Pilgrim Fathers, who is also believed to have brought one with him from home.

American craftsmen also made Windsor stick-back chairs. These had thick, solid wood, saddle-shaped seats on four turned spindle legs, which were positioned at a rake angle and sometimes strengthened by a stretcher arrangement. From the top of the seat, at carefully calculated positions, more spindles projected upwards, slanting backwards to form a curve, and held in position by a top rail. These were first made in America in about 1720, in Philadelphia. Over the years they acquired additions of style, such as ball feet, and in the 19th century craftsmen began to mount them on rockers. These were the forerunners of the rocking chairs which are almost part of American 19th-century folklore. The best Windsor-type chairs were made of hardwood and had nine or more spindles.

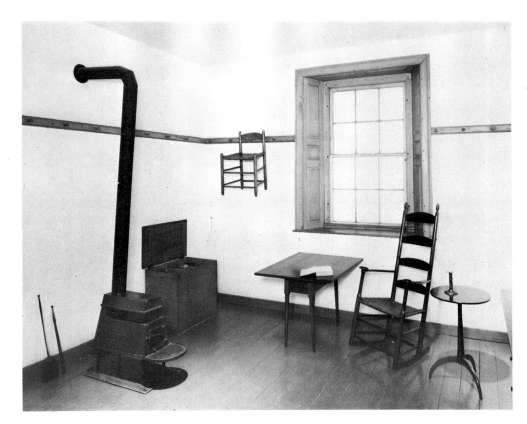

This is the 'Shaker' room at the American Museum in Britain, Bath. Note the extreme simplicity of the furniture style.

Ceramics: Porcelain and Pottery

Articles of old porcelain and pottery are among the most decorative antiques that you can buy. In most cases you can also use them, for, apart from specially made ornaments such as portrait figures, models of animals, plaques for wall hanging and so on, they were all made for use as well as to look nice. Such a quantity of both pottery and porcelain has been made over many centuries in so many lands that ceramics represent far the widest field of antiques for collecting.

Pottery goes back to prehistoric times, not only in Europe but also in the Near East and the Far East. In museums you can see Minoan pottery jugs of the 2nd millennium BC, ancient Greek pottery amphorae (storage jars), Roman red-glazed pottery bowls, Chinese black earthenware of the Shang period (2nd millennium BC), and you can even pick up damaged pieces or fragments of pieces of these ancient wares from dealers specializing in 'antiquities'. Porcelain is a much more recent innovation: it was first produced by the Chinese about 2000 years ago, and was not produced at all in Europe until its secret was independently discovered in the late 16th century in Italy (Medici porcelain), and even that was what we now call artificial porcelain. True porcelain was discovered in the first years of the 18th century in Germany by the craftsman Böttger who worked at Meissen.

In the Victorian era – which is outside the scope of this book – there was a tremendous output of both types of porcelain in Britain, as in most European countries. Much of it was original in design, and if not always very attractive or artistic, it was often gay, colourful and arresting. Much was reproduction of preceding styles, done well and, to the inexperienced eye, hard to distinguish from the original. Detection is not helped by the fact that not all pieces were marked by makers' stamps, and even when they were, they could have been copied or forged.

Antique porcelain is on the whole more expensive to buy than antique pottery, with several notable exceptions, to which we will return. For a long time, indeed, pottery was widely regarded as the poor man's porcelain, but happily for new collectors this attitude has been changing in recent years. The two are very different: porcelain is a finer product; it is normally translucent, pieces are generally lighter and thinner than pottery pieces of the same size, and the decoration is often of better quality. Cups, bowls and plates have a resonant ring to them, rather like good glass (though some ironstone china also has resonance). Much porcelain was made specially to order by the best craftsmen in the field, often in sets for the dinner- or tea-table, coffee sets and dressing-table toilet sets, rather as furniture would be ordered for a drawing-room or dining-room from craftsmen like Chippendale or Gillow.

There are three basic types of porcelain: true (hard-paste), artificial (soft paste), and bone china. True porcelain is made from china clay and natural rock. The clay should be a refractory white clay called kaolin, and the rock is generally feldspar, which fuses at a very high temperature (about 1450° C) into a kind of glass. Feldspar, which is known as *pai-tun-tzu* in China and *petuntse* in France, is what gives the porcelain its hardness and translucency. The article is shaped in the kaolin and rendered into the glass-like state when it is fired with the feldspar. Porcelain is usually white, unless it has been deliberately coloured with dyes, but even without dyes there is sometimes a tendency to discolouration due to the processes. There are several methods of decorating it, such as painting prior to glazing (known as underglaze colouring, for which cobalt blue is particularly suitable); transfer-printing (a British invention done by inking an engraved copper plate, transferring the design to paper, pressing this on to the piece while still wet, and then fixing by firing); and sprigging (attaching separately made low-relief ornament with thin slip). If you should be unlucky enough to break a piece of antique true porcelain, the edges of the fragments should feel smooth and glossy, a clean break as it were. But it is not necessary to go to this extreme to determine whether a piece is true: just look for a bare, unglazed spot on the underside and feel if it is hard.

The most famous porcelain is that made in China, where this true variety was invented in its translucent form in the 800s AD. This form was a development of what is often called protoporcelain, a ceramic ware of porcellaneous nature made first during the Han dynasty in the 2nd century BC. This had used feldspar without kaolin. The best pieces continued to come from China after the secret of porcelain making was discovered in Europe, and there are today enormous opportunities for collecting Chinese porcelain. However, it is a big field, and one filled with traps, for only a tiny number of people in the West are really knowledgeable about it; even the most reputable dealers in oriental porcelain will tell you that after thirty or forty years they are still only beginning to learn about it.

For a long time, craftsmen in Europe tried to find the secret of true porcelain making. They had discovered how to produce artificial, or soft paste, porcelain, which is made by using kaolin and powdered glass in place of feldspar. It is produced at significantly lower temperatures than true porcelain, namely, at about 1200°C. It is also translucent, but much less consistently so than true porcelain, and you can test whether it is artificial by rubbing a file or a sharp knife across an unglazed area; this should produce scratches. Artificial porcelain was made in Italy in the late 16th century (the Medici are mentioned earlier), but it did not take off and was not revived until the later 17th century, this time in France. The French artificial porcelain was known as *porcelaine de France* or *paté tendre*, and there was a small amount also made in England.

Meissen, Vincennes and Sèvres

In 1708, a German chemist in the service of Augustus II, Elector of Saxony and king of Poland, discovered how to make true porcelain more or less in the Chinese manner. He was Johann Freidrich Böttger (1682–1719), who was working at Meissen, near Dresden, and the porcelain was successul enough to encourage the Elector to sponsor a factory at Meissen for making Böttger ware. It was at this time that the practice of inscribing factory marks under the glaze of the porcelain was introduced into Europe and, curiously, the first such mark was an imitation of a Chinese one. This was replaced in about 1724 by the famous crossed swords of Meissen. Böttger made splendid pieces that were admired and copied all over Europe. They included figures as well as pieces modelled on current silverware, such as coffeepots, tea jars and flasks. Böttger kept his secret for a time, and it was maintained by his successors at Meissen, who included Johann Gregor Höroldt (1696–1776) and Gottlieb Kirchner (b.c. 1706).

Another of Böttger's successors was Johann Joachim Kaendler (1706–75) who became *modellmeister* (chief modeller) in 1733 and remained so almost to his death. Kaendler was the pioneer of a range of glorious porcelain artefacts, notably large-scale sculpture which included the new idea of applying figures on the surfaces of vessels, plates, tureens, etc. He was extremely good at animal sculpture, and some of his bird figures are great works of art. At the same time he excelled in human figures, real and imaginary. One authority had described his figures of the Commedia dell' arte characters, such as Harlequin, Scaramouche and Pantaloon, as seeming to 'dance on the shelves of cabinets'. Meissen porcelain rapidly became very famous for its richness of colour and decoration, and it was imitated very widely.

The Meissen business suffered badly when during the Seven Years War (1756–63) Frederick the Great of Prussia took over the town and shipped the best pieces, which were ready and waiting for delivery to clients, together with moulds and tools, to Berlin where he had already sponsored another porcelain factory. There, these Meissen models were copied in profusion. The old Meissen works, meanwhile, was never to be the same again, although some good products were made by Kaendler's successor Marcolini. In the 19th century, Meissen ware, now known as Dresden ware, was markedly inferior and can be bought today even at prices open to the average-income collector. Eighteenth-century Meissen has an atmosphere of romance and magic attached to

J. J. Kaendler, chief modeller at the Meissen factory from 1733 to the 1770s, specialized in porcelain figures, real and imaginary. This is a monkey band by Kaendler, of the mid-18th century.

it, suggesting that it cannot be found except at five- or six-figure prices, but although that may be so for the best items, in 1983 a crinoline group by Kaendler of 1746–50 fetched less than £800, though it had been restored after damage. If you don't mind damaged pieces, you could get old masters' work within average collecting budgets. A Kaendler piece, for example, may not have been made personally by the master but by one of his team, and it would be worth having for that.

In France, not to be outdone by the German porcelain pioneers, ceramics producers started to make artificial porcelain in a disused royal residence, at Vincennes, in 1737/8, following some not very successful manufacturing attempts in earlier decades at other small factories at St Cloud, Rouen and elsewhere. Early Vincennes pieces can be found in sales or at dealers specializing in porcelain, and a pair of slightly damaged small pots with lids of about 1753/4 with the Vincennes mark of crossed 'Ls' went for under £500 at a 1983 sale. Quite good porcelain imitations of oriental wares were, meanwhile, being made at the Prince of Condé's estates at Chantilly from about 1725.

A flower pot in porcelain, from the St Cloud factory, about 1730.

The Vincennes business was patronized by King Louis XV, who in 1753 became the main shareholder, and in that year it was decided to move the business to the village of Sèvres, between Paris and Versailles. Three years later, a new factory was ready to produce the first Sèvres porcelain. Thereafter, up to the Revolution (1789–94) the best French porcelain was made at Sèvres, and in these years the famous Sèvres porcelain plaques were introduced, pictures within frames of gilt on rectangular, square or other shaped panels. These panels adorned furni-

Right: *A jardinière, about 7¾ in. (19.7 cm.) tall, made at Vincennes about 1754.*

Below: *A covered bowl and stand, in soft-paste porcelain, made at Vincennes, c. 1745, and painted by Capelle.*

ture, clocks, ornaments, mirrors and so on, and were often signed by the maker, in the way in which the Paris *ébénistes* and *menuisiers* had long been signing their pieces of furniture. The greatest artists of the time provided drawings for the plaques, notably François Boucher, E. M. Falconet and Jacques Fontaine. In 1769, potters from Sèvres had discovered how to make true porcelain, and from that date the factory began to produce it. All kinds of the most beautiful pieces were made, with rich blues and pinks predominating among the colours.

Don't be alarmed by the name – such pieces as an original Sèvres jug of relatively simple design and floral decoration can still be found for less than £300, and in 1983 several teapots from the period 1760–70, in varying conditions, were sold for between £150 and £250. Ironically, you can sometimes pay more for good 19th-century Sèvres factory reproductions of their own 18th-century styles.

Below: *Sèvres porcelain ewer and basin, decorated in* jaune jonquille *(a daffodil yellow enamel). This colour was introduced in 1753, the approximate date of the ewer and basin.*

Right: *A lovely Sèvres porcelain vase and cover, of about 1775.*

'The Education of Love', an exquisite group figure in porcelain by Falconet, after Boucher, made for the Sèvres factory, c. 1763.

British porcelain

In Britain, artificial porcelain was first made at the Chelsea factory in about 1744, the earliest articles being jugs. Articles were produced for about twenty-five years or so, before the business was bought by the Derby potters. In that time there were four distinct periods, as follows: to 1749, copies of contemporary silver articles, mostly uncoloured, marked with an incised triangle; 1750–53, marked with a small relief anchor on an oval medallion, articles including figures (especially Meissen type) and some oriental copywork; 1753–57, marked with a painted red anchor, producing boxes, good Meissen copies, animals, monochrome landscapes, and botanical pictures; and 1758–69, the gold-anchor period, making copies of Sèvres work, with greater colour range, especially in the blues. The principal craftsman was a Flemish silversmith turned potter, Nicholas Sprimont (1716–1771). He was the first to experiment with bone ash as an extra constituent, in the hope of finding the secret of true porcelain, but he never made it. Chelsea articles are rare, even if damaged, and if damaged will still cost several hundreds.

Two very fine early Chelsea figures: on the left a beggar, and on the right La Nourrice. Mid 18th century.

Another maker of early artificial porcelain was the Bow factory, which in 1745 began to produce porcelain, some of it heavy and not very translucent. Bow was best known for figures, many of which are extremely fine; some are quite original in design, and some are good copies of Meissen and others. The factory was closed in the late 1770s, and so pieces are not easy to find.

Obviously, this book cannot hope to cover all the various porcelain makers of the 18th and early 19th centuries in Britain, so a selection must suffice, but it is important to state that much British porcelain, whether true, artificial or of the third kind, bone china (which was invented in England), stands comparison with the best from any other nation, and is still eagerly sought by international collectors. Coalport is a famous name, and their products are not hard to find. They are often very beautiful and clean. They were made in great quantities from about 1796, the date of the founding of the factory at Coalport, Shropshire by John Rose (d. 1841). He had once worked at the Caughley factory across the Severn in the same county, which specialized in pieces carrying Chinese motifs, and in 1799 he took over his former employers' business and eventually closed it down. Coalport china of the early 19th century had very bright colours and floral patterns, imitations of Meissen and Sèvres as well as more original native British designs. Even

Below: *A very pleasing porcelain* *cup and saucer, of about 1810, from* *the Coalport factory.*

pieces from these early years can be bought relatively cheaply.

Derby porcelain is very well known and collected widely. Interest in the old styles has been enhanced by the excellent modern reproductions of these styles produced by the Derby works today. The earliest Derby pieces, such as cream jugs, were in artificial porcelain, and date from the 1750s. The firm also began to make beautiful figures, some of them of well-known people of the day. There was much copying of Meissen and Sèvres, but the firm also produced a range of entirely British inspiration, household articles and tableware, which were highly decorated with flowers, scrolls and lattice borders, with occasional

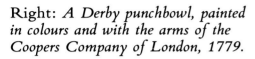
Right: *A Derby punchbowl, painted in colours and with the arms of the Coopers Company of London, 1779.*

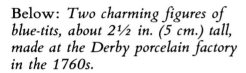
Below: *Two charming figures of blue-tits, about 2½ in. (5 cm.) tall, made at the Derby porcelain factory in the 1760s.*

Some interesting examples of early Lowestoft porcelain: a teapot, inscribed 'Maria Hoyle', and 'Norwich, 1774'; a cream jug, of 1775; and a cup and saucer made for Robert Browne's wedding, about 1775.

Chinese landscapes. After about 1784, Derby pieces began to be marked with a crown surmounting a pair of crossed batons and a capital 'D'. The mark varied in colour up to about 1811, and this is called the Crown Derby Period. The Derby works was closed in 1848, but some of the redundant workmen opened a new business which they called The Old Crown Derby China Works, which made small coloured figures etc. And in 1876, the Royal Crown Derby Porcelain Co was established, which absorbed the Old Crown Derby firm. This has continued the tradition from the 1750s to the present day.

Another very interesting firm was the Lowestoft business, which from the 1750s to about 1802 produced artificial porcelain ware, largely in blue and white. This ware was chiefly for the table and occasionally for souvenirs, for instance teacaddies, jugs and so on, some of which were marked 'Trifle from Lowestoft', and some of which were also dated. Much Lowestoft porcelain was sold locally in East Suffolk, and it was also exported to the Low Countries. It is collected with enthusiasm today. Thomas Minton (1766–1836) was a successful potter of the late 18th century who founded the firm bearing his name in 1793. In his later years he used a good bone china, and produced tableware and ornamental pieces that are in great demand.

Among the craftsmen who worked with Rose at Coalport was William Billingsley (1760–1828), a decorator and entrepreneur who had a most eccentric and erratic career in the pottery business. He had been employed at the Derby works as a china painter of great artistry, and he had also discovered a particular type of very white, translucent artificial porcelain that was extremely costly to make. For a time he ran a pottery which he himself founded at Nantgarw in South Wales in

A Nantgarw porcelain sugar bowl with cover and stand, of c. 1815.

This cup and saucer from the Spode factory, c. 1815 (Josiah Spode II), features Chinese motifs.

1813, and over the next nine years produced this uneconomic porcelain which was, however, most exquisitely painted, especially the floral patterns. Billingsley was marvellous with a brush and a kiln, but he was hopeless with money. The process of making his extremely clear porcelain involved the destruction during firing of a large percentage of the output, and the surviving wares were thus sold at loss. Much of his porcelain was supplied direct to other firms unpainted for them to complete. The Nantgarw business had a chequered existence even during its short life, and then Coalport took it over, complete with moulds, designs, and everything else. Nantgarw ware is much sought after, and if you can find it, even if cracked or repaired, do buy it, for it is an exceptional example of British ceramic art.

We should turn now to the beginning of the 19th century and the pottery founded by Josiah Spode II (1754–1827), the inventor of bone china. This is made of china clay and feldspar, with one third to two fifths of calcinated bone added, which produces an excellent quality china, hard and translucent. Spode's original mix was successful and has with little variation lasted to the present day. A considerable range of pieces was made in many colours: green, dark blue, yellow and red, with flowers, fruit, animal patterns and landscapes, including classical scenes from engravings by Piranesi and his contemporaries. Many pieces were made in deep blue, a style that continued for years, into the period beginning 1833 when the firm was bought by Copeland.

W. T. Copeland (1797–1868) moved in after Josiah Spode II's son, Josiah III, died in 1829.

Last in this short list of leading names in British porcelain manufacture is one of the very greatest, the Worcester business. The Worcester Porcelain Co. was founded in 1751, and the first pieces are associated with Dr John Wall (1708–76), a physician and spare-time artist. The firm produced an artificial porcelain using soaprock (or steatite) as a constituent, which gave a thin, hard-looking and creamy white-to-grey-white tint. It was described by a contemporary as being 'scarcely inferior to that of Eastern China'. From the start the potters experimented boldly with both colour and decoration, producing yellows, apple-green, powder blue, deep blues, deep red and purple with a thinnish glaze, and executing landscapes, fine floral patterns and gilt lattice work. They followed oriental, Meissen and Sèvres wares, and also imitated native British styles such as Chelsea (especially when some of the old Chelsea staff joined Dr Wall in the late 1760s). The pottery

Above: *Unusual earthenware blue and white plate by Spode, about 1815.*

Opposite page: *A porcelain cabbage-leaf mask jug on yellow ground, made at the Worcester porcelain factory during the period of Dr Wall (1751-76).*

was bought in 1783 by Thomas Flight, the firm's London agent, for his two sons John and Joseph, and for about six years the china was generally marked with the name 'Flight' in blue; from about 1789 to 1792 with 'Flight' in red, under a crown. In 1792 Joseph Flight (John had died) was joined by Martin Barr, and up to about 1807 the ware was marked 'Flight & Barr' under a crown, or alternatively, a simple 'B'. From 1807 to 1813, when Barr's son joined the firm, the incised mark 'B.F.B.' (under a crown) was used, and from 1813 to 1840 it was 'F.B.B.'. Other marks were used too, one of the 1820s being a 'B' with a reversed small 'c' at the left of the 'B'. When the Flight take-over took place in 1783 one of the artists, Robert Chamberlain, had left to found his own business in competition, but in the 1840s his firm was amalgamated with that of Worcester, and in 1862 the firm became the Royal Worcester Porcelain Co., which it remains.

Worcester is characterized by its high quality, its interesting glazes and its decoration, though in some quarters the figures are regarded as inferior to those produced by other leading factories. Worcester excelled in the use of the various shades of blue, and this has made that particular range of products highly collectable. Often the blues are combined with gilt friezes in the Chinese manner. You can still pick up a Flight, Barr and Barr plate for under £50, but Dr Wall's period pieces are rare, and a bowl would probably go for over £400 if in very good condition.

Among the many other firms whose products were usually of the very high standards that distinguish British porcelain of the mid-18th to mid-19th centuries, we should mention Bristol (the pottery was bought by the Worcester firm), Caughley (bought by Coalport), Longton Hall, New Hall, Rockingham (bone china from the 1820s to 1842) and Davenport (19th century).

A Worcester teapot of c. 1755 (Dr Wall's period), painted blue with chinoiserie scenes.

European porcelain

In Europe, the Royal Danish Porcelain Factory in Copenhagen (which has been making exceptionally fine true porcelain ware since 1775) has been famous for its lovely enamel colourings, especially its blues, and its superb statuettes and figures as well as decorations on pots, vases, ice pails and so forth. One product of this firm was the Flora Danica service, consisting of nearly 2000 pieces, each decorated with a flower native to Denmark and painted by the German artist Bayer. The service had been intended for Catherine the Great of Russia, but was never finished nor presented.

While there is no space to look at all the principal European porcelain factories of the 18th and early 19th centuries, mention must be made of one further source, and that is Italy. In the 18th century Italy was not yet a united country but a conglomerate of states often in rivalry, some of them independent, like Venice, some of them dependencies of other European states such as France, Spain, Savoy and Austria. Indeed, it was Austrian influence that generated the first porcelain manufacture of the 18th century in the peninsula. One of the best-known firms was at Doccia, near Florence, where artificial porcelain was made from about 1735 and true porcelain from the 1790s. Doccia was founded by the Ginori family, whose name was sometimes stamped on the underside of pieces (another Doccia mark was a six-pointed star, in red, gold or blue), and it produced tablewares, in design and colourings largely copied either from oriental styles or from Meissen and Sèvres. The wares were extremely well executed and are now very rare though the firm imitated the styles, as well as the Capodimonte ones, in the 19th century.

Capodimonte is the most famous of all Italian porcelains. The name comes from the palace of the then king of Naples, who in 1743 set up a factory in the grounds to manufacture artificial porcelain. This was distinctive both in its yellowish hue and in its relief decoration; its speciality was figures and groups. The Capodimonte mark was a fleur-

Doccia porcelain: (left), figure of dancing girl after a Meissen original; (centre), pastoral group; (right), figure of a girl: all of mid-18th century.

Tea bowl and saucer, pretty examples of Vezzi porcelain of the 1730s.

de-lys. Examples of this ware are scarce because in 1759 the king became king of Spain and decided to move the factory lock stock and barrel, including the craftsmen, to Buen Retiro near Madrid, where for the next fifty years the business continued to produce artificial porcelain so similar to the Naples variety that it is hard to tell the difference.

Another leading Italian porcelain factory was that operated by the Vezzi family in Venice, founded in 1720 by Francesco Vezzi (1651–1740), who employed a true porcelain specialist from Meissen, C. K. Hunger. The business lasted less than ten years because Hunger decided to return to Meissen. Evidently there was some bad feeling, because supplies of Meissen kaolin to the Vezzi factory were thenceforth stopped. Yet in that short period some very distinctive wares appeared, mainly for the tea-table. There is a fine Vezzi teapot of about 1725 at the National Museum of Wales in Cardiff.

Opposite page: Capodimonte Italian Comedy figure, by Giuseppe Gricci, the chief modeller at the original Capodimonte factory in Naples. Mid-18th century.

American porcelain

In the United States of America, little porcelain was made before the mid-19th century, and those wanting it had to import it from Europe. Among the earliest experiments in porcelain were those by Andrew Duché (1709–78), a Philadelphian potter who, late in the 18th century, made a good, crisp, translucent product using kaolin, but never went into commercial production. It was not till the 1820s that fine indigenous porcelain began to be produced for sale in America, and that came from the potter William Tucker (1800–32), also from Philadelphia. He used kaolin that he discovered not far from his workshop and produced a hard paste that withstood extreme heat. He displayed his first wares in 1826, much of it pure imitation Sèvres, with delicate flower designs and plenty of gilt. He made all kinds of tableware, pitchers and vases. He began to win prizes for his products, and certainly the exhibits excited a lot of interest. Tuckerware, as it is called, was sold on both sides of the Atlantic and is still obtainable in Britain and the USA, but it is not cheap.

Another kind of porcelain made on both sides of the Atlantic was parian ware, an unglazed (or biscuit, as it is called) white product invented in the 1840s at the Copeland factory. It was used primarily for figures and busts, and intended to resemble marble, hence its name. It was introduced into the USA later in the decade by C. W. Fenton, of the well-established Bennington factory in Vermont. Bennington pottery itself became renowned in the 1850s for fine glazed porcelain. Bennington parian was extremely popular in a land where heroes were especially celebrated, and in the 1860s the firm began to make it tinted in various shades. Bennington 'blue and white' was a spectacular success, and is much collected today.

Opposite page: *Biscuit porcelain vase, about 7½ in. (19 cm.) tall, made at the United States Pottery at Bennington, Vermont, USA, in about 1850.*

Left: *A typical Tucker porcelain jug, of about 1828, made by W. E. Tucker and hand-painted and gilded.*

Tin-glazed earthenware

The term pottery covers everything in the ceramic world that is not porcelain, and it is a much larger field for collecting than porcelain, since it encompasses earthenware and stoneware of many different varieties made by many different people since prehistoric times. This survey, however, is confined to products from the 15th/16th centuries to the early 19th century, beginning with the emergence in Western Europe of what is called tin-glazed earthenware. This is otherwise known as *maiolica* in Italy, *faience* in France, *fayence* in Germany, and delftware in the Low Countries and Britain.

Tin-glazed earthenware is produced by applying a white opaque glaze to the fired red or buff clay base, the glaze consisting of a mix of sand and lead oxide with tin oxide. The fired article is dipped into the mix (which has been stirred into water), which deposits itself more or less evenly over the surface, and which when fired turns to a dense white glaze. If the article is to be decorated with coloured designs, these are applied once the item is dry, and the whole is then fired again. This fuses the glaze and can often enrich the colouring. The processes vary in small details from country to country, indeed from factory to factory, but basically they are the same.

Tin-glazed earthenware was made by the Assyrians in the early 1st

This faience *vase, from the French* faience *pottery at Nevers, has Old Testament scenes, and was made probably in the 17th century.*

An Italian maiolica plate made at the workshop of Giorgio Andreoli at Gubbio in Urbino, in the 16th century.

millennium BC, but it was not taken up by Greece or Rome, and it re-emerged in Islamic Persia in the 800s AD. The Moors brought the techniques to Spain in the 10th or 11th century, but these did not spread any further until the late 14th or early 15th century, by which time they were widely practised in Spain and Portugal, notably in Spain at Valencia. From Spain tin glaze came to Italy in the very late 15th century via the Balearic island of Majorca, which was known in those days as Maiolica, hence the Italian name for the ware. The French and German names for the ware are both taken from a major Italian tin-glaze manufactory at Faenza. The Dutch began to make tin-glaze in several areas, but one in particular, at Delft, has given its name to a wide range of the pottery. When similar pottery was produced in Britain, the same name was used (only with a small 'd') because the techniques were brought to England by emigrant Dutch craftsmen. The first British delftware was produced at Norwich in the mid-16th century; later it was made at Southwark in London, and later still at Bristol, Glasgow, Dublin and Limerick. By the end of the 17th century, or perhaps some time before, tin-glaze was being made in numerous potteries throughout Western Europe, and for a long while was the dominant form of ceramic ware.

Italian *maiolica* flourished in the 16th century and well into the 17th, the main designs being flowers, portraits and religious subjects, especially on large plates. You can still find single plates of this period, but you may have to pay over £1000, though the 17th-century pieces are appreciably less. Jugs, jars for ointments, vases, paving stones for floors and tiles for wall decoration were sometimes beautifully produced, with geometric patterns or coats-of-arms, in blues, greens, browns, oranges, purples and occasionally gold. Many fine pieces have survived, though most of them have been damaged.

French *faience* copied Italian styles in the 16th century, and often developed them to a high degree of artistry. In the 17th century, Chinese and other oriental themes began to take over, but by the end of the century, native French styles had emerged, which were to be superbly developed in the 18th century, appearing in the palaces and great houses up to the middle of the century when the Vincennes-Sèvres porcelain vogue supplanted tin-glaze as the 'in' ceramic ware. One pre-porcelain style that was widely enjoyed by those with the resources to buy it was the *style rayonnant*, which was introduced in factories at Rouen where *faience* had been made since the mid-16th century. *Style rayonnant* has been described as a rich embroidery of lines in blue on a white ground, or the other way about, an apt description, though it was to be enriched by the use of polychrome. Among pieces of distinction were huge plates, known as Rouen dishes, between 2 and 3 ft (60 and 91 cm) across, which used to be loaded with fruit or other food – a contemporary account mentions '18 to 20 partridges'. Sometimes the decoration followed the tracery one more usually finds in contemporary wrought ironwork. Other articles of *faience* included trays, globes,

This is an early 18th-century Rouen dish of tin-glazed earthenware, in style rayonnant. It is nearly 22 in. (55.9 cm.) in diameter.

A Delft blue and white punchbowl made to commemorate the Peace of Ryswick, 1697.

dolphin fountains, statuary and even wall clocks, some of the 18th century ones being in Rococo style, and very arresting to look at. These wall clocks were a speciality of *faience* makers in Strasbourg.

Dutch Delftware had its beginnings in Antwerp and other centres in what is now Belgium early in the 16th century, and some delightfully colourful pieces were produced, including many varieties of wall and floor tiles. Typical colourings were dark blue, rich green, orange and yellow. By the start of the 17th century, when the Northern Provinces were on the way to full independence from Spain, potters at Delft had begun to produce their own versions of *maiolica*, and they were to be markedly influenced by the decorative styles of China throughout the first half of the 17th century. But alongside this oriental trend, the native love of flowers, especially tulips, comes out time and time again in the decorative treatment of articles, and indeed in the types of article made, such as vases of all shapes, special tulip vases that had several spouts, one each for an individual bloom. Most of this ware was in blue and white, with occasional subsidiary colourings, and at the end of the 17th century Baroque features also began to appear in the decorative treatment. Delftware, especially the blue and white varieties, became famous throughout Western Europe, and indeed it dominated the tin-glaze markets for decades. Perhaps its influence was more pronounced in Britain than anywhere else outside the Netherlands.

English delftware was notable for its designs in deep blue. Decoration took the form of landscapes, family scenes and flowers, in European and oriental styles, and there was a big market for floor and wall tiles, mostly in the manner of those produced in the Netherlands. Experts can generally – though not always – tell the difference between

73

Dutch and English, but new collectors need to be careful. English delftware is being collected more widely every year, though there are signs of a growing scarcity of articles in good condition. The London producers continued to manufacture from the late 16th to the early 19th century, a long period, and much of it was turned out at the Lambeth factories during the 18th century. The bodywork of delftware is pretty fragile and it gets easily damaged, and so there is not much original ware that has survived completely intact.

Other types of pottery

The predominance of tin-glazed ware in the 16th to 18th centuries was ended not only by the introduction of porcelains (which tin-glazed ware could not hope to imitate), but also as a result of the development of other types of pottery such as salt-glazed stoneware (stoneware glazed with salt in the glazing mix, forming a thin coat), which enjoyed popularity from about 1690 to about 1770, and cream-coloured earthenware, known more briefly as creamware. This was a very fine pottery that emerged in Staffordshire in the 1730s, and was made from white clay from Devonshire and Cornwall mixed with calcined flintstone, with a lead glaze. Creamware was to prove so successful that it seriously affected the whole European tin-glazed ware industry, and in the end supplanted it, partly by massive importing from Britain and partly by home manufacture in Europe. The glaze of creamware was brilliant, often with a golden tinge, and it was decorated with a variety of designs, piercings, mouldings, with enamelling, or with printed designs. The greatest exponent of creamware was the Wedgwood business (see below).

A particularly attractive ware to collect is Leeds pottery. The first factories were set up in Leeds in 1750s and the Leeds industry lasted for over a century, adding new factories from time to time. Early products were creamware table pieces and also figures, which are remarkable for their rich, creamy white colour and fine glaze with a very faint green tinge to it and their lovely texture. One feature often associated with Leeds ware, and which appears in many articles, is basket work, that is, pierced interlaced reeds. The Leeds firms printed catalogues, surviving examples of which can help in identification today, since Leeds did not as a rule use marks. Another Leeds feature is lattice work as edging for plates, though this was not exclusive to the ware. The flat surface decorations included landscapes, willow pattern, notable buildings and Chinese subjects.

Staffordshire pottery is a household name, but it is a term, and not a product of one factory or even one town. By the end of the 18th century there were more than twenty places at which quantities of gaily decorated and, on the whole, well-made tableware, ornaments and figures were being produced. Among the pottery centres were Longton Stoke on Trent, Newcastle under Lyme, Hanley, Fenton, Burslem, Brownhills, Tunstall, Longport and Etruria (the centre of Wedgwood's pottery). Individual articles of tableware, tea ware and dressing table sets are very collectable and widely available today, but the prices vary enormously. It is advisable to consult some of the detailed books about Staffordshire pottery to help towards successful collecting.

A pioneer in the Staffordshire wares of the mid-18th century was Thomas Whieldon (1719–95), whose products are now commanding good prices – it would be hard to find an authenticated Whieldon piece for less than £300, unless damaged. He set up a pottery at Fenton in 1740, and created a most successful business, retiring in the 1780s. Among the potters who studied under him were Josiah Spode and

Opposite page: *An early creamware bowl with pierced lid, made at the Leeds Pottery about 1770.*

Above:*Three charming figures in early Longton Hall porcelain (1750s), the first factory to produce porcelain in Staffordshire.*

Josiah Wedgwood (who later became a partner before setting up on his own). Whieldon was to be a major influence on British pottery. His earthenware was remarkable for its galaxy of colours, achieved with different coloured clays or dyeing the glazing. Though producing much tableware distinctive for its simplicity, Whieldon is also known for figures of people, real and imaginary, and animals. He worked in several pottery media, such as agate ware, marbled ware, 'tortoiseshell' ware, blackware, salt-glazed stoneware, red stoneware and of course cream-ware. Whether he initiated the vogue for pottery figures or not, he was certainly involved in the early exploitation of their popularity. Among these were the famous Toby jugs, that is, jugs shaped like a seated man wearing a tricorn hat (the hat brim being the lip of the jug), a motif introduced in the 1760s and so called from Toby Fillpot, a popular nickname of a well-known drunk whose habits were recorded in contemporary etchings. A Whieldon Toby jug of about 1770 recently sold for £400.

Another Staffordshire pottery family who had a business at Fenton and at nearby Lane Delph was the Pratt family, whose business was begun towards the end of the 18th century. This firm made earthen-wares decorated in relief, using what are often described as 'muddy' or 'drab' opaque colours – blue, yellow, orange, green – and made Toby jugs that today command £150 or so, which seems a lot.

Before looking at the greatest British pottery firm of the 18th century – Wedgwood – we should also mention a few others whose articles are always in demand. Mason's Ironstone china was invented in about 1813 by C. J. Mason (1791–1856) at a family business at Lane Delph, near Stoke on Trent. It is a hard white earthenware which probably contained some iron slag, and was produced as a fair imitation of porcelain. It certainly rings like porcelain. Typical pieces which can still be found relatively cheaply are jugs, vases (often in pairs) and dinner and dessert services in sets of up to a hundred or more pieces. Mason produced until the late 1840s, when things went wrong and he was declared bankrupt. He started again, but by 1854 the firm was at an end, and Morley bought the moulds and design plates and sold them soon afterwards to G. Ashworth, who continued to make Mason's Ironstone (though under the Ashworth name). The author inherited an incomplete service of this Ashworth ware a few years ago.

The Rockingham business has already been mentioned as a manufacturer of porcelain, and they also made creamware of high quality as well as brown china (a hard, white earthenware covered with a mottled brownish glaze which may have contained iron). The firm was linked for a time with the Leeds potteries, but it was then bought by William Brameld who, with his family, produced wares until the 1840s. John Walton (fl. *c.* 1805–50) made pottery figures and groups, human and animal, at a business in Burslem. These were often given a background of trees or foliage, known in French as *bocage*, and surviving pieces of this ware, produced in vivid-coloured enamels, and bearing a scroll at the front with the name of the scene or figure and at the rear, Walton's name, are in demand among collectors. Another Burslem potter of interest is Obadiah Sherratt (fl. *c.* 1814–46) who with his wife Martha began to make rustic figures and groups from about 1815. Sherratt was succeeded by his son, Hamlet, but the firm wound up in the 1850s. Walton and Sherratt were among the best pioneers of Staffordshire figures, which were later in the 19th century to be produced in such colossal quantities for commemoration, decoration, Christmas and birthday presents and so forth.

Opposite page: *The Nelson jug, designed by Alfred Crowquill and made by Samuel Alcock of Burslem in about 1851. The jug is in parian ware, and is 15 in. (38 cm.) tall. The main part of the jug is decorated with relief scenes taken from Nelson's column in Trafalgar Square.*

Above: *A jardinière in the Chinese style, designed by John Davenport and produced in his pottery in the 1820s.*

Below: *A typical late-18th-century Staffordshire creamware teapot.*

Wedgwood wares

Josiah Wedgwood's career is briefly outlined in the short biography on p. 312. From 1759 when he set up his first factory at Ivy House, Burslem, to the 1790s, he was responsible for pioneering major improvements in many types of pottery manufacture in Staffordshire, and he created a brand image that has lasted to this day. Even his factories were models for their time. One of his first interests (from 1762) was creamware, which was particularly fine. It is known as 'Queen's Ware' because he made special articles for George III's wife, Queen Charlotte. Most pieces are marked with the Wedgwood name, and items can be bought today. His descendants have copied his original wares, but it is relatively easy to learn to tell the difference. In 1768 Wedgwood introduced his black 'basaltes' (though he did not invent the idea), a stoneware that could be decorated by cutting and polishing, and was employed for ornamental and domestic purposes. In 1774 he produced his now world-famous jasperware, which was made by mixing clay with large amounts of barytes and barium carbonate to produce a hard stone that could be wheel-polished. The stoneware was unglazed and some pieces appear translucent. At first the colouring agents were mixed in with the clay and the chemicals, but later the colours, such as pale blue, green, lilac and yellow, were applied on the surface (known as dip jasper). Many articles, such as plaques, vases, jugs, and urns were two-toned, that is, with white relief sculpture or decoration on the coloured background. From the 1780s, this hitherto distinctive Wedgwood style was copied by many other potteries in England and abroad.

One of Wedgwood's brightest business ideas was to profit from the revival of interest in classical artefacts following the excavations at Pompeii and Herculaneum and the classical revival in architecture and interior decoration that they stimulated. He created new styles of pottery, known as Etruria ware from the name of his Etruria factory, predominantly reproduction Etruscan, Greek and Roman style urns, vases, pillars, cameos, ewers and so forth. The most famous of the artefacts, the Portland Vase, was copied and a limited edition of the copies produced.

The Wedgwood tradition was carried on by his son Josiah II (1769–1843), but with much less success, partly due to general recession in the wake of the French Revolution and the Napoleonic wars, and partly due to his own inexpertise and indolence. However, in 1812 he did begin to experiment with bone china and manufacturered it on a modest scale for about ten years. For a time, the Wedgwood business languished, a shadow of its greatness under the first Wedgwood, but it was revived in the 1870s and flourishes today.

Below: Wedgwood's famous 'Queen's Ware' (cream-coloured earthenware made for George III's wife, Queen Charlotte) was copied by other Staffordshire potters from about 1780. This chestnut basket, with cover, is a Staffordshire creamware copy of 'Queen's Ware', dated about 1780.

A selection of 18th and early 19th century Wedgwood pieces.

American pottery

Pottery in the USA hardly progressed until after the War of Independence beyond the making of simple, useful articles such as pots, vases and jugs by potters in the various embryo settlements. Much of the earlier ware was in red clay, and pre-Independence 'redware' is collected. Some of it was lead-glaze decorated, in brown, yellow, black and green. In the later 18th century some emigrants from Staffordshire, who had been working in the potteries, set up small businesses, and their redware products are collectors' items, though rare. Emigrant potters from other European countries also set up works and made interesting pottery. One such was Pennsylvania Dutch ware (the Dutch

is a contraction of Deutsch – German, for the ware was made by German emigrants from the 1730s), and articles included pie dishes, flower pots, tobacco jars, some decorated in *sgraffiato* (scratch decoration achieved by coating the article in slip and then cutting into the clay through the slip when it was still moist). Many articles were signed and even dated. Creamware modelled on that from Britain and Europe was introduced by the Bartlam pottery at Charleston in the 1770s, but it took some time to be accepted, for people preferred the original articles from Leeds or Staffordshire, Wedgwood or factories in Europe. In fact, indigenous American pottery manufacture did not really get off the ground on any scale until the 1820s, more or less contemporaneously with Tucker's early porcelain.

American redware and slipware dish and cup, both of the 1780s.

Glassware

Glassware is one field of antique collecting which is still open to those with modest means, although the earlier articles, that is, those made in the 17th century and before, are becoming increasingly hard to find and are very dear. A great deal of glassware was made in Britain and Europe in the 18th century, as it was early in the 19th century, before the invention of pressed glass, and the variety of articles was enormous: drinking glasses, jugs, sugar bowls, salt cellars, scent bottles, sweet dishes, cream jugs, finger bowls, wine coolers, cake stands, fruit bowls, candlesticks, vases, decanters, ornaments, chandeliers, *épergnes*, plates, and of course bottles. Many of the styles of the time were imitated in the later 19th century in great quantity, and although specialists can usually distinguish the copies from originals, some of the imitations are fine pieces in their own right and are worth collecting, or just owning.

Glass has been made by craftsmen since the 4th millennium BC, in ancient Egypt and Babylonia. For centuries it was produced as a glaze for jewellery, but in the mid-2nd millennium, Egyptian glaziers learned how to make hollow utensils out of a form of glass. They did this by winding coils of molten glass round a core of clay and sand which

A fine, well-preserved Egyptian glass amphora, of the 4th-3rd century BC.

corresponded to the desired shape. Variations in colouring were achieved by adding certain chemicals. It seems the Egyptians also made the earliest sheet glass, perhaps by fabricating glass cylinders and then opening them out under heat to lie flat.

In the 2nd century BC, again in the Middle East, someone discovered how to blow glass to specific shapes. A gob, or 'gather', of molten glass lifted out of a furnace on one end of a hollow iron tube was taken to a clay mould and then blown to fill it. This led to rapid production of hollow glassware, and glassworks began to open up in the Middle East and in Mediterranean areas. The first glassware thus produced seems to have been coloured and only slightly translucent, but over the years, Roman craftsmen in particular developed almost colourless and very translucent glass by experimenting with various additives such as manganese. They also introduced the idea of cutting and engraving glass, and a few craftsmen also made some elementary *millefiori* ornaments. The Romans brought glass blowing to Britain in the first century AD. It is possible to buy odd items of Roman glassware in Britain at a few specialist dealers, and articles occasionally come up at sales, but they are almost always damaged or incomplete. Fragments of Roman glass can be found almost anywhere in England and Wales.

In the Middle Ages, glassmaking flourished in several European countries, particularly France and Italy. Craftsmen were decorating glassware with very fine engraving, gilding it and staining it (some of

Below right:
The celebrated Portland Vase, now in the British Museum. This is a glass-cameo vase, made in Egypt in about 50 BC. It was bought from the famous Italian family of Barberini in 1770 by Sir William Hamilton, later to be husband of Nelson's Emma, who sold it to the Duchess of Portland. In 1810 it was loaned to the British Museum, but in 1845 a lunatic smashed it. Its restoration (as in the picture) was possible because sometime in the decade 1780-90, Wedgwood had copied it in jasperware (see page 80). It was finally bought by the British Museum in 1946.

A fragment of Roman glass, gilded, with a portrait of Orfitus and his wife Constantia. 4th century AD. The small figure between them is of Hercules, suggesting the couple were pagans.

85

the loveliest stained glass in the world is in the windows of Chartres Cathedral). In Venice, glassmakers were producing glass with almost water-like transparency. In Britain, much glass was imported, but there were a few areas where home-based industries produced coarseware, as in the Sussex Weald.

The principal constituent of glass is silica, a common mineral found in sandstone, quartz, flint and other rocks, and of course in sand itself. It has to be melted, but the melting point is extremely high, about 3092°F (1700°C), too high for many furnaces, so fluxes had to be added to reduce the temperature. Soda ash was the commonest, and cut the temperature down to about 1472°F (800°C), but it needed another flux to retain stability, and the most usual additive was lime. This type of glass, quite coarse and heavy, was used for windows, bottles and cheap tableware.

The other two glass mixes were lead crystal glass and borosilicate glass. The first was devised by George Ravenscroft (1618–81) in the 1670s, and the flux he used was lead oxide, which produced a glass of exceptional brilliance. Borosilicate glass was discovered about 150 years later by Michael Faraday (1791–1867), who mixed silica with boric acid and produced a glassware whose expand-and-contract ratio was very small. Glassware of this mix was perfect for household ovenware and also for scientific apparatus and vessels.

Drinking vessels

By the 17th century, glass was used for a variety of utensils and decorative articles, but its greatest application was for drinking purposes. You can generally find good examples of 18th-century and early 19th-century glass drinking vessels and drink containers in salerooms and antique shops. Sets of six, eight or twelve glasses may be harder to pick up than twos or threes, and when you do find the larger sets you need to be assured they are not made-up sets, that is, consisting of some genuine and some good 19th-century imitations. Drinking glasses are the most popular pieces of glass to collect, and have been for years.

The average 18th-century glass was made in two or three parts, that is, bowl and stem in one piece joined to a foot, or bowl, stem and foot as separate parts joined together. The stem in a great many cases is the key feature, for by its shape you can roughly – but only roughly – put a date to the glass. The shaped bulges in the stem are called knops, and these varied during the 18th century, the different styles overlapping. The most sought-after glasses of the 18th century are those with air-twist stems, although the baluster stems are rarer. Also sought are opaque-twist stems. These are often, but mistakenly, thought to be

Below: *A collection of 18th-century English twist-stem wine glasses.*

Below right: *Some mid-18th-century glasses, including a large goblet of 1760 (on the left), and an unusual mead glass (on the right).*

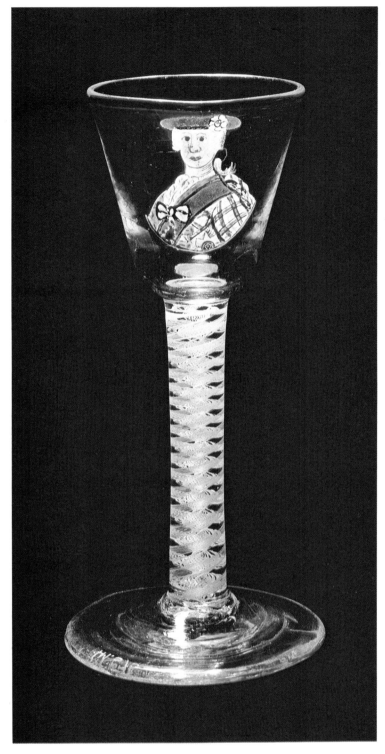

Above: *Three wine glasses with straight-sided bowls and straight opaque white-twist stems, enamelled in white with flowers. The end two glasses also bear names, and are of about 1770. The centre glass is dated 1764. All are products of William and Mary Beilby's works in Newcastle upon Tyne.*

Left: *A mid-18th-century air-twist stem wine glass, with enamelled portrait of Bonnie Prince Charlie, the Young Pretender, possibly decorated by William Beilby.*

Below: *An 18th-century engraved glass posset cup and cover, dated 1774.*

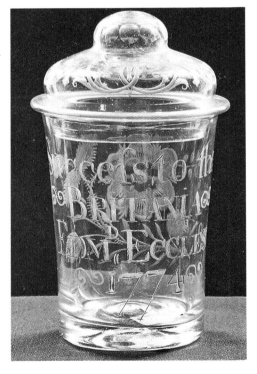

Jacobean, but in fact the air-twist stem did not emerge before about 1730, and the opaque twist, created by using enamel (either white or coloured), did not occur until about twenty years later.

A mid-18th-century variation of these most attractive twist stems is the incised twist, where the stem is decorated externally by a number of close-rowed twisted ribs, an idea that originated in Venice. Another variation is the mixed colour twist, produced between about 1755 and 1775. Meanwhile, the cut stem, which lasted from about 1740 to the end of the century, was often in diamond or hexagon facets. It was very popular, and has been copied profusely from the mid-19th century onwards.

A particular feature of 18th-century glasses is their sparkle. Before about 1675, when George Ravenscroft discovered his lead oxide flux

Right: *An example of the rare posset pot of about 1680 and moulded with the seal of George Ravenscroft.*

Far right: *Another George Ravenscroft posset of similar period.*

process and produced the first clear glassware, English glass had been heavy and dull in shading. In a short time Ravenscroft was manufacturing fine glasses, and purchasers no doubt amused themselves by testing their soundness by striking them gently to produce a bell-like clang (this test can still be applied to good glass today!). The addition of lead increased the density of the glass and so enhanced its capacity to disperse light. Ravenscroft glassware does not appear very often in sales, but 17th-century glass of other makers using his technique is obtainable.

Glasses continued to be made in a heavy style until 1745, when a Glass Excise Bill was passed putting a tax on the materials used in glassmaking. Thereafter, glassware became much thinner and lighter – and more fragile – and before long the industry was seriously affected.

Faking methods

Glass, like most decorative domestic artefacts, has been subject to faking. There are a number of ways of telling fakes, though it requires rather more than the application of one or more of the rules below, and specialist advice would be the best course. Up to the mid 18th century, when a glass was made a jagged surface was left behind on the base where the blowpipe was snapped off. This mark is the pontil. After about 1750 glassmakers tended to grind the edges away to finish the product tidily, and in the 19th century little trace of pontil could be found. Pontils can be faked and faked well: therefore, you should look for scratches across the base of the glass, which suggest years and years of being drawn across tables or other surfaces. These scratches can also be imitated by using emery, but it is not so easy to fabricate the haphazard usage of years. The opaque twists of the 18th century could also be imitated, but the experienced eye can usually spot the differences. The enamel used in the genuine article was dense white, with a faint touch of blue at the end of the twist, but 19th-century copies have a wishy-washy look, and the spaces between the spirals are uneven. This is probably because to copy the patterns accurately would have taken more time than the faking justified.

One way to acquire some judgment in these matters is to examine known fakes beside known genuine glasses, where the differences become apparent. In the last resort, a glass can be examined by special light rays or ultra-violent radiation, revealing the stress patterns created in the manufacture; the 18th-century patterns are quite different from those of the 19th and 20th centuries.

Bottles and decanters

Wine and spirit bottles and decanters are also a satisfying field for collecting. They have been made in great quantity and variety over the past three centuries or more. The earliest British glass bottles go back to the end of the 16th century, and glass bottles are actually listed in some inventories of the period, for instance one mentioned '2 glasse bottles couerde [covered] with leather'. For many years they were more or less the same shape, namely globular, with either a round base or a flat base. They had a short neck and an untidy lip. If the base was rounded, the bottle was enclosed at the lower end in wickerwork or leather to enable it to stand up (rather like the present-day Chianti bottle). They were also, as a rule, made of greenish glass. Many were fitted with a seal-like pad of glass on the upper curve of the globe, on which would be stamped by means of a brass stamp the name of the owner or the publican, for in those days it was customary to order wine from a supplier and provide your own bottles to be filled from the supplier's cask. Sometimes the seal space was filled with wax bearing the initials and a device. Such a bottle, of the 17th century and in good condition, would today fetch several hundred pounds, but as soon as you reach the bottles of the 18th century the prices drop dramatically – to well under £100. The shape of the bottle begins to change after the 1720s, and it becomes thicker and taller, but also narrower in the body, not unlike the Drambuie bottle we know today. The seal continued to be used, indeed did so into the 19th century. The colour remained a shade of green, but in the mid-18th century other colours emerged, particularly reds introduced from Germany. Round about 1780, the bottles begin to get more like the sherry bottles we use today.

Much more variety is found in decanters, which first appeared in the late 17th century. They have the same function as the bottle, but were much better designed and finished because they were decorative ornaments as well as utilitarian vessels. Decanters were provided with stoppers of glass, and as much artistry went into the stopper as the body itself. The first stoppers were hollow blown, then after about 1700 they were pinched solid glass with decorative tops, and from the mid–18th century the ends were ground, as were the insides of the decanter mouths, so that a tight fit was obtained. Early decanters also had a beak spout and some had a loop handle as well. Ravenscroft's brilliant lead crystal glass elevated a mere alcohol container into an object of beauty, and some of the first decanters were true works of art.

In the middle of the 18th century, decanters began to be labelled for the particular liquor they contained, indeed, they were often advertised as such. The labelling was done by enamel paint, perhaps white on clear glass or gold on blue glass. A set of three Bristol blue glass decanters with the names 'Rum', 'Brandy' and 'Hollands' (Dutch gin) in gilt, dating to about 1790, were valued in 1983 at about £300, and were set in a lacquer stand. Sometimes the name of the liquor was actually engraved on the surface of the body, and in a few cases there was an additional engraving, a slogan or a family motto, such as 'Truth & Loyalty'. One of the leading glass decorators of the mid–18th century, William Beilby of Newcastle-upon-Tyne (1740–1819), labelled many of his decanters. He and his sister Mary worked as enamellers for about twenty years, often signing their designs with a butterfly device. Beilby-decorated glass is a field of collecting on its own.

A collection of gilt and enamelled glasses of the later 18th century.

Another way of labelling decanters was to hang round their necks a silver label suspended on two short silver chains, the label bearing the liquor name and usually surrounded by fine etching. Silver wine labels (PORT, BRANDY, BURGUNDY and so on) are themselves collectables.

Decanters were made in a fascinating variety of body shapes over and above the usual cylinders, ovoids and barrels. There were the 'mallet' decanters of the early 18th century, that is, six- or eight-sided, with long neck; there were narrow- or broad-shouldered decanters of the later 18th century, with the body slanting out or in towards the bottom, often decorated with deep cut faceting; and there were ship's

Pair of English early 19th-century cut-glass decanters, standing in silver wine coasters of 1776, the PORT label by J. Wilson, 1800, and the SHERRY label of 1790.

An 18th-century mallet shape decanter.

decanters, of the period *c.* 1780–1830, specially shaped with an enormously wide base tapering up and inwards into the neck (triangular in profile) to stop it falling over when the seas were rough. Ship's decanters were made of heavy glass for extra stability. Another type was the square-shaped body with a large faceted ball-top stopper or flat mushroom top with cut grooves, both copied widely in the 19th century. These square decanters often appeared in pairs, or threes, set in line in a stand with a bar that could be locked into position to prevent removal, an arrangement known as a tantalus. And the more conventional decanter shapes, globular and cylindrical, barrel and ovoid, were made in great quantities decorated all over with massive deep-cut patterns.

A pair of late-18th-century ship's decanters.

Irish-made decanters are especially interesting to collectors because they were very finely made. Several factories produced quantities of high-quality vessels, and particularly notable were the Cork Glass Co., the Waterloo Co., and those at Waterford and at Belfast. These decanters were usually of barrel shape, wider at the top than the base, with three rings round the neck and with mushroom stopper, cut in flutes. Although the basic design was similar, each factory had its own highly individual characteristics of engraved décor.

Irish glass

Altogether, Irish glass deserves some notice. Glass was used in Early Christian Ireland, and some of the first manuscripts discuss the transparency and purity of glass in use at the time. But in the Middle Ages most of the glassmaking in Ireland was directed to window glazing, and any artefacts made in those years have since disappeared. Glasshouses (factories) were first set up in the reign of Elizabeth I, according to surviving letters. A glassmaker from the famous centre of Stourbridge in Worcestershire built a factory in Portarlington in the late 1660s. The earliest flint glass from Waterford appears to have been made in the late 1720s, and from the 1780s to the 1820s, the quality of Irish-made glass was extremely high, examples of it being much sought today. Though of high quality, the articles were on the whole much cheaper than their

Irish early-19th-century cut glass water jug.

English counterparts, because for half a century or so Ireland was excluded from the glass tax. It was often tougher, stronger and heavier than English, and it was found that it could be dropped without much risk of breakage. Items to look for from this high period include cut-glass bowls, some with turned-down edge, girandoles, pickle jars with lids from the Dublin works, candlesticks with urn stems on square bases, bowls mounted on three legs, and, of course, the decanters already mentioned. You could find a pair of Irish made rummers (short-stem drinking glass with ovoid bowl) for £50, or the single one for £20 or so, engraved or plain, and a pickle jar with lid from one of the Cork factories could be obtained for about £80.

The supremacy of Irish glass was short-lived, however, as in 1825 the Glass Excise Acts were extended to include Ireland, and the glasshouses were ruined. Waterford, the last to go, closed down in 1851.

Left: *An Irish pitcher, decorated in prismatic cutting, produced in about 1810, during the high period of Irish glass manufacture.*

Below: *An Irish cut glass canoe-shaped bowl on pedestal, of the early 19th century.*

Coloured glass

So far we have discussed mainly colourless or bottle glass, but coloured glass is another fascinating field for collecting. After the introduction of the glass tax of 1745/6, a number of glassmakers in Bristol, who had for a long time been making window panes, bottles and other household goods, turned to lighter-weight articles to obviate the worst effects of the tax, and also decided to feature coloured glass as a new decorative feature that would perhaps make up for the disappearance of heavy colourless glass. Before long, other makers in England went into

Candy-striped glass bell in the Nailsea (Bristol) manner. This piece is of the early 19th century.

A cruet set in opaque white glass, decorated with floral patterns, made in Bristol in the mid-18th century. Several Bristol glassmakers of this period produced opaque white ware to compete with porcelain.

coloured glass, not only at Nailsea in Somerset (on the outskirts of Bristol), but also in the Midlands, in Yorkshire and in Newcastle. The principal manufactory of coloured glass, however, was Bristol, and though several colours were featured, the favourite was blue glass. One decorator of Bristol glass was Michael Edkins (1734–1811), and some of his designs have been preserved in the British Museum. Edkins painted clear colourless glass and also coloured glass from about 1760 to about 1787, working for several firms, and concentrating on natural subjects for decoration, such as birds and flowers.

Genuine Bristol coloured glass of the 18th century is not easy to find today, and you could easily be asked over £300 for two coloured wine glasses on hollow stems. Much blue glass described as Bristol glass is not in fact Bristol made. The term is often used to describe the colour.

Coloured glass stemmed from Europe. In Roman times it had been made in the area of what is now Venice, and it was in that same district that glass manufacture was reborn in the Middle Ages. From about 1000 AD, bottles of many kinds were made there, and from about 1350

Some late-18th-century blue glass: a decanter of c. 1780; a custard glass of c. 1760; and a wine glass with facet-cut stem of c. 1780.

97

or so some of the glassmakers were using manganese to produce a clear glass that they called *cristallo*, much like the best glass of Roman times. This *cristallo* attracted great attention and was soon in demand in Europe, and the export trade that followed was one of the many contributing factors to the legendary Venetian wealth in the late Middle Ages and beyond. Venetian glassmakers were also making looking-glasses for the first time, from glass silvered by an amalgam of mercury and tin. Venetian glass was the finest in Europe for at least two centuries, the craftsmen being splendidly bold in their designs and the intricacy with which they worked. Chandeliers of this period were particularly exquisite. After about 1700, the industry declined as the overall power and wealth of the republic waned. However, the traumatic years of Napoleon's dominion in Europe and the general recession afterwards were followed by a revival in the 1830s and 1840s, and a great demand developed for reproductions of the articles of the 18th century and earlier. These 19th-century imitations, which were well made and are eminently collectable, include bowls, cups, vases, *épergnes*, candlesticks and girandoles. Look for articles made by Salviati.

Opposite page: *A boat-shaped ewer in Venetian opaque glass, with turquoise medallions round the side. The design is attributed to the Venetian artist Armenia Vivarini, 16th century.*

Below: *Two interesting examples of 16th-century Venetian glass: a wine glass consisting of a bell-shaped bowl on a squat baluster stem and folded foot, decorated with* latticinio *work (threads of opaque white or coloured glass drawn into a network and melted into the surfaces of the clear glass vessel); and a* tazza *(wine cup with shallow bowl) with ribbed foot.*

There were other centres of glass manufacture in Europe that flourished over the centuries, among them being Bohemia (a part of today's Czechoslovakia). In the Middle Ages, fine coloured ornamental glass, chiefly green and yellow, was made here in some quantity, and was bought all round Europe. In the late 17th century, Bohemian craftsmen began to etch finished articles with designs using hydrofluoric acid and wax, a skill still practised today. This engraved glassware was for a long time among the best in Europe, and British glassmakers frequently sent pieces of their own finished ware to Bohemian etchers for decoration. One of the principal centres was Breslau. From the beginning of the 19th century, the Bohemian manufacturers started to make coloured

A very fine two-handled glass casket with lid, of mid-16th century Venetian make.

A mug in hyalith glass (an oval type glass), from the factory of F. Egermann, the Bohemian glass-makers, c. 1830.

Bohemian cameo glass of about 1840, decorated with double overlay pink on white clear glass.

A selection of early-19th-century coloured wine glasses made in Stourbridge, with overlay staining and enamelling.

glassware in quantity but without any decline in quality and artistry. They copied British porcelain and pottery articles, like some of the famous Wedgwood wares which they copied in jet-black glass. They also produced much cased glass, that is, glass articles made by applying one layer of glass of one colour on to a layer of a different colour, the layers being clear or opaque. Articles in cased glass included decanters, finger bowls, fruit dishes, vases, cups, plates and glasses. The designs were often cut through the top layer down to the under layer or layers.

Glassmaking also flourished in France, notably in the early 19th century, and here in the mid-1840s there appeared the first major examples of *millefiori* paperweights.

American glass

Glassmaking in the United States began before the founding of the republic. The early colonists fabricated simple glassware in the styles of the lands from which they came, but by the 1740s some distinctively new 'American' styles had begun to emerge in the eastern districts. Among the earliest was glassware made in the factory near Salem, New Jersey by Caspar Wistar (1695–1752), who specialized in window glass, bottles and jars. Some of this ware, notably bottles which had thin threading round the neck, is known as South Jersey ware. In the mid 1760s a fresh style appeared in Pennsylvania, introduced by a German emigrant, William Henry Stiegel (1729–85), who had returned to Europe to entice German craftsmen to come back with him. He produced soda-ash glass, flint-glass in blue and purple, moulded glass with network patterns, and enamelled pieces.

The principal innovation in America, however, was pressed glass, successfully tried out in the late 1820s. This was made by squeezing molten glass into shape under pressure. The inside of a mould was shaped to correspond to the desired outside, and the molten glass forced in. This technique resulted in some excellent reproductions of cut-glass styles. It also enabled a host of patterns and objects to be made in a new medium, leading to a dramatic increase in the overall production of glass in Europe and North America from about the 1840s, as other countries adopted the techniques. Cheaper table and domestic ware was now available to an ever-increasing buying public.

Pressed glass was introduced in the USA in the 1820s, and was the first new glassmaking technique for many centuries. Much of the pressed glass of the early 19th century was of very high quality, like this opalescent sauce dish.

Silver and Silver Plate

Anyone who collects objects made of the precious metal silver starts with some distinct advantages. Silver articles are generally attractive to look at and have often been made with considerable skill and artistry. More often than not they are also functional, so they can actually be used. Because they are made of precious metal, they have intrinsic monetary value as well as antique value. The metal itself is almost indestructible, which means that there is still a lot of old silver about for collecting. And finally, in the UK at any rate, it is generally possible to date pieces accurately, certainly from the end of the 17th century, because of the hallmarks (to which we will return).

A James I silver-gilt wine cup of 1608. The maker's mark is stamped 'CB' as a monogram.

A Charles I wine cup of silver, 4¼ in. (11.4 cm) high, made in 1635. The maker's mark is indistinct, but looks like M.G. It was sold at Christie's for £2,300.

Two mid-17th century silver tankards. The left-hand tankard is finely decorated and bears the maker's mark.

This handsome assemblage of benefits, however, has to be weighed against the fact that the value, and therefore the cost, of much antique silver is subject to the prevailing world demand for the raw material itself. Silver articles are generally divided into two types: those of high artistic quality and rarity, and those less artistic pieces (outnumbering the high-quality pieces many times over) which are often not worth much more than their 'melt down' price. This 'melt down' price is related to the value of silver on the bullion market, which fluctuates enormously over the years. For example, during the period from November 1967 (when sterling was devalued) to December 1968, antique silver prices rocketed up by 300 per cent or more, then over the following six months they plummeted by about 50 per cent. In 1983, the melt price of silver fluctuated between £2.75 and about £7.25 per ounce, and ended at just over £6 (December 1983). This intrinsic value fluctuation is a significant factor in silver collecting, but it ought not to be regarded as a deterrent, especially in the case of table silver, teapots, coffeepots, jugs, tankards and so forth, as it is extremely useful as well as decorative. I am inclined to think that in the long term, silver collecting is a good investment, quite apart from the other advantages.

Types of silver: making a choice

When starting out to collect silver, there are several courses open to you. Either you can collect items simply because you like the look of them, and because they will adorn your home – perhaps even impress your friends and neighbours. In this case, you could specialize, for example, in silver snuffboxes (later Georgian ones of the period *c.* 1800–30 can still be bought for under £100) or in silver figures, which generally cost at least a few hundred pounds but if beautifully made are an investment as well. Or you can go in for building up a set of table silver – tablespoons, large dinner forks, dessertspoons and forks, teaspoons – collecting enough to equip you with six, eight or twelve of each. Or you could simply collect teaspoons. These are the most prolific of all spoons. They were not made in sets much before the 18th century, but the designs have been adventurous and interesting. Spoon ends were foliage patterned, stump-ended, trefid-ended, dog-nosed or Apostle-ended. Apostle spoons have ends with a figure of Christ or one of his disciples, a motif dating from the Renaissance period and lasting in England to the time of James II (and copied in much later times). Teaspoon bowls were egg-shaped, pear-drop, round, nut-shaped, oval on the horizontal plane. So many teaspoons were made that it could still be quite easy to build up a good collection of them.

You may decide to accumulate silver which has more definite appreciation value. For this you will need to study silver closely, to find out what well-informed dealers and experienced collectors are

Very fine James II silver two-handled porringer with cover, of 1688.

Below: *A Queen Anne Irish silver porringer, probably by A. Sinclair, Dublin, 1708.*

Above: *A silver shallow porringer of 1693. These are sometimes called bleeding, or cupping, bowls, although they were not as a rule used for this medical purpose.*

looking for, and concentrate on a few pieces that really do have quality. Bowls, for example, were made in many shapes and sizes, often with the most interesting handles on which much skill was lavished. Bleeding bowls (also known as cupping bowls) were produced throughout the 17th century and for much of the 18th. They were made for various substances, such as porridge, posset, soup and so on, and are more generally known as porringers. The term bleeding bowl came to be used for the shallower type of porringer. The handles (single or one each side) were pierced as a form of insulation when the contents of the bowl were very hot, or more simply to provide something to hang

them by. Charles II porringers are not cheap; they can cost over £1000, and even the later 18th century ones will be several hundreds.

Silver has been made in a great many countries. The whole of the British Isles has produced it, and this has on the whole been among the best made of all silver, with particularly well-made items coming from the top Scottish silversmiths. Much American silver is also of good quality, especially that of the 18th and early 19th centuries, but it is not hallmarked, which is an interesting collecting point.

The variety of silver articles is extensive. For centuries, rich people regarded the metal almost as a status symbol, and filled their homes with silver ornaments, utensils and containers. In France, in the headier days of Louis XIV, the court and some of the wealthiest nobles even had items of furniture made with heavy silver decoration, such as inlays, mounts, borders and so forth. (Incidentally, when the long series of wars waged by France in the Sun King's reign had cut deep into the nation's wealth, much of this silver-embellished furniture was broken up and the metal melted down to provide bullion).

Articles commonly found in great and even some not-so-great houses in Britain of the 17th and 18th centuries included knives, forks, spoons, sauceboats, saltcellars, pepper pots, sugar casters, entrée dishes, cream jugs, candlesticks, wine coasters, salvers, teapots and coffeepots, cups, porringers, toast racks, bannock racks, dishes, plates, tureens, snuffboxes, card cases, tankards, beakers, cake baskets, rose bowls, tobacco boxes, fruitstands, centrepieces, wine cups, chalices, oyster-

Above: *A fairly typical octagonal-shaped silver tea service of the Queen Anne period, made by R. Watts, London, 1712.*

Opposite page, above: *'A Family at Tea', by Richard Collins, early 18th-century.*

Opposite page, below: *George I round tea pot by James Taitt, of Edinburgh, 1726, and a matching sugar bowl with lid.*

108

Above: *These spoons are American made, and distinctive for what is called their coffin ends. The salt spoon (at the bottom) is by T. du Bois, New York, 1797-9, and the two tablespoons are by J. & P. Targee, also of New York, dated 1811.*

Left: *Two silver teaspoon handles, at left, of 1782, and at right, of 1791.*

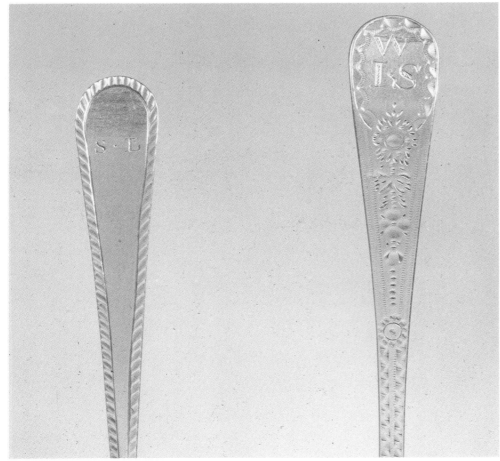

shell butter dishes, inkstands, trays, inkwells, brandy saucepans, fish servers, teacaddies, wine labels and candlesnuffers. Of these, spoons are the most widely surviving items, because probably more than thirty different types of spoons could be in use in one household at a time. Among the more obvious types of spoon – which are still collectable – are caddy spoons, usually short-handled, often designed in shapes such as leaves, birds and even jockey-cap or open-handed patterns. You might have to pay over £100 for a jockey-cap spoon of the later Georgian period today.

Another kind of spoon that lends itself to collecting is the long-handled marrow spoon, straight and usually with a very narrow bowl. This was used to scoop out the marrow from bones, and the spoon often had two ends, of different size.

Right: *Marrow scoops, from the early 18th century onwards, were used for eating bone marrow. This silver scoop was made in 1778.*

Right: *A group of silver items. Left to right: skewer by Eley & Fearn, 1801; sauce ladle, Edinburgh, 1800; soup ladle by C. Haines, Dublin, 1774; sauce ladle with King's pattern end, J. McKay, Edinburgh, 1851; and marrow scoop, c. 1750.*

111

Three silver caddy spoons, one in the
form of a hand, and a fish slice. The
fish slice is by John Younge of
Sheffield, dated 1783.

This is an example of the superb craftsmanship of the great silversmith Paul de Lamerie. It is a silver basket, of 1739, pierced and engraved, the feet in the form of grotesque heads, and with swing handle.

Silvermaking has had its share of very fine craftsmen over the centuries. Among the best known in British silver history were Paul de Lamerie (1688–1751), Paul Storr (1771–1844), the Scotsman Robertson, and the enterprising woman silversmith, Hester Bateman (fl. 1761–93). De Lamerie was the leading silversmith craftsman of the early 18th century, while at the other end of the century Paul Storr dominated the craft in Britain, and continued to do so well into the 19th century.

113

This tea-urn of 1809, with ivory tap knob, is a splendid example of the skills of the late Georgian silversmith, Paul Storr.

Hallmarks

This may be an appropriate point at which to look briefly at the hallmarking of silver in Britain, for it is essential to know about hallmarks if you are going to spend any time collecting the silver of the four nations that make up the British Isles.

There are five possible marks to be found on what is described as properly assayed silver, that is, silver that has been tested by an assay office. By law, British silver has had to be assayed since the Middle Ages, and among the earliest marks were those indicating the year of assay, the place and the maker's name. The hallmark is strictly speaking the mark establishing the hall, or assay office, of the town where the piece was assayed. London's mark is a leopard's head, and was introduced as far back as the reign of Edward IV (1461–83). It has continued to be used up to the present, except for an interval of twenty-two years (1697–1719). Assay offices were established in several cities in Britain, some of which are no longer operating. The offices are (or were):

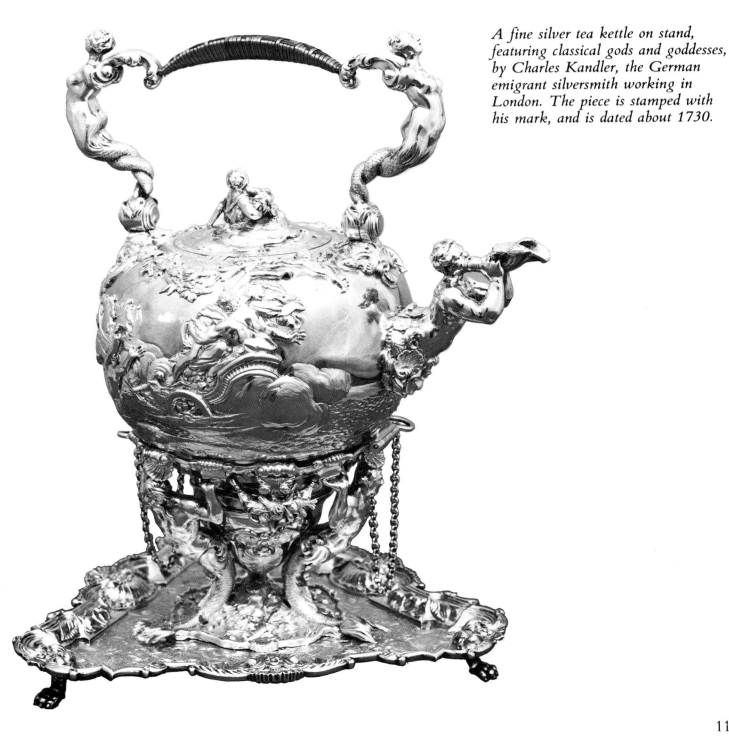

A fine silver tea kettle on stand, featuring classical gods and goddesses, by Charles Kandler, the German emigrant silversmith working in London. The piece is stamped with his mark, and is dated about 1730.

115

One-pint silver baluster-shaped tankard by William Shaw & William Priest, London, 1746, decorated in Rococo style.

Birmingham (since 1773), Chester (1680–1962), Dublin (since 1638), Edinburgh (since 1552), Exeter (1570–1882), Glasgow (1681–1964), Newcastle (1658–1883), Sheffield (since 1773), Norwich (1565–1701) and York (1560–1856).

The term hallmark has now come to embrace the whole set of marks found on silver, including the maker's mark, the date letter, the standard mark, and from 1784 to 1890 the sovereign's head, used as a duty mark to indicate that the tax raised on silver manufacture during this period was paid. The maker's mark, up to about 1840, was his (or her) initials, or in some cases the initials of the firm employing the maker. Before about 1720, maker's marks were a little more varied: for a period from the end of the 17th century to about 1720, the maker would stamp the first two letters of his name and add a symbol. In the 16th century a symbol alone sufficed.

The date letter established the year of assay, which usually meant the year of manufacture as well, and it is a letter of the alphabet decreed to distinguish the year of assay, a single letter in a certain print face inside a shield of one shape or another. Not all the letters of the alphabet were used in every city of assay, except one or two series from Birmingham and Glasgow. The date lettering requires some careful studying before an accurate dating of a piece can be made. The order

of date lettering varies. Because the letters are so small it is possible to confuse one in one cycle with another in a later, or earlier, cycle. For example, a capital Roman 'O' which is the London letter for 1809, is much like the small 'o' for 1820. The difference in this case is established by reference to the town mark: in the former year the leopard's head had a crown on it, and in 1829 it did not.

The standard mark indicates that the article has been made to the correct quality of silver, that is, the sterling standard, of 925 parts of pure silver in 1000, a standard established at the beginning of the 14th century and maintained until 1697 when the standard was raised to 958 per 1000. The standard mark was a lion passant (introduced in 1544). The raising of the standard was to stop silversmiths melting down silver coins to make articles, and the new standard applied until 1720, during which time the lion passant mark was abandoned and a figure of Britannia used in its place. When the new standard was no longer compulsory (from 1720) the lion passant was restored as the standard mark. The Britannia mark was, however, retained for pieces made of the higher standard, and is still used today, though it is limited to expensive presentation articles.

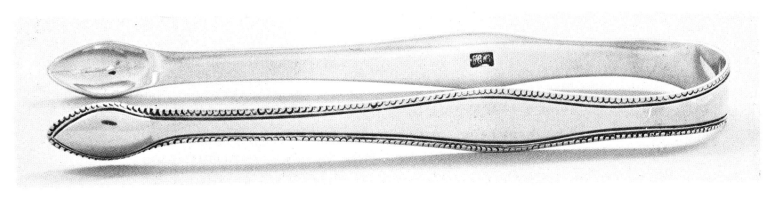

The complicated business of hallmarking might seem to preclude forgery, but in fact our Victorian ancestors went in for forging on a large scale. Earlier generations also tampered with marks, but generally for different reasons. False marks are imitations of old marks. They were (and still are) perpetrated by forgers for the express purpose of deceiving, and thereby acquiring money dishonestly. Detecting false marks is not easy, and is only possible after years of experience in handling antique silver. A false mark may look too new for the alleged age of the piece, that is, it may not show enough wear round the edges where it was stamped on the metal. But even this could be overcome, by claiming, for example, that the faked set of forks was made for Lord X in 1765 but that he died before using them and they have remained wrapped in soft cloth in a drawer ever since. This kind of claim was believed in Victorian times, but we are perhaps more cynical, and far more substantial proof would be required for us. An easier type of forgery to detect is the article made, for example, in 1890, but alleged to be of 1750 vintage and given the required marks, but which does not fit into the styles of silver of the mid-18th century. There are not many of these about, but they do offer a field for the collector.

The other major kind of mark tampering was transposition. Transposed marks are those lifted out of a genuine piece and moulded into another faked or reproduced piece. Transposition is not a new dodge. If it was done in the early days of silvermaking, it would often be because the silversmith did not want to incur the expense of having an article assayed. This was of course illegal, but perhaps the chance of being caught was an outside one. Victorian forgers learned this technique and adapted it to deliberate misrepresentation, and some were done so well that it is today hard to detect the forgery.

Left: *A silver centrepiece by Paul Storr, executed in 1838, towards the end of his long career.*

European silver

Although British silver is among the best in the world, we should not overlook the very fine silverwork from Europe, particularly Italy and France. Italian silver is a favourite with collectors, but it is very expensive. The silversmith's art flourished during the Renaissance in several centres, such as Florence, Genoa, Turin and Venice, but nowhere perhaps more prominently than in Rome where in the early years of the 16th century the silversmiths, reorganizing themselves into a guild, actually erected a church and dedicated it to St Eligius, patron saint of silversmiths. Their silver was largely for ecclesiastical use and adornment and followed the prevailing architectural styles. But many very fine pieces were made for secular and domestic use. Among the craftsmen was the sculptor and engraver Benvenuto Cellini (1500–71),

Opposite page: *This interesting page from* An Illustrated Cyclopaedia of the Great Exhibition of 1851 *shows two sugar spoons by Lias, a candelabrum flanked by a ewer and a mug, and a cut glass claret jug.*

SUGAR SPOONS.—LIAS.

CUT GLASS CLARET JUG. BY GREEN.

THIS very magnificent jug, which is of the purest glass, is very beautifully engraved with the Royal arms, and the national emblems of the three kingdoms.

SUGAR SPOONS. BY LIAS.

THE design of these spoons is novel and pretty, and we have no doubt will become popular.

CANDELABRUM, ETC. BY HARVEY AND CO.

THIS candelabrum is extremely fanciful, and pretty in design. It is composed entirely of shell-work, mineral plants, and water. The principal figure is that of Venus, on one side of whom is a syren singing to her lover: on the other hand is another of the same class of beings, entwined in a net, who is presenting the Goddess of Beauty with a string of coral. On the stem is a young Triton covering her with pearls; and on the summit a Cupid shooting at every heart. The workmanship is very careful, and the whole has a pleasing effect. The silver ewer of antique fashion, and the mug, which is silver gilt, of the cinque-cento style, are both very beautifully executed.

CANDELABRUM, ETC.—HARVEY AND CO.

who was also a leading gold- and silversmith, working in Florence and Mantua as well as Rome. Genoese silver was noted for its high-quality filigree work.

Over the 17th and 18th centuries there followed a stream of superb silversmiths, making quantities of lovely silverware, in the Baroque, Rococo and Neo-Classical styles respectively. These were all imitated on a large scale and with equal skill in the 19th century, in many instances so well that it is wellnigh impossible to tell the difference. These 19th-century copies are much in demand for collecting, for though expensive, they are not at the same level as the earlier pieces.

We have seen that the silver decoration on French furniture in many palaces and great houses in the time of Louis XIV had to be stripped out for melting down to provide bullion for financing French wars. This melting down affected the whole silver craft in France, and on several occasions the people were exhorted (no doubt compelled in some districts) to surrender their silverware for the national war effort. As a result, very little French silverware of the 17th century has survived, and what has was mainly those articles that were sold or presented to customers abroad. These surviving pieces, however, show very clearly that French silversmiths were capable of the highest craftsmanship; there is a glorious example in the shape of a toilet set in the Royal Scottish Museum in Edinburgh. There was a revival of silversmithing in the 18th century, particularly in the best years of Louis XV, and much was in the Rococo style pioneered by Juste-Aurèle Meissonnier (1695–1750); instantly recognizable by its accent on asymmetry. But the need for solid silver for bullion arose again during and immediately after the French Revolution, from about 1789 to the end of the century, and the great bulk of the lovely silverware, so much of which complemented the unique furniture of the century, was consigned to melting furnaces. In the quieter times of the 19th century

A 19th-century silver four-piece tea and coffee set in 'Cellini' pattern, that is, roughly in the manner of Benvenuto Cellini (1500-1571), the Italian artist, sculptor and goldsmith.

Opposite page: A well-made European silver coffee pot of the late 19th century.

French silversmiths got to work again and once more began to turn out fine articles, many of them in older styles. These are now collected.

American silver

American silver in its earlier years closely followed British styles, and was fashioned by craftsmen who had served their apprenticeships in London or the provinces, or in Scotland or Ireland, and had then emigrated to the New World. It seems that few items of these times have survived, partly because of the colonists' need to melt silver down for money during the War of Independence in the 1770s and 1780s, and partly because life for the first settlers was so harsh and uncertain, and articles simply disappeared. Even the simplest pieces of the 17th and early 18th centuries, such as spoons and porringers, are very hard to find and are extremely costly.

Once the British were defeated and the new American republic founded, Americans began to make their own silverware again, and in great quantities. They copied British styles (even if it hurt to do so to begin with, as it had certainly hurt their fellow craftsmen in wood), but they also adapted European styles, perhaps more widely than British. American silver was not as a rule marked in the way in which British silver has been for so long, but the silver standard was every bit as

Opposite page: Silver lidded creampot by Paul Revere, 1784.

Below: An excellent illustration of the high skills of early American silversmithing. This is a two-handled cup, with cover, made in New York at the end of the 17th century. The shape is English, but the ornament is Dutch, notably the coat of arms.

high. Makers in the new America stamped pieces with their initials, but generally no other marks were required, though at the beginning of the 19th century some silverware made in Baltimore was given date stamps as well, from about 1814 to 1830. These pieces are relatively rare and offer an interesting field for collecting.

The easiest pieces of American silver to acquire are probably the commemorative spoons that started to be made in quantity in the 18th century. Many had the most original handles, such as crocodiles, 'Red Indian' figures, spades and other utensils. Other articles for collecting are sugar tongs, soap tins and punch strainers. Many American silversmiths were extremely highly skilled, just as good as their British counterparts, the most famous being Paul Revere (1735–1818), a specialist in Rococo and Neo-Classical styles. He is sometimes called the American Paul de Lamerie. Revere is in fact better known to the world for his daring ride through the night from Boston to Lexington in 1775 to warn the 'rebel' colonists that the British forces were on the march against them, a ride that saved the colonists and was later commemorated in a great poem by Longfellow, *The Midnight Ride of Paul Revere*. Of Huguenot descent, he was an engraver as well as a skilled goldsmith and silversmith, and when not occupied in harassing the British forces in the war, he designed the first official seal of the colonists and he designed and printed their first money. Much of Revere's silver, made in the later part of his life, when he could settle down to pursue his craft, is marked with his name enclosed in a rectangle. Leading collectors seldom miss the chance to bid for a Revere article, but they are as a rule very expensive.

A Paul Revere teapot and stand, about 1786.

126

Sheffield plate

When collecting silver, it is worth considering Sheffield plate. It was introduced in the early 1740s by Thomas Bolsover (1706–88) – it seems by chance. A sheet of very hot silver was accidentally placed by him upon a bar of copper in his workshop, and in moments the two metals had fused. Bolsover played around with the mix, pushed it through rolling bars, hammered it, reducing its overall thickness, but noticed that its overall proportions remained the same. He realized he had found an excellent substitute for real silver. By the 1760s this 'copper-rolled plate', as he described it, had become a serious rival to silver for the less rich market. Bolsover himself made small items, such as little boxes with pull-off lids, knife handles, thimbles, buttons and buckles, but it was not long before other makers were producing a huge variety of articles, particularly the larger ones like tureens, entrée dishes, candlesticks, coffeepots, kettles and so on. The term Sheffield plate is thought to have come into use in 1771 when an advertisement contained the phrase. Sheffield plate lent itself well to ornament, as can be seen from the variety of cruet stands, tea-urns, claret jugs, tobacco jars and so on that can generally be found in shops and also come up regularly at sales. Good 18th-century plate is not cheap to buy, and you could have to spend two or three hundred for an elaborate tea-urn. But at the other end, you can still find Sheffield plate snuffboxes of considerable artistic appeal for £70 to £90.

Sheffield plate, which held the stage for a long time for those who could not, or did not want to, spend money on real silver, met a major rival in the 1840s with the invention of electro-plating, by which a piece made in base metal was coated with silver by electrolysis. This was the beginning of electro-plated nickel silver (known as E P N S). The silver coating of E P N S wears off quite quickly from pieces that are in continual use, such as table silver.

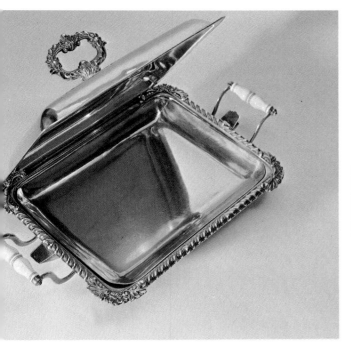

Below: *A Sheffield plate serving dish of 1805, with hot water compartment under the low tray. Note the small funnels on the shorter sides; this is where hot water was poured in.*

Right: *A Sheffield plate cheese toaster of 1805, with hot water compartment. The funnel with cap is at the inner end of the handle.*

127

Metalwork

Metals have played a part in man's economy since the Copper and Bronze Ages, and through the centuries, as a result of increasing technological knowledge, metals have been refined and blended to produce many different materials. In the field of antiques, metalwork is used in two ways: either as a filling or as a mechanism in primarily non-metal objects, or by itself as a result of practical or decorative necessity. Into the latter category come such things as firedogs, saucepans, trivets and so on. Since metals have very different properties, the simplest way to discuss metalwork is to take each metal in turn and look at its uses.

Bronze

The Sumerians and Egyptians used copper for tools and utensils, but it was the invention of bronze – an alloy of copper and tin – at least 5,000 years ago that is of real significance. In Europe from ancient Greek times this alloy was favoured for casting fine sculpture, and in the 16th century AD, the French and the Germans made caskets and clock cases from it. These were finely chiselled and then gilded. The craft of gilded bronze work reached its height in the French ormolu work of the late 17th and 18th centuries, and in England in the later 18th century in the work of Matthew Boulton and others. Bronze has always been favoured by artists for the casting of anything from huge public sculptures commemorating great men or battles to small decorative pieces of the salon, which sometimes imitated these heroic subjects.

It seems, however, that the ancient technique of casting large bronzes was temporarily lost during the Middle Ages, and its revival was led by the Frenchman Giovanni de Bologna (or Jean de Boulogne). Bronze first appeared as an embellishment for furniture at the time of André Charles Boulle in the late 17th century. Other artist craftsmen abounded after this date, among them the great artists Jacques Caffieri (1673–1755), Jean-Claude Duplessis (d. 1774), Galliène and Pierre Gouthière (1732–c. 1812).

Bronze sculptures, provided they are not too large, are an excellent field for the collector. There is a profusion of different forms and styles to choose from, plus the chance of famous signatures and the interest of different editions. Modern demand for the works of well-known sculptors like Rodin or Pradier always outstrips the supply. The same is true of the ever popular 'animalier' artists such as Bargé, Rosa, Pompon and P. J. Mène. This demand invites forgeries which are always circulating the salerooms and less reputable shops. The faker has two problems when making a spurious bronze. He must either take a mould from an existing piece, which would arouse the suspicion of those who know the 'edition', especially as bronze shrinks with age,

A pair of bronze figures by the 18th-century Italian sculptor, Francesco Richetti. The figures are (left) Actaeon and (right) Bacchus.

129

A French Empire-style candelabra in bronze and ormolu by P. P. Thomire, the well-known 18th-century Paris bronze-caster, often employed by the Crown and by individual Paris cabinet-makers.

and size difference would show in any comparison. The second problem arises if the faker tries to create an altogether 'new' sculpture. Not only must he be a consummate artist of his chosen style, but he must also be able to convince the purchaser of the hitherto undiscovered edition to which this piece belongs. This of course does not apply to unsigned bronzes, but they fetch much less, and forgers rarely settle for less.

Patina is all-important in the study of bronze, and there are different sorts of oxidisation, corrosion and wear that can produce varied colours and textures. Far Eastern bronzes often have an almost silky black appearance, whilst ancient objects from Greece and Rome are frequently covered with a blue-green surface. Then there is what is called 'Renaissance rose', describing the beautiful brown colour of many 15th- and 16th-century bronzes. Fakers claim to be able to create all these surfaces, either by dipping a hot bronze into mineral oil and then polishing or, more drastically, by using sulphuric acid, whose effects are fixed with beeswax. Only experience will teach the collector to beware of such artificially produced finishes. Unlike copper and brass, the patina of genuine antique bronze must be respected. Cleaning should be undertaken only with soapy water and a soft brush. Hot melted beeswax can then be applied which, when quite cool, may be rubbed with a soft woollen duster. Mention should be made here of the many copies of bronzes made during the 19th century in a zinc alloy called spelter. These are light and hollow and do not acquire a fine patina. They will only deceive the extreme amateur.

A lovely Italian bronze sculpture by Andrea Riccio of the early 16th century. The subject is a shepherd milking a goat.

A 16th-century German iron casket with a very complicated locking system on the underside of the lid.

Iron and steel

Iron was hardly used, even by the Egyptians and the Hittites, much before 2000 BC, and then only for very important tools and decoration. In fact, because of its rarity, it figured in rich jewellery along with gold and precious stones. In Roman times Pliny the Elder noted that iron was as valuable as silver. Civilizations advanced tremendously when improvements in metallurgy allowed iron to come into general use for agricultural implements, weapons, craft tools and fittings for furniture and buildings. Unfortunately, because iron decays so quickly in damp conditions, very little early domestic work has come down to us. Mediaeval blacksmithing can be seen to best advantage in churches. Doors, in particular, are often covered with applied scrollwork of chiselled leaf design in the Gothic style. However, some more utilitarian objects survive from this period, notably hinges on chests or cupboards, and locks which are in themselves works of fine engineering and which may have highly decorative escutcheon plates around the keyholes. A well-known type of box that occasionally appears in shops and sales is the so-called 'Armada chest'. These rectangular iron strong-boxes have handles at each end and are criss-crossed with a grid work of iron straps rivetted onto the plates. Their locks are often highly complicated mechanisms whereby one key activates many mortises around the inside of the lid. Such boxes are hard to date, and must have been made in many countries from the 16th to the 18th century.

The iron firedog, or andiron, appears to have been used in Roman times, but the earliest known examples date from the later Middle Ages. Medieval firedogs were fairly simple (incidentally the term 'andirons' is usually applied to dogs standing 3 ft/91 cm or more high), but as the fireplace assumed more importance as a focal point they became more decorative. In the 15th and 16th centuries they were made of cast iron and the influence of the Renaissance gave them a classical appearance. The classical column is a popular motif for the upright. One can still find simple firedogs made by the local blacksmith in the 17th century for use in cottage or yeomans' kitchen. These are of wrought iron and may have a series of hooks at the front for spits, and possible 'cressetts' (like iron baskets) at their tops for holding the basting pans. To protect the brickwork behind the fire, cast firebacks were made. These come in a variety of designs, with low relief modelling of popular subjects,

Pair of late 17th-century English cast-iron firedogs with brass finials, the front two feet cast in the form of scaly human legs and feet.

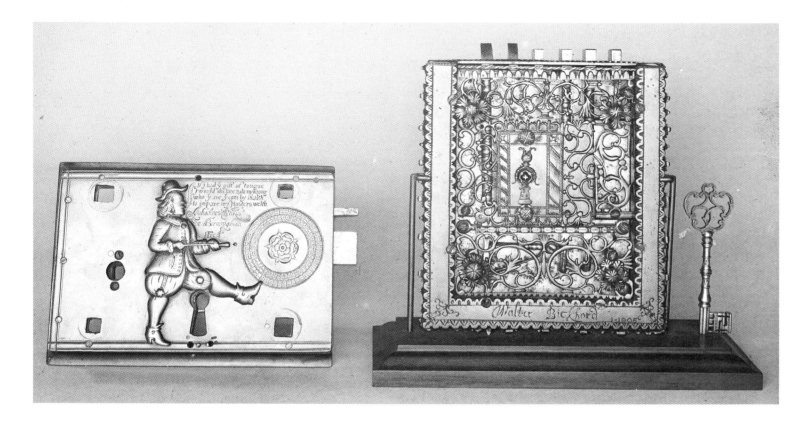

such as Adam and Eve, the oak tree (Charles II) or the Royal Arms. Like the cast firedogs, these have been reproduced for half a century or more, and originals can be difficult to distinguish.

By skilful tempering of iron, various different sorts of steel could be produced, from springs to blades. Many household objects, such as scissors or fire tongs, pokers, etc., were made, particularly in the 18th century. Very fine embellishments were possible on this hard material. Sometimes engraved lines were inlaid with gold or silver – a process originating in the East but perfected by the craftsmen of Italy and Germany and called damascening (from Damascus).

Locks and keys, mentioned earlier as fittings, are now collected in their own right. Amazingly, there are some numbers of medieval and even Roman keys in existence, so a very comprehensive collection can be assembled. Early keys are mostly plain, but a medieval example might be recognized by a Gothic-shaped bow. Any more elaboration suggests the imagination of the Victorian rather than the medieval mind. During the 16th and 17th centuries keys became very ornamental, the French being masters of elaborate Renaissance designs. These French keys often had shanks of triangular or clover-shaped section, and bows with winged figures and Ionic supports. In this field, one should beware of late 19th-century copies. English keys, the most complicated of which may have aristocratic ciphers in their bows, were mostly simple yet elegant, and 18th-century 'kidney bow' keys in different sizes can form an attractive collection.

The basic principles of lock-making changed little from the early Middle Ages until the beginning of Victoria's reign. Plate locks were used on doors in the 18th century, and 'stock locks' (plate locks set into rectangular blocks of oak) were still being used in the 1830s. Brass or steel case rim-locks were characteristic in the middle-class homes of the 18th century. Despite the complexity of some medieval locks, the simple types seemed perfectly serviceable for most purposes.

There is an increasing number of dealers who specialize in architectural fittings rescued from demolished buildings. Whilst such things can rarely look so good as in the context for which they were designed,

Above: *Two very finely made locks: on the left, an English late 17th-century steel lock in a case of engraved brass, signed by Walter Bickford; and on the right, a cast and engraved brass lock signed Johannes Wilkes de Birmingham fecit, of about 1680.*

Above: *A pleasing wrought-iron bracket of the mid-18th century.*

Opposite page: *A fine English painted ironwork door grille of the first quarter of the 18th century.*

The Golden Gates (Sanctuary Screen) at St Paul's Cathedral in London. They were executed in 1698-99 by the great architectural ironsmith Jean Tijou, who worked in England from about 1690 to 1712.

Occasionally, 19th-century furniture was made of cast iron. This is a Victorian wash-stand of the 1850s.

we must at least be thankful that they are now being saved, whereas twenty years ago they were usually destroyed on site. Although the majority of demolition material is of Victorian date, one may occasionally be surprised to find some fine pieces of period ironwork whose provenance connects it with a certain designer or factory. Three names stand out in the history of British wrought ironwork – those of the Huguenot Jean Tijou, the Davies brothers, and Robert Bakewell of Derby (fl. 1707–52). Tijou introduced to England the elaborate decorative styles of French wrought ironwork. The best known example of his work is the screen of the fountain garden at Hampton Court, Middlesex. Tijou's drawings in his '*The New Booke of Drawings Invented and Designed by John Tijou*' (1693) were disseminated throughout England and imitations can be found throughout the country. Bakewell's works include a garden arbour at Melbourne Hall, near Derby and the chancel screen at Derby Cathedral. The Davies brothers of Wales made some exotic Baroque gates for Chirk Castle, near Llangollen, but their later work shows more restraint, and this approach was to characterize British wrought ironwork in future. By the end of the 18th century the industrial revolution was tolling the death knell for many of the smaller firms of artist-craftsmen smiths.

Cast iron was the great structural material of the Victorians – from mass-produced fireplaces to the great frames for railway stations. The interest in industrial archeology has caused the prices of some of these things to rise sharply. Nevertheless, those who can afford the time may sometimes come across attractive pieces of cast-iron work for a modest price and such things as Gothic supports or grill work from old industrial buildings can be incorporated successfully into modern structures.

The gates, transom panel and overthrow at the Clarendon Building in Oxford, executed in about 1710.

Copper

Copper was one of the first metals worked by man. Among its assets are its good conduction of heat, its malleability and, not least, its attractive appearance. From the 17th century, copper was used widely for cooking utensils, measures, warming pans, etc., until in the beginning of the 20th century aluminium and stainless steel cornered the mass market in kitchen ware. Copper saucepans and kettles appear regularly in antique shops. Originally, copper pans were tin-plated inside to offset the bad-tasting (and possibly poisonous) effect of the metal, but this coating has usually been removed. Because of the difficulty in casting copper, the handles, knobs and hinges of copper articles were made of cast brass or iron. Copper was, however, often used as a basis for enamel work and of course in the production of Sheffield plate later from the mid–18th century onwards.

To a certain extent it is possible to date copper by the way in which an individual piece has been worked. 17th-century copper ware was beaten somewhat crudely and was thick when compared with the products of the late 18th century, which were made of rolled metal in uniform thickness. Early copper also tends to be pale compared with the reddish colour of later examples.

A good set of period ale measures (which are hugely expensive), with the light reflecting on the dented rosy surface, is one of the finest adornments of a country inn. Many copies have been made of these sets, which run from the gallon down to the dram, but even they are unnecessarily expensive.

A pair of candle vases, decorated in ormolu and blue john, produced by the Boulton & Fothergill metal firm in the early 1770s. Blue john, known also as Derbyshire spar, is a form of calcium fluoride in violet-blue crystals used in the later 18th century for decorative purposes, especially for vases. The vases above are copies of designs originally produced for George III.

Two 19th-century English iron skillets.

Below: Some mid-19th-century articles of copperware: kettle, ham brazier and coal scuttle.

Brass

Brass, an alloy of copper and zinc, is one of the most important metal alloys known to man. It is harder than copper, it is ductile and malleable, it takes a high polish, it is easily joined and it does not disintegrate rapidly when exposed to the elements. The proportions of copper and zinc used in the alloy, together with many impurities in early times, give antique brass a lustrous glow beloved of collectors. Another alloy similar to brass, but including lead and tin in various combinations, is referred to as 'latten' in medieval and Elizabethan inventories. This metal was usually beaten into flat plates, one of its applications being in the making of monumental 'brasses'. Brass had such a wide variety of uses in the days before it became too expensive for engineering and household fittings that most of the utensils commonly made of copper or iron were also made of brass. Antique shops are full of brass fire tools, fenders, dogs, skillets and coal scuttles, and the golden lustre of the metal puts their value above their equally serviceable and interesting counterparts in iron. On the whole though, a 19th-century spun-brass saucepan or kettle will not fetch so much as a similar item in copper. Coal scuttles or hods are much in demand and because of the hard wear they come in for, the demand usually outstrips the supply of old ones. Few survive from before about 1800, hence the large industry in reproductions from the Midlands. Sometimes one finds a variation from the usual 'helmet' or cone-shaped container, in the form of a nautilus shell or urn with a lid. This genteel modification of a utilitarian object was meant to beautify the hearth, and the Victorians euphemistically called it a 'coal vase'.

Another lovely adornment to the fireplace are brass fire dogs. Some magnificent examples were made in the 17th and 18th centuries, with classical acanthus, swags, flambeaux and ball and claw feet. Small plain Victorian ones are very common. Sometimes wrought-iron dogs would

Above: *A very beautiful pierced and decorated brass warming pan of Dutch make, dated 1602.*

Right: *A fine English brass curfew of the later 17th century. A curfew (couvre-feu) was used to cover an unattended fire or to help it stay in overnight.*

be highlighted with the occasional brass finial or roundel.

The brilliance of polished brass made it eminently suitable for light fittings. Candlesticks and oil lamps are the most easily found of these. The first candlesticks were of 'pricket' type, with a spike for the candle. The socket form started to come into general use at the end of the Middle Ages, but pricket candlesticks continued to be used in churches and for large domestic candles. 16th and 17th century ones can be of triangular section with three feet, or turned, with circular spun tops and bases. Domestic candlesticks, whether of brass, pewter or silver, tended to follow the prevailing taste, and development can be traced from this. A rare design of the 16th century had a broad dished base to catch the grease, but later in the century and in the early 17th century, the grease pan was moved to a position halfway up the stem. The only decoration on the English sticks of this date is a series of grooves turned on the stem. Contemporary Continental candlesticks had already adopted the elegant baluster shape the English were to use later. 18th century candlesticks changed from being octagonal baluster in the first quarter, shell base and vase baluster in the middle of the century and finally the Neo–classical square base and section of the late 18th century. Some of the latter period are in the form of a classical column. The 17th century candlesticks were cast in one piece, with base attached by means of a tenon or screw. From the 1670s to the early 19th century

A mid to late 18th-century English brass trivet, placed in front of a fire to support cooking vessels.

A group of early Victorian brass domestic articles: a pair of candlesticks, a china-handled trivet; and a watercan.

they were made in sections, with a return to the earlier method after this.

Despite popular belief, not all old brass chandeliers are Dutch, although it is probable that the first ones were made in the Netherlands. In the Low Countries they were in far more widespread use for domestic lighting, whereas in England they are usually found in public buildings or churches. Some English chandeliers come on to the market, having been removed to private houses when gas ousted them from many churches. There are certain differences between the styles of the two countries. In the late 17th and early 18th centuries the branches of the chandeliers from both England and Holland were attached to the rims of trays projecting from the central stem. The English ones, however, hook into these trays, whereas the Dutch used tenons which pass through holes and are secured with pins. Dutch chandeliers also look heavier and have more elaborate ornament at the jointure between the scrolls of the branches. These are commonly in the form of foliage, fish or a human head. Mid-18th century English craftsmen began to bolt the pieces of the chandelier together, and so the pendant has to be made up of more parts. A flame-like casting at the top serves to hide the suspension device. Needless to say, important period chandeliers very rarely come the way of the small collector. They represent the height of the brassfounders' craft.

The list of brass objects around today in antique and junk shops is almost unending. The vast majority of these pieces are trifles from this or the last century, often made as souvenirs or as attempts to copy past styles. The collector will learn to judge between the flashy rawness of modern metal and the deep lustre of old brass. An example of the need for careful examination is in the field of horsebrasses – a minefield for the small collector. Before the 19th century, working horses were hardly ever decorated with more than a single 'sun flash' domed brass on the head. Up to the 1860s brass containing calamine was used for castings and the results show in minute pitting on the surface and a warm gold colour. After this date the industry centred on Walsall in the English West Midlands. The brass has great brilliance and the basic rough castings were carefully drilled, filed and finished by hand. The 'gets' – two small projections remaining from where the casting left the mould – were painstakingly removed on early brasses, but on modern reproductions these often show as distinct blemishes. In the last quarter of the century horsebrasses were made of pressed brass in some cases, but these were always well finished. From 1900 to the present many copies have been made. Some are faithful and of good quality, others are coarse, heavily pitted and depict subjects never employed by older makers. The better fakes can be detected by subtle details, such as lack of the correct wear in the strap-loops and at the bottom inside edge where it should have rubbed the leather harness. There is a 'feel' to originals that can be acquired with practice.

A group of martingales (a strap to connect a horse's girth to its noseband, bit or reins), with brasses. Horse brasses, as they are called, are collected widely. Few, however, are older than mid to late 18th century, and most surviving examples are later 19th and early 20th century.

Pewter

Tin is the basic constituent of the alloy pewter, but the proportion in which it is mixed with lead, brass and antimony varies greatly. Although pewter goes back to the Roman occupation in Britain, it is rare to find anything earlier than the 17th century on the antique market today. All sorts of table ware, as well as tobacco boxes, apothecaries' equipment, candlesticks and church vessels, were made of pewter in the same designs as the more expensive silver versions. The strict controls of the Pewterers Company over quality meant that British pewter attained a high standard and reputation. Each master pewterer had to invent a touchmark and register it on a plate at Pewterers Hall in London, or in the case of Scotland, the Edinburgh Hammermens' Guild in that city. Unlike silver, however, pewterers did not employ a date-letter, so it is impossible to tell exactly when an object was made. Sometimes a series of 'hallmarks' is found on pewter, but these marks have no meaning and were used to give the object a superficial resemblance to silver.

Two pewter measures of the 18th century, the left one from Scotland, the right one English.

Spoons are probably the earliest utensils to be found in pewter.

Before the 18th century, these had pear-shaped bowls and a variety of decorative knops at the ends of the handles. The best known of these is the 'apostle' design, but there are also acorns, horned heads, and abstract geometric patterns. There are a fair number of such spoons that date from the early 16th century. Plates of various sizes, tankards and measures, are the commonest type of period pewter to be found in the average antique shop. Huge numbers of pewter drinking vessels and flagons were made in the years before glass came into general use in alehouses. These measures come in various capacities and shapes – the baluster shape being a popular form. Such pieces are often of a low grade pewter with a high lead content. The fine metal with mostly tin was reserved for the very best work. Pewter dishes and chargers can form an attractive display, especially when set off by the warm glow of early oak. 17th-century plates often had double or triple reeded rims. In the field of candlesticks, salts, porringers etc., pewterers followed the styles of the silversmiths, and it was only with the introduction of cheap pottery in the later 18th century that pewter declined in everyday household use. Much early pewter was melted down, making what remains rarer than some silver pieces.

By the first decades of the 19th century the industrial process had developed a new type of metal called 'Britannia' which it was hoped would compete with cheap china. This new metal, made of pure tin and antimony, was much harder than traditional pewter. It was very easily worked cold, or it could be die-stamped, thus obviating the need for casting. It was often spun on the lathe. The trade was centred on Sheffield, and the makers, whose names were stamped on the underside of the objects, include James Dixon & Sons, Broadhead and Atkin, Wolstenholme and Ashberry. Purist pewter collectors used to despise Britannia, but in recent years there has been a cautious acceptance of some of the finer pieces that can be appreciated for their aesthetic qualities.

Pewter is easier to fake than some other collectables such as fine paintings or clocks. There has been a steady flow of fakes onto the market since the 19th century, although the objects of the fakers' art have changed since those times. Well known in the trade are what are known as 'Billies and Charlies', named after two mid-19th-century fakers, William Smith and Charles Eaton. Their favoured area for faking was in medieval medallions and pilgrim's badges. They were crudely cast and had only a superficial appearance of antiquity. They are now over a hundred years old and so form an interesting subject for collecting in their own right. Later fakes have been of rare 16th- and 17th-century types, some of which were produced by partly recasting or reshaping damaged genuine pieces with original touchmarks.

Japanned work

Japanned metalware goes back to the time of George I, and was produced first at Wolverhampton and then by Edward Allgood in Pontypool. The latter firm, a small family business, made boxes, salvers and candlesticks, all with a beautiful smooth rock-hard surface achieved by repeated stoving at low temperatures. Undecorated japanned ware could be placed in a fire without damage, so this made it suitable for charcoal burners, urns, kettles and snuffers. The Allgood business was finally closed in 1820. The Midlands manufacturers continued to make a cheaper decorated ware which was exported all over the world. Collectors can choose between a wide range of ware including trays, tea canisters, cake baskets, charcoal brazier sets and knife cases. These come in a wide range of styles from 18th century Rococo to Adam classical and even Chinese.

Above: *Three American mechanical cast-iron money banks: on the left, the Punch and Judy type, 1884; in the centre Williput, 1875; and on the right, Magic Bank, 1870s.*

Right: *A fascinating early-19th-century American weathervane, in the form of an American Indian, decorated in gold-leaf répoussé.*

American metalwork

Little brass or copper was made in America before the War of Independence, and what was needed was generally imported from Europe. But after 1783 there was a spontaneous rush to design and make a range of household and decorative objects in both alloys. In about 1780 James Emerson fused zinc and copper in the ratio one to two and evolved a very high-quality brass with a golden hue. Emerson pieces are rare, but his formula was copied and articles made from this can be bought. And the great silversmith and patriot-hero, Paul Revere (see p. 126), designed and made a variety of brass articles. Copperware of the 18th century is equally hard to find, but one artefact that is still available, though at a price, is the weathervane, the most popular style of which was fabricated from two or more sheets of copper brazed together at the edges, and cut out to form the required figures, such as cockerels, ships, horses and even grasshoppers. American-made copper kettles of the late 18th and early 19th century can occasionally be found, and they often have swinging handles.

Amercian pewter must be mentioned, as it formed an important part of life from the first days of Colonies. Much pewter went out with the first settlers, but because of the duty on bar tin this was often reworked by the craftsmen of later years. For this reason not many of the very early articles survive. Boston was the centre for a thriving industry by the late 17th century, and craftsmen came to work there from England, Holland and Sweden. American pewter made by the Dutch retained its national characteristic of round sturdiness. Generally, styles were copied in America twenty or thirty years after their introduction in England.

Two American pewter tankards: on the left, an 18th-century tankard attributed to J. Skinner of Boston, and on the right, a lidded tankard in 17th-century shape.

Arms and Armour

Above: *This iron backplate is possibly from the Civil War; the style is of the 17th century.*

By the end of the Middle Ages, European armour had become much less effective for war, and was made thereafter more for display, for ceremonial wear, for tournaments and in some instances to impress conquered peoples in other parts of the world, such as that worn by the Conquistadores in Mexico and South America. Suits of armour had always been expensive to make even when they were essential for battle, and they cost no less when their war function gave way to the more decorative purposes of the 16th and 17th centuries. It is not perhaps without significance that a suit made for Henry Wriothesley, Earl of Southampton, in the reign of Elizabeth I, recently fetched almost £1 million at a London sale. Specimens of body armour of the Middle Ages, and indeed of the 16th century, very rarely come on to the market, and when they do they can be expected to attract very high bidding. Most of the surviving suits or pieces are to be found in museums, and in the UK particularly at the Tower of London Armouries. There is, however, still a good deal of mid-17th-century English Civil War armour to be had, usually consisting of breast plates, back plates and helmets.

A chapter on arms and armour in a book of this nature is thus more appropriately centred upon hand weapons, many of which have survived, and present an interesting field for collecting. At an antiques fair at Bury St Edmunds in March 1984 I saw an Italian stonebow, or prodd, which is a version of crossbow that shoots stones, marked up at £450. It was about 400 years old and in excellent condition. Prodds were generally used for hunting game, but since crossbows were still being used in sieges and other kinds of fighting in the 16th century, no doubt stonebows played their part in the business of killing or injuring enemies.

Hand weapons were made for war, tournament, duelling and ceremonials, and we can divide them into two main groups, firearms and hand weapons not activated by gunpowder. To take the second group first, we are talking about, among other things, swords, daggers, maces, battle axes, polearms and bows and arrows. Examples of all these appear in salerooms regularly, can be found in antique shops and are often for sale on stands at antique fairs, in varying conditions. Polearms have generally had their wooden parts replaced or shortened, and bows and arrows are invariably represented only by crossbows, but although this may detract a little from their cash value, it need not affect their collectability.

Opposite page: *This splendidly decorated suit of armour for foot-jousting was made for Elector Christian I of Saxony (1586-91) in about 1590. It was one of twelve such suits made by Anton Pfeffenhauser at Augsburg.*

Below: *A 17th-century iron breastplate unearthed in Cambridgeshire. The dent in the heart region may have been caused by a musket ball.*

Swords

Two European swords of the 18th century. The larger one (possibly English or French) has a gilt-brass hilt and gold inlay on the blade. The smaller one may have been a boy's sword. The blade is Solingen made (the stamp can be seen, about half an inch to the right of the knuckle bow).

Swords are a huge field in themselves, for although at first sight there do not appear to be more than a dozen or so varieties, in fact every sword was an individually made weapon, and so differed in some respect from the next. Even confining ourselves to European swords from the 16th and 19th centuries (the most numerous grouping of surviving examples that are still available to collectors), there are several types for various uses. From the 12th century onwards, swords were made by bladesmiths, a new branch of the ironsmithing craft specializing in sword-making, following some uncomfortable experiences endured by early Crusaders, whose broad and blunt swords proved to be no match for the superior Muslim weapons. By the time of the third Crusade (1189–92), professional sword-making businesses had been established in Italy, Germany and Christian Spain, at sites close to iron-ore sources, such as at Milan, Solingen and Toledo. Soon, other craftsmen known as cutters began to specialize in making decorated hilts for the blades, and they introduced all sorts of new styles of hilt. For a long time swords were made in two parts by the two different craftsmen.

Italy, Germany and Spain remained the three principal areas in which sword blades were produced, both for home consumption and for export to other countries, including Britain, whose home products at that time are generally regarded by specialists as markedly inferior. This situation lasted right into the 17th century, when the Stuart kings encouraged German bladesmiths to set up in business in England and Scotland. In 1629, for example, the Hounslow School of Swordsmiths was established by Charles I, with German emigrant craftsmen instructing English smiths. New schools were opened elsewhere, as at Birmingham and Shotley Bridge. It was, however, some time before the British product was really good enough for top military men, and it is interesting that several of the leaders in the Civil War of the 1640s continued to buy their swords from abroad. Two swords attributed to Oliver Cromwell (and now in the Cromwell Museum at Huntingdon) were made in Germany.

Typical of the blades produced in the 17th to 19th centuries are rapiers (thrusting weapons, of Renaissance origin); hangers (short, light, all-purpose swords used by soldiers and sailors, precursors of the British cutlass for the navy, which was a heavier sword with a broad guard); special swords for naval officers, war duty and ceremonial alike, with straight blade and highly decorated scabbard; and the broadswords such as those used by the Parliamentarians in the Civil War, with a wide, double-edged blade and heavy pommel. There were others, for example, those specially manufactured for presentation purposes. The sword hilts were also more varied in design. The term hilt describes the whole assembly of a sword above the blade, including the subject of much decorative treatment. Guards came in various guises, the two main kinds being the basket hilt, resembling a small basket or cage structure that protected the whole hand from slashing, if not always from well-aimed thrusting, and the cup hilt which was shaped like a cup or bowl and which protected only the fingers. Prices of swords over the past year or two have varied enormously. A Scottish basket-hilt sword of the 18th century might cost anything from about £150 to about £400; German duelling rapiers of the 17th century are seldom less than £400; French small-swords of the 18th century, curiously somewhat rare, are much sought after but can be bought for £200 or so.

Sword blades were also the subject of the highest decorative treatment, particularly on the flat part nearest the hilt, and many owners had their names etched on them inside profuse surrounding illumination. The makers also imprinted their trade marks. The Solingen school of bladesmiths in Germany (one of the most famous of all) used the emblem of a wolf; the two Cromwell swords already mentioned have the Solingen wolf mark. Solingen swords do occasionally emerge for sale, but fetch high prices.

A 17th-century cavalry sword, 43½ in. (110.5 cm.) long. This was discovered in the thatch of a cottage at Catworth in Cambridgeshire. It may have been hidden there by a Civil War trooper on the run.

151

Polearms

Polearms are cut-and-thrust weapons mounted on long hand poles. There were several kinds, and each was the subject of a variety of individual treatments and refinements aimed at causing as much injury and unpleasantness as possible to the opponent at the receiving end. The best known in the public mind, probably because of period films and historical television features, are the pike, the bill and the halberd, and certainly all three were major war weapons for a long time. The pike was the infantryman's device for meeting the cavalry charge. It

was a spear-like weapon whose head was about a foot (30 cm) long and resembled that of an assegai, with many small variations in the contours from maker to maker. The shaft was anything from about 15 ft (4.6 m) to about 20 ft (6m), and it was held in both hands forwards at chest level by infantrymen generally drawn up in ranks. Pikes were eventually replaced by bayonets at the end of the 17th century.

The bill was a spiked axe-type bladed weapon with a sharp hook on one side of the blade, fixed on a long shaft, and it preceded the pike, although for a time it also continued to be used alongside. The halberd had a similar style of blade to the bill, but the axe part was shorter but broader with no hook, though it had at least two spikes, one vertical, one horizontal (assuming the weapon to be standing vertically with its head upright). The shaft of a halberd was much shorter, 6 to 7 ft (1.8 to 2.1 m). The horizontal spike, known as the fluke, was more pronounced than the bill spike. The halberd was a cut-and-thrust weapon, equally effective when wielded as an axe to cut through armour as when jabbed into the flanks of an onrushing knight or his mount.

All three types come up for sale, though very rarely with their original wooden shafts, more often with replacement shafts or simply as shaftless blades. It is unlikely that a shafted polearm could be bought for under £100.

Less commonly found, because they were weapons more exclusive to leading men in battle, especially mounted knights, are maces. The mace can be described as a sophisticated club. It was a thick straight stick with one or other of a variety of murderous heads. The two most familiar heads were the solid sphere of iron whose surface was covered with very sharp spikes, up to two dozen of them on one orb, and the elliptical profile head consisting of several steel wings, or flanges, with sharp cutting edges spaced equidistantly round the ellipse. Mace heads were decorated, as were the handles, often elaborately, with goldwork, enamels, intricate chasing on metal and so forth, and thus the mace subsequently made for symbolizing authority in parliaments, local councils, judicial establishments and so on, is invariably a highly decorated and valuable artefact.

Akin to the mace is the war hammer, rarely seen outside a museum these days. This was a weapon for smashing open plate armour, and it probably did it very well. The blunt hammer part was balanced by a beak-like point (in some cases looking much like a falcon's beak (in French, *bec-de-faucon*) or a raven's beak (in German, *rabenschnabel*).

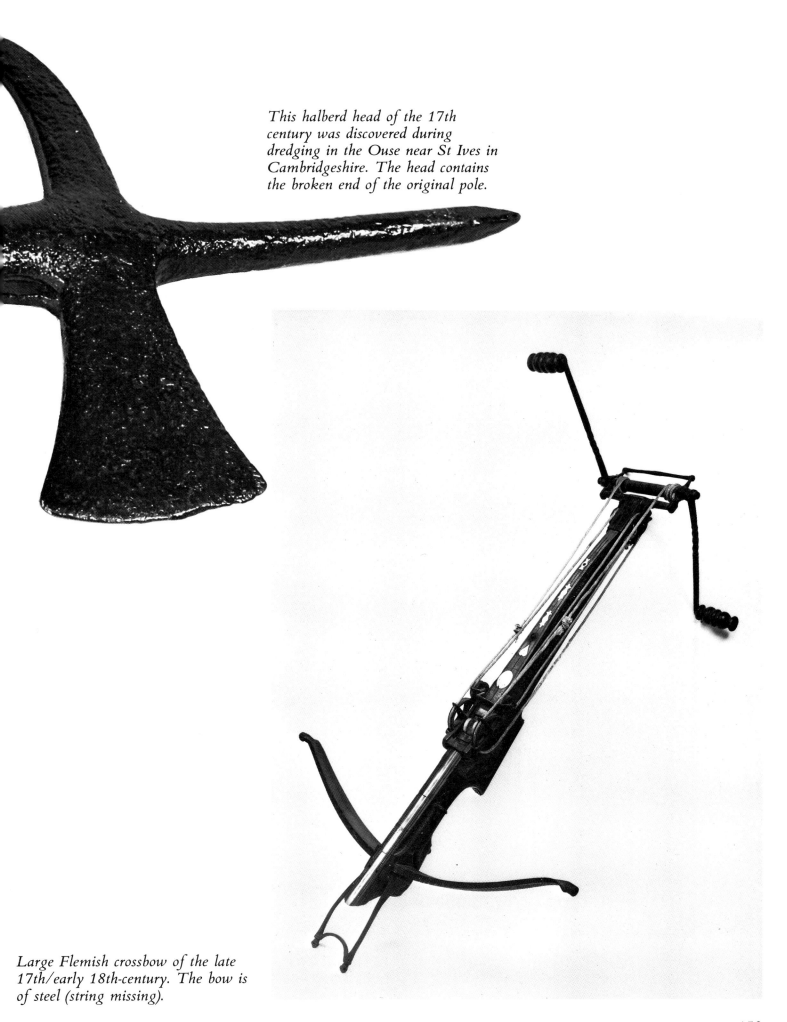

This halberd head of the 17th century was discovered during dredging in the Ouse near St Ives in Cambridgeshire. The head contains the broken end of the original pole.

Large Flemish crossbow of the late 17th/early 18th-century. The bow is of steel (string missing).

Bows and arrows

As we have seen, the only type of antique weapon likely to be available to the collector in this field is the crossbow and its relative, the stonebow, or prodd. Crossbows were devised towards the end of the 11th century (perhaps earlier, but the first records are in the last years of the century), and consisted of a metal bow fixed transversely upon a stock, with a wind-up mechanism to pull back the string and a trigger to release the missile, a short arrow or bolt generally known as a quarrel. The crossbow was extremely accurate and had a range greater (350+ yards or 320+ m) than the alternative hand short bow (150 to 200 yards or 137 to 182 m), though about six arrows could be fired from a short bow in the same number of seconds as one quarrel from a crossbow. The longbow was an improvement on the range of the shortbow, and was more effective on impact, but could not match the crossbow's accuracy. The crossbow survived as an important weapon of war for at least five centuries, despite the emergence of hand guns and artillery. Much artistry was put into the making and decoration of the stock, and many improvements were devised for the loading and firing mechanism.

Crossbows were used for hunting as well as warfare, and so continued to be manufactured long after their disappearance from the battlefield. Crossbow archery, if such a phrase may be used, was a popular sport for a long time in several parts of Europe, up to the present century in some areas – and indeed it is not unknown today. The crossbow that fired a bullet type of missile was made by some

Below: *An Italian stonebow (or prodd) with slender steel bow, folding arch back-sight, two fore-sight pillars, slender stock of rectangular section with curved neck, tapering butt with baluster pommel. It is 41¾ in. (106 cm.) long and was made in the late 16th century.*

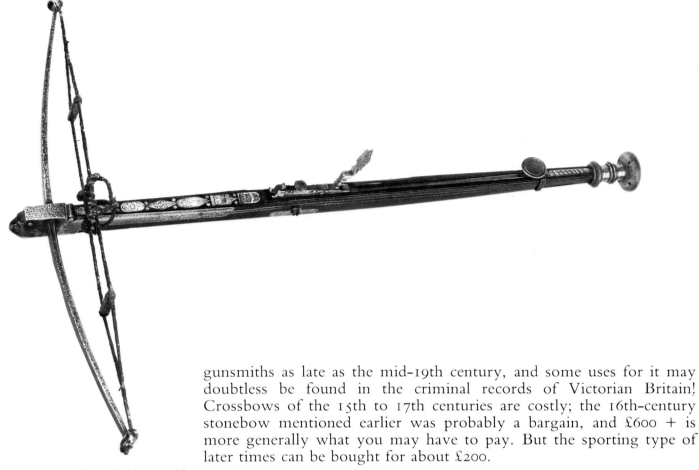

Above: A rare English child's prodd (stone-bow) of the mid-17th-century. This fetched over £1500 at auction in May 1983.

Below: A late 15th-century European hand-cannon which fired bolts rather than balls. Note the uncovered priming pan in the centre. The wooden stock is not original.

gunsmiths as late as the mid-19th century, and some uses for it may doubtless be found in the criminal records of Victorian Britain! Crossbows of the 15th to 17th centuries are costly; the 16th-century stonebow mentioned earlier was probably a bargain, and £600 + is more generally what you may have to pay. But the sporting type of later times can be bought for about £200.

Firearms

Firearms have been collected almost since they first were invented in the 14th century, probably because from the late 15th century they were as a rule finely made and often richly decorated, and most of them, like swords, were highly individual weapons, each differing in some way from the next. The fact that they have been collected by emperors, kings, nobles and commoners should not obscure the fact that firearms were made largely for offensive and defensive uses (and less widely for sporting and hunting use), and not for house decoration, personal adornment, or as works of art for posterity.

There have been numerous different types of gun through the history of firearms, and since we have space only to consider a few of the key examples we shall confine this survey to hand-guns, that is, weapons that discharge missiles, using gunpowder, air or gas.

The first hand-gun needed a stand to rest it on for firing. It was no more than a miniature cannon, of bronze or wrought iron, strapped to a pole with iron or leather bands. The earliest barrels were vase shaped (like the first cannons), and had straightened out into uniform cylinders before the end of the 14th century, the length of the cylinder being extended as military engineers discovered the relationship between length and accuracy of fire. The gun was loaded with ball and powder

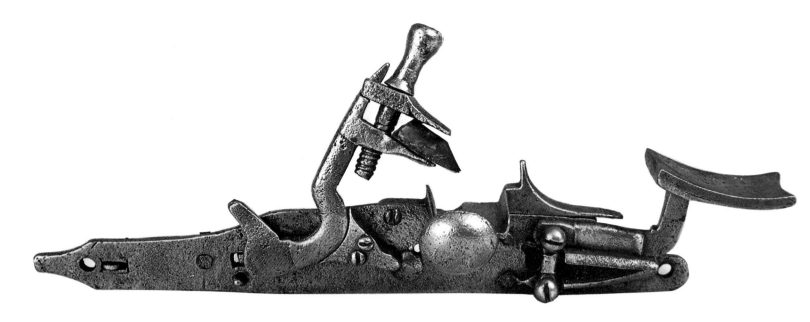

at one end and fired by igniting the powder with a taper touched at a hole in the top of the barrel. Eventually, barrels were fitted with a stock, and the weapon was fired from the shoulder, with what must have been an extremely powerful recoil. To lessen this problem, a hook was fitted near the muzzle (open) end which could be attached to a wall top or some other support while firing. Such adaptations were called, in German *hakenbusche* (hook-gun), in French *harquebus* and in English arquebus, from the French. You can see one or two 16th-century arque-buses in the Armouries of the Tower of London. Two examples of 15th-century hand-guns went through the saleroom three years ago. Because they were both plain and crudely made (one bronze, the other iron) they made only about £300 each.

The firing mechanism of the arquebus was improved at the begin-ning of the 15th century by the matchlock system, an S-shaped lever fitted to the outside of the stock, one tail of which held the taper while the other was the trigger. This device was the subject of much experiment and modification, but it remained basically the same for

Above: *An early type of flintlock mechanism where the steel is separate from the pan cover. Late 16th century.*

Opposite page: *Looking down on the mechanism of German wheellock rifle, probably made by Peter Opel of Regensburg at the end of the 16th century.*

Below: *A 17th-century German wheel-lock rifle, the carved stock embellished with paintwork. The chiselled lock shows a rural scene of merrymaking.*

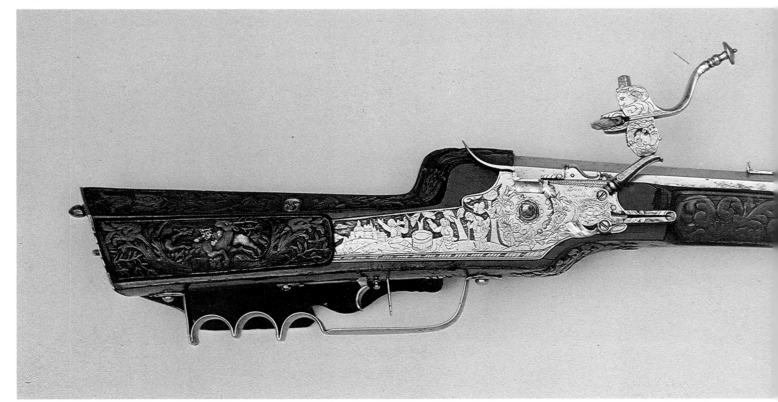

about two centuries. The matchlock device was applied to the arquebus before the arquebus had been modified for shoulder-position firing.

In the last years of the 15th century, a new kind of mechanism was introduced for firing hand-guns, the wheel-lock. Its introduction is generally ascribed to that universal genius of the Renaissance, Leonardo da Vinci, and he certainly drew several sketches of what is quite clearly a wheel-lock device for guns. It was essentially a steel wheel which was wound up against a spring, and which spun round when the trigger was pulled. In so doing it struck a spark to ignite the powder. The sparks were created by the rubbing of the wheel against a piece of iron pyrites. At some time in the middle of the 16th century a simpler mechanism was tried. An arm resembling a miniature vice into which a piece of flint was screwed was pulled back against a strong spring and latched into position. When the trigger was pulled the spring smashed the vice holding the flint down against a piece of hardened steel swivelled above the priming pan. The resulting shower of sparks ignited the priming and fired the gun. Guns operated by flintstone mechanism were known as flintlock operated, and from the 16th century until the invention of the percussion cap in the 19th century, flintlocks were the principal hand-gun mechanisms used in war, for hunting and for other sport. Of course there were improvements and variations, developed in different countries over the years, and to some extent the outcome of at least some battles was influenced by the relative effectiveness of these guns. At the same time, and perhaps curiously, matchlocks continued to be used for decades after the superiority of flintlocks had been amply proved.

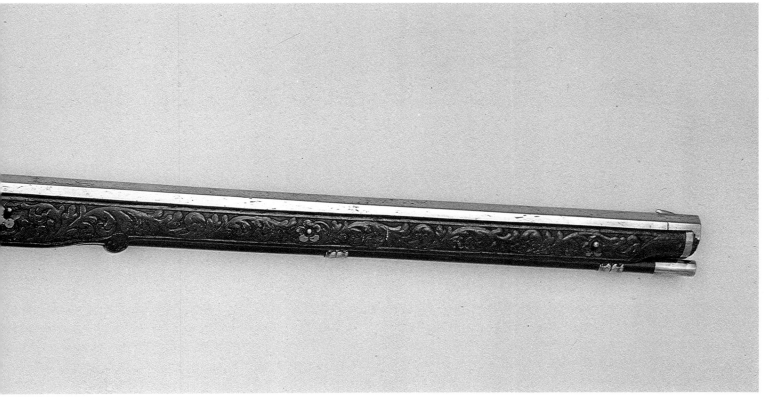

The arquebus was followed, though not necessarily superseded, by a lighter and smaller gun, the musket, sometime in the first quarter of the 16th century (though it is impossible to be precise in these matters). The word musket is said to have been taken from the Italian *moschetto*, which means a sparrow-hawk. In its earliest form it had a long barrel, longer than an arquebus, and it had to be supported by a rest. It fired a ball nearly 1 in (2.5 cm) across. Soon, this large gun was complemented by smaller versions that did not need rests, and which fired smaller balls. One was the petronel, invented in the early 17th century, a sort of cross between arquebus and pistol, and used by cavalrymen. Muskets remained a major weapon for warfare for at least two centuries. The most popular version in Britain was the 'Brown Bess', of which several types were produced over the years. Introduced in the 1720s, it was the principal hand-gun of the British army for the rest of the 18th, and the first forty years of the 19th century.

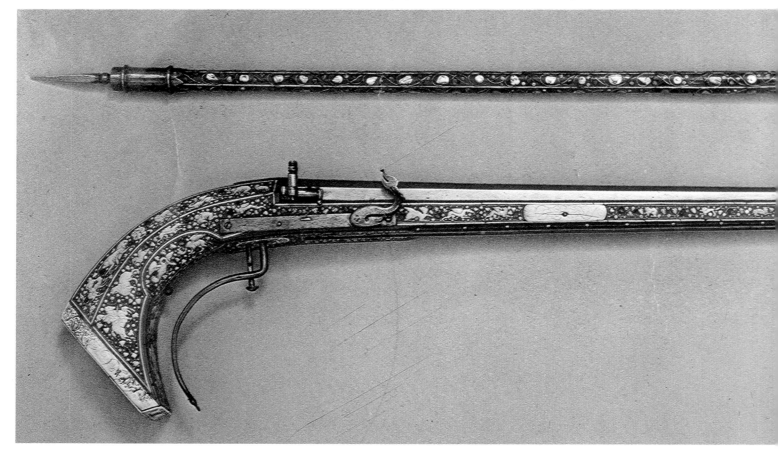

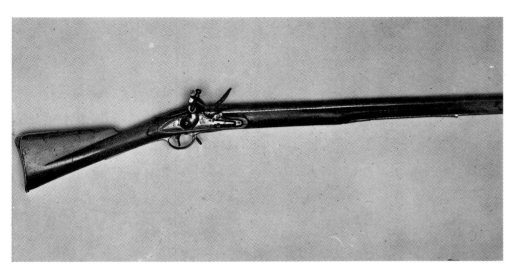

A good example of the famous 'Brown Bess' musket. This model of about 1810 is in the collection of the Ministry of Defence's Enfield Pattern Room.

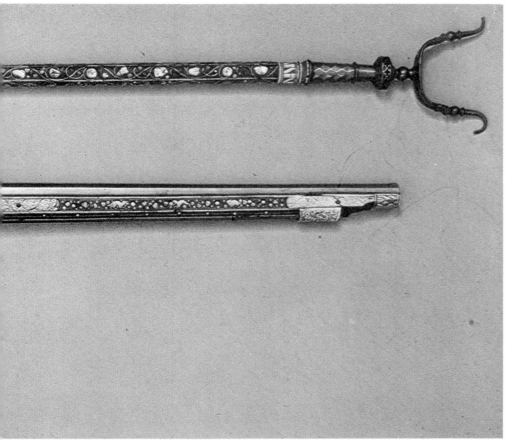

An English musket rest of about 1630, the wooden shaft inlaid with mother-of-pearl and engraved staghorn. (Below), a French matchlock of c. 1570, the walnut stock inlaid with engraved and stained staghorn.

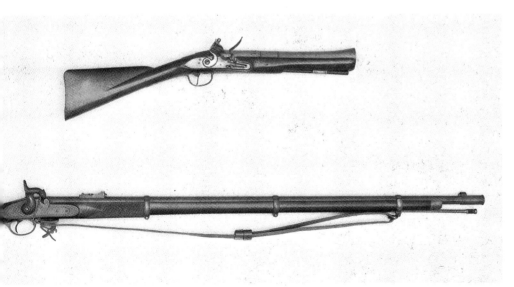

Eighteenth-century blunderbuss (top) and rifle from a private collection.

Pistols appeared in the 16th century. They were small one-hand weapons and were produced as a direct result of the introduction of the spark-producing wheel-lock mechanism. The flintlock pistol may have been introduced before the end of the 16th century. This had a long barrel with a small bore. (When we use the term 'flintlock' here, it includes all the snapping, spark-producing locks.) Another short weapon to emerge in the late 16th century was the blunderbuss, a kind of short musket with a gradually widening barrel (a little like a trumpet bell), which was intended to discharge a number of balls at one firing and acted as much as a 'terror' weapon as a life preserver. The blunderbuss was very popular in Europe for domestic protection, and when the stage coach arrrived, with its concomitant drawback of being subject to attack by highwaymen it became a favourite weapon for coach guards.

The principle of rifling the barrel of the hand-gun was worked out by German gunsmiths in the late 15th century. Rifling means making spiral grooves inside the barrel, enabling the ball to be spun on its way outwards, which greatly improved its capacity to travel straight towards target. The earliest rifling, however, was a very difficult skill to carry out, and it also made loading the barrel more time-consuming than the smooth bore. Thus until the later 17th century rifled barrels were not in common use in hand-guns for warfare, though guns made for sporting uses were often rifled earlier in the century. One of the first British service rifles was the Baker .625. This was introduced in about 1800, it had a seven-groove barrel and it was the standard British army rifle for about forty years. In America, the colonists who fought and won

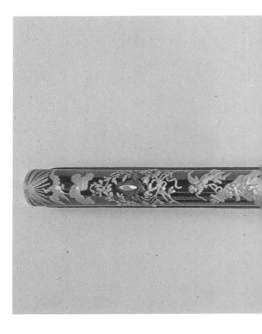

Two European ball-butted pistols of German pattern, the stocks of both engraved with staghorn. Late 16th-early 17th century.

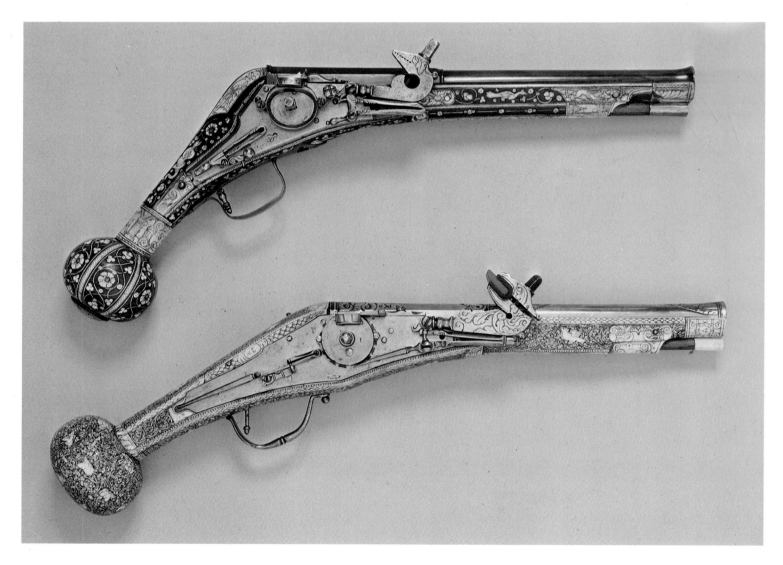

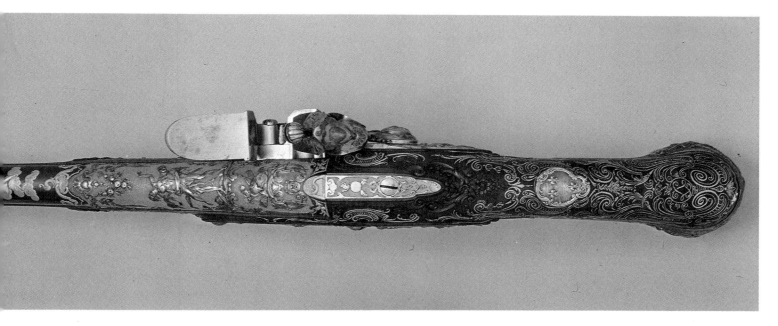

Above: *A late-17th-century French flintlock pistol.*

Below: *An interesting pair of Scottish fishtail pistols of the 17th century, with snaphaunce locks.*

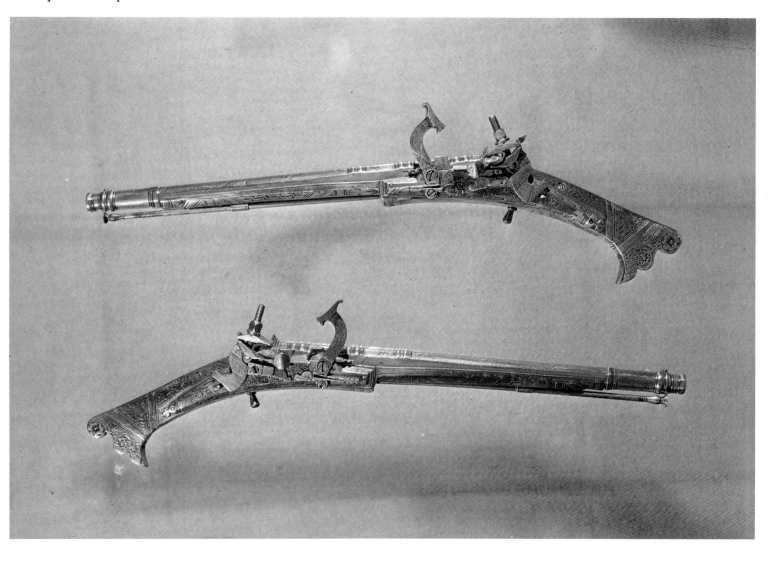

the great War of Independence (1774–83) had developed one or two rifles, in particular, the Pennsylvania Long Rifle, which was superior to anything the British infantryman carried into battle in that war, with the exception of the breech-loading 'Ferguson' rifle, which was decades ahead of its time.

Hand-guns, like swords, were for several centuries the receivers of the widest and most attractive variety of decorative treatments. The earliest stocks, for example, were decorated with all kinds of inlays, such as silver, ivory or mother-of-pearl. The match- and wheel-lock mechanisms were engraved, or moulded into special animal or fantasy shapes, executed with the greatest skills. Sporting and hunting guns thus elaborately decorated generally indicated the wealth or rank of the owner. Some guns were decorated to designs specially provided by leading artists of the time who worked in other fields, such as the German jewellery designer Virgil Solis (1514–62), who produced books of jewellery design and sheets of gun décor patterns, used all round

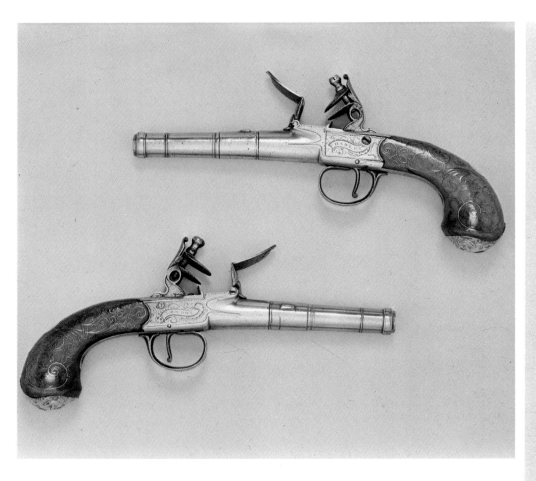

Above: *A pair of English late 18th-century flintlock pocket pistols with box locks and brass turn-off barrels, stamped 'Hadley, London'.*

Right: *A finely decorated pair of flintlock pistols, now in the Armouries of H.M. Tower of London.*

Europe, and the Dutch engraver Pieter Flötner (*c.* 1485–1546) better known for his designs which were executed by craftsmen on goldware and silverware. Special books of patterns for firearms were produced in the later 16th and the 17th centuries. There is one by the Paris maker, Nicholas Guérard, in the Victoria and Albert Museum in London. Many gunsmiths etched or engraved their names on the barrel top or on the lockplate (holding the wheel- or flintlock). It was the German gunsmiths who first employed the skills of artists and designers on firearms, but in the 17th century the initiative had passed to France and to workshops in Italy (especially at Brescia, between Milan and Padua, in north Italy). On the whole, continental hand-guns were much more elaborately decorated than their British counterparts, though there is no special reason for this; the skills were certainly obtainable in Britain. One view is that in England, gunsmiths preferred clean lines, efficiency of design and restrained quality of workmanship to the showy, sometimes meretricious 'tinselling' of some Continental gunsmiths.

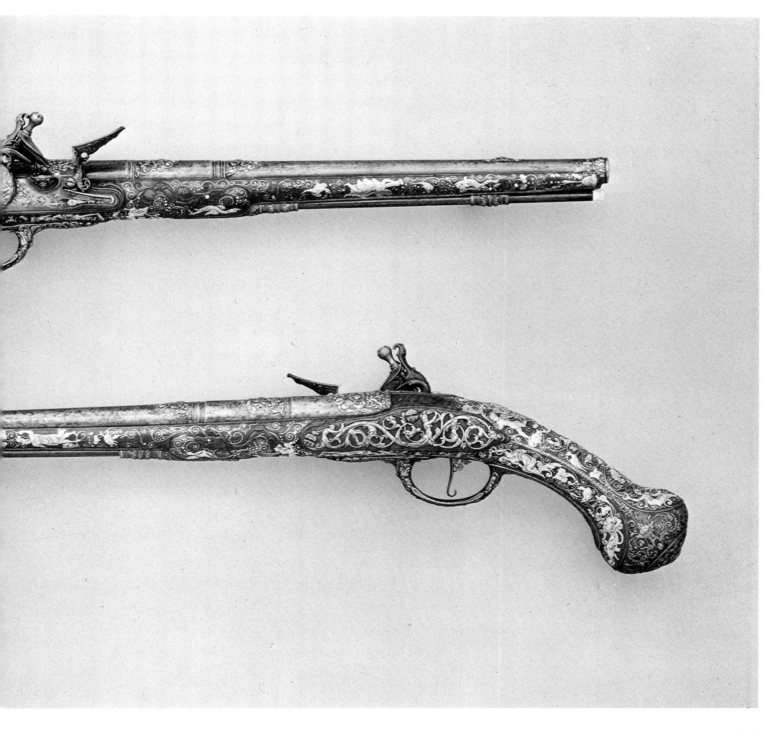

Clocks
and Watches

We do not know exactly when the geared mechanical clock first came into being, but from the earliest periods of civilization there have been numerous inventions directed to the accurate measurement of time. Apart from the sundial, which must in its crudest form have occurred to the very earliest men of knowledge, there have been various types of water-clock, particularly those invented by the ancient Chinese and ancient Assyrians.

The sort of clock mechanism we are familiar with today was probably first seen in the Middle Ages: there is an 11th-century Chinese record of what appears to have been a primitive escapement. In Europe, early monastic records use the term 'horologium', but it is not yet known whether this refers to a sundial, a water-clock or a mechanical

An early 18th-century German alarm clock. The bell rings and the candle is lit by means of a small charge of gunpowder ignited by a self-acting mechanism.

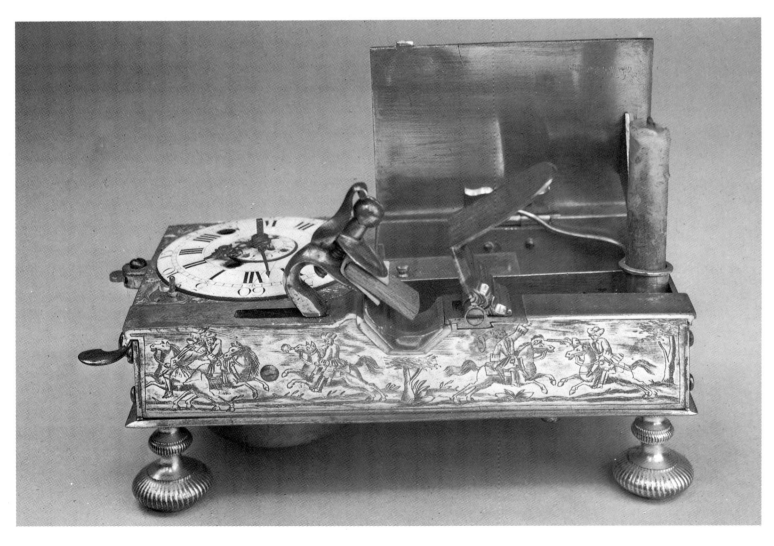

This German drum clock was made in Nuremburg in about 1590, and is housed in a silver-gilt case. The hours are shown by a single hour hand.

clock. By the mid-14th century, there are descriptions giving details of various astronomical devices that showed the courses of the sun, moon and planets, as well as the hours of the day; Dante mentions one such in his *Paradiso* (*c.* 1321). These appear to have been turret clocks (the domestic timepiece was not to emerge until the later 15th century), and they were driven by weights and regulated by what is called a 'foliot' escapement, whereby a balance with a weight hung on the end of each arm swung to and fro on the impulse of the pallets in the crown wheel. The oldest movement of this type in Britain is dated to about 1385/6 and can still be seen at Salisbury Cathedral. The mechanical clock at Strasbourg Cathedral is about thirty years older.

The development of more efficient springs led to the proliferation of smaller portable clocks, chiefly in Europe. At the same time, attempts were being made to counter the inevitable slowing down of the motion as the coiled spring lost power in opening. The 'fusee' was one device. It was a spiral round which a chain or gut line ran from the spring barrel. When fully wound, the line was bearing on the largest diameter of the spiral, and it moved progressively to the smaller end as the spring unwound itself. This device remained in use in much the same form right to the present century, especially in English clock movements. The round, or drop-dial, wall clock, often seen in antique shops, usually has a fusee mechanism.

If you intend to buy a clock, or to start collecting clocks, always check that they are working properly, for repairs are very costly and the people who really understand the older clocks are few and far between. Despite the enormous variety of dials, case shapes and movements, clocks since about 1600 fit neatly into five main categories: lantern clocks, bracket and mantel clocks, longcase clocks, carriage clocks and wall clocks. (The borderline between some small clocks and watches is blurred, but the book deals with watches separately later in this chapter.)

Apart from the turret clocks already mentioned, there is not much evidence of English clockmaking before about 1600. As in other fields, the English relied very much on immigrant Flemish or German craftsmen in the early years. The oldest surviving pieces, mostly of the early 17th century, are lantern types. Some of these were originally spring-driven, but these are now very rare, the majority having been converted to pendulum regulation later in their life. These clocks were made to be attached high on a wall on spikes or to stand on a table, and thus they can be said to be the forerunners of both the longcase clock and the bracket clock. Despite their appearances – and they changed but little over the long period of years in which they were made – they are by no means all ancient. In some country districts lantern clocks were still being made new in the early 19th century. In the late 17th century, when other more refined types of clock were becoming more fashionable, some well-known makers continued to make lantern clocks.

Apart from the rare balance-wheel variety, the earliest lantern clocks had 'verge' escapements of crown wheel and short, rapid-swinging 'bob' pendulum. Many of these were converted to 'anchor' escapement after the late 17th century, so an unaltered piece is much sought after, with prices running into thousands of pounds. Some 'converted' examples have more recently been 'returned' to their original verge form, and so the potential purchaser should examine carefully the brass plates for signs of disguised holes or marks.

In 1656, the Dutch physicist Christian Huyghens made one of the most dramatic contributions to clockmaking, by perfecting the long pendulum to a degree where great accuracy was possible. About fifteen years later, William Clement invented the anchor escapement, which was to be virtually a standard mechanism for longcase, wall and bracket clocks for the next two and a half centuries.

Longcase clocks

The exact origin of the longcase clock is still a matter of argument, but it seems to have appeared as a style of clock in both the Low Countries and England in the 1670s. The casing of a brass movement would probably have occurred much earlier if the short bob pendulum had not had such a wide swing. Once the long pendulum had been introduced, the need to enclose it became more obvious, not least in order to keep the dust out of the finer movements of the mechanism. Changes in cabinet-making techniques and a fashionable desire for grand proportions would in any case have helped to alter the appearance of clocks from the somewhat insignificant lantern clock.

Makers of distinction at this time include the Fromanteels, Joseph Knibb, Thomas Tompion (1639–1713), Edward East (1602–95) and William Clement (d. 1695), who were all leaders in what is recognized as a golden age of English clockmaking.

The first longcase clocks were about 6 ft (1.8 m) tall, frequently having an architectural pediment to the hood. The slender trunks were usually of oak, ebonized in the fashionable continental manner and divided into panels. The dials were small, 6¼ in (15.8 cm) to 9 in (22.8 cm) with corner spandrels of winged cherubs' heads. Another sure sign of a clock having been made before about 1700 is that the moulding beneath the hood is convex, whereas after that date it became

English early 18th-century longcase clock, with floral marquetry decoration, by James Cox.

An English mid-18th-century longcase clock in black lacquer case, the movement by Martineau of London.

A German table clock in hexagonal shape, made by Johannes Martin (1642-1720), of Augsburg. It has a thirty-hour movement, with alarm mechanism.

concave. The hoods of these clocks often slide upwards rather than forwards, as is more common later. This is a point to watch for when trying to examine the movement inside!

Unaltered clocks by any of the early makers are extremely valuable, but perhaps the best name of all is Thomas Tompion, and his work, whether with longcase clocks, bracket clocks or watches, at present commands the highest prices at salerooms. His fame rests largely upon his ability to produce extremely complicated and long-duration movements inside casing with the very finest finish. His early cases were in the ebonized style, but by the 1680s he was fitting his mechanisms into beautiful and simple cases of well-chosen figured walnut (he always preferred plain veneers to marquetry). Clockmakers were on the whole very conservative craftsmen, and the adventurous spirit in creative invention was often kept in check by the conservatism of the craft guild, the Clockmakers' Company. As a result, fashions were slow to affect the outward appearance of clocks. Ebonized examples were being produced long after the demise of this finish in other articles of furniture. The same happened with lacquer work. Chinoiserie was really out of vogue by the 1720s, yet clocks continued to be decorated with it right to the 1780s. On the other hand, mahogany for clock cases did

A thirty-hour longcase clock with country-made case and brass dial bearing a single hand. Early 18th century.

not come into popular use until the 1750s and even then it was worked in the styles more relevant to the walnut styles of the previous generations.

Longcase clocks, like other furniture, began to be decorated with marquetry work in the last two decades of the 17th century. The Dutch craftsmen who introduced it favoured designs of birds and flowers in bright colours, with the use of inlaid bone dyed green. This kind of marquetry was usually laid out in panels edged with boxwood stringing and set into a plain walnut ground. Later (after about 1700) the seaweed or arabesque pattern, with fewer colours, became fashionable. After about 1715, we see the use of arched top dials for tall clocks. The extra dial space provided by this allowed makers to add to the clock's functions, including moon phases, strike/silent control and, late in the 18th century, decorative novelties such as moving ships or Father Time swinging his scythe. The demand for this new type of dial became so strong in the early years that in order to meet it, square dials already in stock had arches riveted on to them. However, in the provinces, plain oak-cased clocks with square dials continued to be produced up to about 1820.

Apart from America, Holland was the only country to produce longcase clocks like those being made in England. Some of the ebonized and walnut examples are almost indistinguishable from their English counterparts – indeed, in the late 17th century, many cases were imported from Holland to house movements fabricated by the leading London makers. Sometimes it is possible to recognize a Dutch clock (assuming there is no name and town of origin) by examining the details of the case design, such as heavier mouldings, use of *bombé* shape at the clock base, or scrolls on the base or at the top front corners of the trunk supporting the hood. Such clocks often have quite large bun- or ogee-shaped feet as well.

French clocks

Although the French were in the forefront in early clock craftsmanship, they never went for the longcase clock as a style. In many ways, the variety of French 18th-century clocks is a limited one. André Charles Boulle's ubiquitous tortoiseshell and brass marquetry was used to decorate elaborate clock cases, and some of these were almost sculptural, being set upon pedestals or wall brackets and featuring as prominently as furnishings. The nearest the French craftsmen got to the longcase clock was the *regulateur*, which in the Louis XV period featured Rococo curves and bombé outline. At this time, bracket clocks and 'cartel' or wall clocks were being made in the same exotic taste, with ormolu and porcelain cases. In the 1730s–40s the dials were made of metal with inset enamel plaques for the numerals, after which came the well-known circular enamel dial, sometimes with metal numerals.

Despite the extravagances of the cases, the movements of French clocks were standardized in type quite early on. The two-train mechanism with plate lock striking (as distinct from the rack strike of 18th century English clocks) was enclosed between circular plates. Similar movements were mass-produced in the 19th century and are to be found in the typical Victorian marble clocks commonly found in British antique shops.

Louis XVI's reign roughly coincided with the Neo-classical period in design, and clock cases became more symmetrical and more slender. There was greater use of 'cool' unglazed porcelain and marble, and human and animal forms of ancient Greek inspiration were popular. The upheavals of the Revolution, which destroyed the strict guild system in France and put an end to royal patronage, were relatively short-lived, and Napoleon's Imperial court generated a fresh impetus in clock-

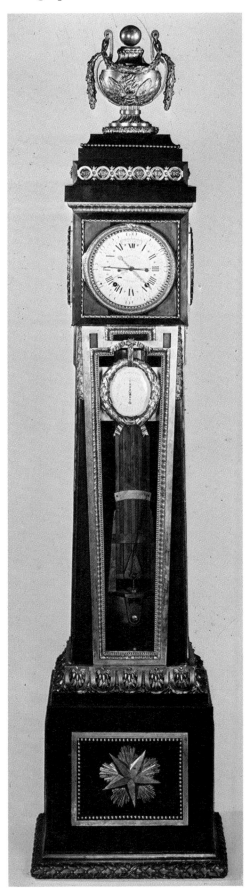

A Louis XVI ebony-veneered equation longcase clock, by Ferdinand Berthoud (1727-1807), of Paris. Berthoud worked for Julien Le Roy in the mid-18th century, before setting up on his own.

making, with many fine timepieces in the new Empire style.

From the 1770s, some fine *regulateurs* had been made, mostly in plain cases of mahogany with glass trunk doors and perhaps a few gilded mounts of classical form. These clocks had various different sorts of pendulum compensated to allow for expansion and contraction, in order to achieve greater accuracy. Some of these had a gridiron of alternating brass and steel rods, others had a glass cylinder containing mercury. The later 19th century in France saw a renewed interest in earlier styles (as in the furniture) and the cases are often of metal alloys like spelter. Despite this, the movements are still of good quality. One often sees marble clocks of the 1870s with visible pin wheel escapement, with ruby pallets. Another common sort was the set *à garniture*, which had accompanying figures, or urns, at either side for display on a mantelpiece.

There were various regional styles in France that were made in almost unchanged design from the late 18th century. One such is the 'Morbier' clock, made near Morez in the Jura mountains. These had lantern type movements, with a sort of upside-down verge escapement and frequently unusual striking combinations. They are easily recognizable by the circular white enamel dial on a decorative pressed-brass face plate. They either hang on the wall or are housed in rather ungainly walnut cases. They are not expensive, considering their attractive appearance.

A fine Rococo gold bracket wall clock by the 18th-century maker Pierre Le Roy of Paris.

A regulator clock in mahogany case, by Barraud of London, c. 1810.

A French 18th-century table clock supported by Chinese figures, made by Godin of Paris.

Advances in English clockmaking

From the 1680s, the accuracy of clocks had so increased that second hands were included on most longcase clocks. The English craftsmen were in the forefront of the clockmaking technology. Clocks with a very long pendulum had been made to run for a year, and Tompion, amazingly, produced a spring-driven year clock – the making of such a spring by hand shows amazing skill. There were also many elaborate striking devices, from the *grand sonnerie* in which the hours and quarters are struck at each quarter to musical clocks of eight, ten or twelve bells. The old circular locking plate control for striking gave way (except in country districts) to the 'rack' mechanism, between dial and front plate, from about 1705. Any clock with a 'Westminster' chime must have been made after 1793, when these chimes were first employed in the turret clock of St Mary the Great, Cambridge.

A clepsydra (water-clock) by Arnold Finchett, of Cheapside, London, of about 1735, now in the British Museum.

The vast majority of 18th century clocks to be found in antique shops today are of the two-train eight-day type or the simple country thirty-hour single train movement, both of which usually do no more than strike the hour. The former are the more valuable, on the basis that the longer the duration of run the more expensive the clock (though this may not apply if the clock is one made by a famous maker, specimens of whose work are rare).

Towards the last quarter of the 18th century the brass dial was replaced in England by the enamel or painted dial. A variation was the one-piece flat engraved dial of steel or brass with no attached spandrels or chapter-ring. Longcase clocks tended to employ the fashionable 'swan-neck' pediment on the hood, and especially in the north they were made increasingly broad with shorter trunks in relation to plinths. Lacquer cases of various colours continued to be made quite late in the century, but the best ones are usually earlier. Pine is only found in the humblest pieces, though with the present vogue these now command unwarrantedly high prices. Apart from London, Yorkshire and Lancashire were the most prolific areas of longcase clock manufacture in the late 18th and early 19th centuries. Many of these clocks are in wide mahogany cases, sometimes lavishly inlaid with stringing and shell motifs and with fussy turned columns on hood and trunk. The dials can be very decorative with painted scenes at the corners. The arched top is often taken up with moon phases or the representation of a ship rocking to the oscillation of the escapement. Because of their size, these clocks are perhaps undervalued today. Carved oak cases are occasionally encountered. These are mostly the work of the Victorians who took a delight in ruining the otherwise simple charms of plain 18th-century oak in order to make it look 'Jacobethan'.

A pretty table clock by J. Ellicott II (1706-72), in a silver-mounted case, the mounts designed and executed by George Michael Moser.

A circular ship's clock by Graham, c. 1735.

173

Apart from the balance-wheel type of lantern clock, most later bracket clocks had verge escapements and short 'bob' pendulums. In appearance the clocks from the 1670s to the 1750s were much like miniature versions of longcase clock hoods with domed tops and carrying handles. At first, of course, they tended to be less accurate, as they were driven by springs. But what they lost in time-keeping they made up for in convenience. There are far fewer pre-1750s bracket clocks than longcase clocks. This is partly due to the fact that the provincial makers tended to adhere to the weight-driven mechanism, which had always been easier to produce, the specialist craft of the spring maker being more associated with large industrial centres. Thus the average farm house was filled with longcase or wall clocks.

In the early 18th century, the need for very accurate time-keeping at sea led to a prize of £10,000 being offered (in 1714) by the British government for a chronometer which would allow longitude to be calculated to within 1°, and £15,000 for longitude to be calculated to within 30°. John Harrison (1693–1776), a Yorkshire carpenter's son, won the £15,000 prize for the latter, and he was followed by John Arnold (1736–99) and Thomas Earnshaw (1749–1829), who achieved even finer results. Such timepieces are in the sphere of scientific instruments (see p. 228) and are expensive to collect. But improvements in time-keeping technology filtered down to more ordinary clock construction. At the end of the 18th century, many more bracket clocks were being produced, now with circular enamel dials and in a variety of cases including 'balloon' and Gothic outlines. Mass-produced copies of both these types were turned out in the later Victorian period. They have standard French circular drum movements inserted into the solid wooden surround.

A well-constructed lantern clock of the late 17th century, by J. Baylis. The time was shown by a single hand, and the hours were struck on a bell above the clock.

An early 19th-century English bracket clock by J. Rose.

Far Right: *An unusual French carriage clock, in oriental style, with enamelled front face, late 18th century.*

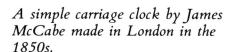

A simple carriage clock by James McCabe made in London in the 1850s.

Eighteenth-century types

The Regency period was very much influenced by French Empire clock styles. The English examples have fusee movements and can be distinguished from their continental cousins at a glance by the high position of their winding holes in the dial.

Reference has already been made to wall clocks of various kinds, but perhaps the best known 18th-century type is the so-called 'Act of Parliament' clock, supposedly the result of William Pitt's tax on clocks and watches, imposed in 1798 to help pay for the protracted struggle with France. These clocks, with enormous dials, were made for public display in places like inns where they could be seen by customers who had had to give up watches because of the tax. A good example of an Act of Parliament clock is in the George Inn at Southwark in London, and there is a fine specimen on the main stairs landing at Wolfson College in Cambridge. The clock at the George is of fairly crude construction underneath its finish of poor-quality black lacquer and gilt numerals. The dials, which might be circular or basically hexagonal, averaged about 3 ft (90 cm) in diameter. Genuine examples fetch large sums to-day, perhaps £2000 or more. Such clocks are the direct ancestors of the common white dial wall clock so familiar in schools, station waiting rooms or old offices. Nineteen-century methods of manufacturing meant that such clocks, sometimes with bells, could be powered by springs and sold cheaply. A version of this design was also made in the Black Forest of southern Germany, and it has a wooden movement.

Travelling and skeleton clocks

Travelling clocks can be as early as the 17th century, though few of these survive. In the 18th century circular dials about 5 in (2 cm) across had verge watch movements fitted, and these were hung in coaches or sedan chairs. The invention of what we know as the glass carriage clock can be attributed to the eminent French clockmaker A.-L. Breguet, in about 1800. From this emerged the brass and glass model so often reproduced today. Most of the 19th-century ones were made on the Swiss borders, and they varied in complexity from simple timepieces to alarm, strike and repeater mechanisms with cylinder and, later, lever escapements. Many were provided with leather-covered cases, some with a button on the top lid which if pressed plunged down to a button

Act of Parliament clock, of the very early 19th century, in japanned oak case, with gilded decoration and numerals. This clock has an eight-day movement.

A late 18th-century English urn clock by Benjamin Vulliamy (fl. 1770-1820), with ormolu mounts attributed to Matthew Boulton. Decorated with Wedgwood-made jasperware plaques which hide the winding and rise and fall apertures. The clock is flanked by a Derby biscuit porcelain figure of a woman, after a model by Jean-Jacques Spengler. The plinth is veneered in satinwood,

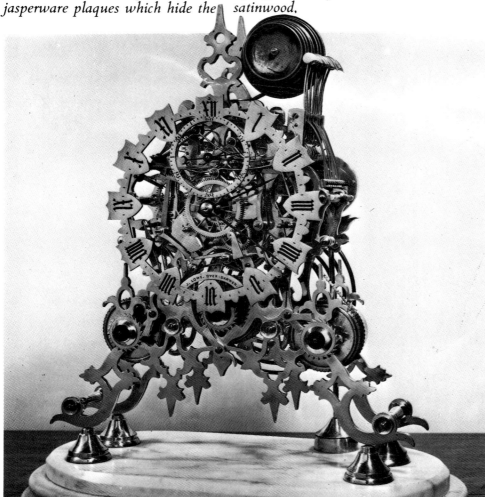

Above: *A fascinating mid-19th-century English skeleton clock, by J. Lowe, of Darwen, Lancashire, with eight-bell quarter-chiming movement and lever escapement. Mid-19th century.*

Left: *English 19th-century skeleton clock with large main wheel to give longer running periods between winding.*

on the clock itself and struck the hour nearest the time on the clock face – a useful feature when travelling in the dark. The value of these travelling clocks these days depends on such extras, together with the style and quality of decoration, and of course the survival of its carrying case. But expect to pay several hundred pounds for a nice travelling clock with case and repeater mechanism.

One form of clock beloved by the Victorians was the skeleton clock. The mechanism was visible under a glass dome, and the plates were shaped and fretted so that the whole effect was one of lightness. Though French in origin, these clocks (usually of some size) were made in great numbers in Britain, with strike chime or musical movements. Like carriage clocks, skeleton clocks are expensive.

American clocks

American clocks provide an interesting field for the collector, and a surprising number of varying kinds and from many periods have found their way over to Britain. In the earlier years, American clocks were very little more than copies of British types. The colonists were fond of longcase clocks – as their present-day descendants seem also to be – and after the War of Independence they began to make them in some quantity. The hoods reflected the furniture styles of the period, and the cases were made of mahogany, pinewood and cherrywood, with a great deal of skill and care put into them. Some craftsmen, wanting to economize, made the moving parts in wood, as was done here and there in parts of Germany, and they made them so well that little loss of accuracy in time-keeping was experienced. Such pieces were made by Cheney of Hartford, Massachusetts, Gideon Roberts, and David Rittenhouse of Pennsylvania. These and others are sought eagerly by collectors.

American clockmakers devoted their skills to wall clocks of many kinds. They introduced two most original and attractive types, the 'banjo' and the 'shelf'. The 'banjo' was first produced by the Willard family firm in Massachusetts at the beginning of the 19th century. These had eight-day movements and they kept very good time. Willard banjo clocks are in demand on both sides of the Atlantic. Many visiting US military and air personnel, stationed in the UK for two or three year periods, have sold these enchanting clocks to local salerooms and shops, and some have replaced them with carriage clocks or other decorated varieties.

The shelf clock is an amusing piece, though not of very high craftsmanship. When shelf clocks were first made, about 150 or so years ago, they were intended for export to Britain and Europe. They can still be found here, often in sales. One of the best-known makers was Eli Terry, of Connecticut, whose products often had wooden working parts. The casing, however, was the point of interest: it stood about 2 to 2½ ft (60 to 76 cm) high, and normally had a kind of architectural front, with pillar sides, broken arch top, or Gothic arch top, or occasionally, swan's-neck pediment. Below the dial was a painting or decorated panel. Sometimes these are referred to as steeple clocks, especially if they had finials rising on either side of the pointed arch over the clock face.

An American longcase clock by Simon Willard, of Willard Brothers, Massachusetts, about 1810.

Eighteenth-century Dutch clocks

We have seen earlier that the Dutch and the English clockmakers were making very similar clocks, especially longcase clocks, for a time. One type of Dutch clock that comes on the market from time to time in England is the 18th-century Friesland clock. This stood on a small bracket on the wall, had a posted movement rather like that of the lantern clock, and was generally most colourfully decorated on its dial. Sometimes there was a fretted canopy above the dial part. The Staart-klok of the later 18th century was a version of the Friesland clock, but with more of a typical longcase style arched hood. If there is any doubt about whether a clock of the 18th century is Dutch or English in origin, the method of striking can often provide a clue. The Dutch used a system whereby two bells were used, one high and one low. The hour was struck on the low bell, first quarter on the high, the half hour by striking the next hour on the high bell and the three quarter hour by one note on the low bell.

Watches

The other timepiece we have yet to look at is the watch. Although nearly everyone has a watch these days, few perhaps realize that craftsmen were making watches 500 years ago. The earliest watches were much larger than today, and were spherical, drum shaped or 'soap-tin' shaped, more like portable clocks. They did not keep good time, for the early mechanisms were mainspring operating through a succession of wheels, but the casings were invariably most beautifully made and decorated.

Watches take many curious forms, and they have many different escapements. Pre-17th-century watches are very rare, with the British lagging far behind the French and German craftsmen in this field, and by the 18th century, the French were leading the world in the making of rich and splendid watch cases. They were worked in gold, rock crystal or enamel, and shaped in many different ways: like crucifixes, skulls, books and tulip blooms, to name only a few. From the start, watchmaking involved two separate crafts, that of the watchmaker and the casemaker, and one often finds, for instance, an English watch in a case made at Blois or another centre in France, or a provincial movement put in a fine-quality case similar to those made in the capital.

The movements of watches are generally of brass. An aid to dating these is the shape of the pillars that separate back and front plates. Tulip-shaped pillars are of the late 17th century, balusters of square or round section are of very late 17th or early 18th century, and are sometimes similar to the turnings on furniture of the same period. The so-called 'Egyptian', or inverted, baluster is typical of the mid-18th century, whereas the straight cylinder turning suggests the greater mass

An English-made coach watch, with alarm and repeat mechanism and silver dial, made by Cabrier in London c. 1775. It has a Dutch-style arcaded minute ring. The outer case (right) is of silver, covered with black fish skin. The scale has been increased to show the detail.

English silver-cased verge watch regulated through the barrel and with partly jewelled train. By Edward Banger, London, c. 1710-20.

production of the late 18th and 19th centuries. In the end, pillars became much squatter as watches were made thinner, and these have a number of protruding bands around them.

As with clocks, English watch case design shows restraint when compared with European models of the same period. Plain silver was favoured from the 17th century onwards. Movements often had a 'feathered' engraved border round the edge. After the invention of the balance spring by Huygens in 1675, the 'cock' that holds one end of the balance pivot was made large to cover the large wheel. These cocks were often works of art in themselves in their fine filigree decoration. The early ones are oval in shape, but later on they became round, the piercing decoration giving way to surface engraving, including grotesque masks.

By the mid-18th century, watch dials were of white enamel, with blued steel bands and Roman or Arabic numerals, or they were silver. The precision work of horologists such as George Graham, the Reverend Edward Barlow, John Ellicott and Thomas Mudge led to great accuracy in watches by the close of the 18th century.

Popular watches for collecting are the 'hunters' and the 'half-hunters', which began to be made in the 18th century. The former has a cover for the front glass and another for the rear part of the watch. The half-hunter is a watch which has a small circle of glass in the middle

of the front cover through which you can see the position of the hands without having to open the cover. Both types are quite common. An almost limitless variety of decoration has been employed on them over the centuries, and this alone makes them worth collecting. Some were made by the great clock-makers such as Tompion and Ellicott, but they are extremely expensive. You would have to pay probably £800 for an early 19th-century hunter with a gold case, a few hundred less for one of silver.

The commonest watches to be found in antique shops today are semi-mass-produced pocket watches of the 19th century. The Swiss, who had been leaders in watch-making since the 16th century, introduced machinery in Geneva workshops as early as 1804, and the English watch trade suffered.

Jewellery

The origins of jewellery are almost as old as those of clothing; surviving jewellery artefacts from the days of the earliest civilizations in the 6000s–5000s BC show how much importance men and women have always placed upon the wearing of ornaments made of brightly coloured stones, shining metal, carved wood and ivory and other materials. They wore them for decoration; for identification; with engraved, carved or moulded symbols for religious or magical purposes; to demonstrate power, wealth, class or nationality; to illustrate the high quality of national craft skills, or simply to draw attention to themselves or underline their social standing. In many societies, the wearing of jewellery was regarded as a privilege, an emblem of rank (hence the strong association of rich jewellery with the first orders of knighthood in medieval Europe), but above all, people have always simply liked jewellery.

Medieval tastes were expensive and showy, and craftsmen were constantly both devising new ways of treating long-known materials and looking for new ones. Precious stones began to be cut and bevelled as well as polished; cameos were revived; new techniques of enamelling, always a popular form of jewellery decoration, were developed, with a much more exciting range of colour treatments. The discovery of new, rich sources of the precious metals gold and silver and of plentiful supplies of precious stones such as emeralds in the New World at the beginning of the 16th century enabled the growing number of craftsmen emerging during the Renaissance to produce a profusion of jewelled pieces of all kinds. Some of the great artists of the day happened also to be goldsmiths or jewellery designers; Ghirlandaio made jewelled garlands; Dürer, better known as engraver and painter, was also a fine goldsmith; Holbein designed jewels for Henry VIII; Benvenuto Cellini's fame is assured forever as a goldsmith along with his other distinctions. Yet little of this earlier jewellery remains outside museums or great collections, and one has to look to the 17th century for the earliest pieces that come within the reach of the collector of average means.

The 17th century

By the 17th century, enamel decoration in jewellery was beginning to give way to settings containing gemstones, such as emeralds, rubies, sapphires and topazes. Jewellery itself gradually ceased to be worn for its own sake and became a complementary part of overall dress. Necklaces, bracelets, ear pendants and rings continued to be worn, and new decorative motifs were introduced. One type of jewellery to flourish in the first half of the 17th century was what is called mourning jewellery, or *memento mori* ('reminder of human mortality'). It was perhaps a reflection of the sad and calamitous times, a period in Europe dominated by

An early 16th-century Italian lapislazuli cameo brooch, bearing the portrait of a Roman emperor.

The Barber Jewel, containing a cameo of Queen Elizabeth I.

the terrible Thirty Years War (1618–48) and in Britain by the disastrous reigns of James I and Charles I, culminating in the Civil War and the latter king's execution in 1649. *Memento mori* jewellery consisted of pendants of skulls and cross-bones, of brooches decorated with, or in the shape of, coffins, sometimes having a lid that opened to reveal a corpse inside. Families of distinguished or wealthy individuals who had just died handed out mourning rings to relatives, friends and retainers, which bore the deceased man's name or an appropriate motto.

Hat brooches, or badges, had been worn since the late Middle Ages, but in 17th-century Britain these became major features of men's decorative attire. Prince Henry (Prince of Wales in James I's reign until his premature death in 1612) had had a hatband of diamonds that cost £4000 in the money of those times (more than £1m today). Men also sported jewelled buttons and carried swords with jewelled hilts, and some men also wore ear-rings or a single ear-ring. For years Charles I

185

This is a superb 18th-century parure, of necklace and ear-pendants, in diamonds and spinel.

A pretty ring of rubies and diamonds set in a bow. English c. 1760.

The Mancini pearls. This is a pair of pearl and diamond earrings given by Louis XIV of France (1643-1715) to his childhood sweetheart, Maria Mancini, niece of his first minister, Cardinal Mazarin.

used to wear a single pearl ear-ring: the one he had on the morning of his execution on 30 January 1649 has survived.

The growing interest in gemstones stimulated lapidaries (gemstone cutters) and jewellers to design and produce many very fine pieces, using a variety of shapes and sizes of stones, setting them more openly and more adventurously. Cut stones in fact dominated jewellery in this period – and continued to do so for two centuries, until there was a reaction in the Art Nouveau age at the end of the 19th century. Faceting of precious stones became more precise and more symmetrical as the craftsmen improved their skills and had better tools and chemicals to work with. Most of the jewellery of the 17th century has not survived because it was broken up to make smaller pieces of different styles in later years, according to changes in fashion, it being much less expensive than buying newly made pieces. What we do have is mainly in museums and well-known private collections. It is rare for 17th-century jewellery of any kind to come to auction, and if it does it is beyond the reach of most collectors. And we have also to rely on surviving pattern books produced by the great designers of the 17th century, such as Gilles Légaré (b. *c.* 1610), jeweller to Louis XIV, who in 1663 published a pattern book that had a very wide influence in and outside France. Légaré's designs included models of the celebrated Sévigné brooch, a bow-shaped brooch balanced with pendant drops, named after Madame de Sévigné (1626–96), the Paris writer who had much influence on fashions of her time. Légaré actually included directions on how to set the various stones to make up the Sévigné brooch, and it is a style that was imitated for many years afterwards, the phrase 'Sévigné brooch' still being used today of modern imitations.

The one stone that was to dominate jewellery from the mid-17th century – and indeed ever since – was the diamond. Although known in Europe in the late 15th century, it was not till the 17th that it came to the forefront, partly as a result of expanding trade with India and Brazil, the two principal sources, and partly because of the development of much better techniques for cutting gemstones in general and diamonds in particular. For a long time, lapidaries had had major difficulties with cutting diamonds into symmetrical facets to make enough planes to produce that unique characteristic of the diamond – the sparkle at every angle. No tools of the period would do the job properly; diamonds were simply too hard. But gradually, craftsmen were able to overcome the problem, and by the second decade of the century the rose cut was achieved, though not perfected. This was a basic hexagon divided into equilateral triangles, resembling a dome whose surface was entirely composed of triangular facets. Some rose cut stones were made in Britain and elsewhere in the decade 1610–20, but it was the decade 1640–50 in which the skill moved forward with a leap, and it took place in France.

Indian dealers selling diamonds to European merchants had tried to explain that the only way to cut diamonds properly was to use diamond chips, and they showed them how to find the most suitable cleavage points. Encouragement came in 1640 from the Italian-born Jules Mazarin (1602–61), secretary to the great Cardinal Richelieu (1585–1642) and in 1642 to become Richelieu's successor as chief minister in France. He was a collector of jewellery and himself no mean specialist in techniques. He appreciated the potential value of rose-cut diamonds for jewels, and under his patronage Paris lapidaries were able to develop their skills. From time to time Mazarin offered to buy good products for his own collection. Thus was perfected the rose-cut diamond, which came to be called the Mazarin cut. It had sixteen facets and two tables (top facets), which produced the greatest brilliance so far achieved in a gemstone. The rose cut was the principal cut over the next half century or so, and it had a dramatic effect on jewellery, boosting the demand for diamonds of all kinds probably as no other innovation in the craft has done before or since, not only in France but over all Europe. In France, Louis XIV, who decided to govern the realm himself when Mazarin died in 1661, was an avid purchaser of jewels, especially of diamonds, and was no doubt delighted when Mazarin left him his jewellery collection in his will.

Although cut stones prevailed in jewellery of the 17th century, enamelling continued to be worked, and there was a ready supply of fine articles made by enamel specialists all over Europe, using new techniques. One process was introduced by the Toutin family of

A pretty mid-18th century necklace of diamonds in a stylized flower and leaf motif.

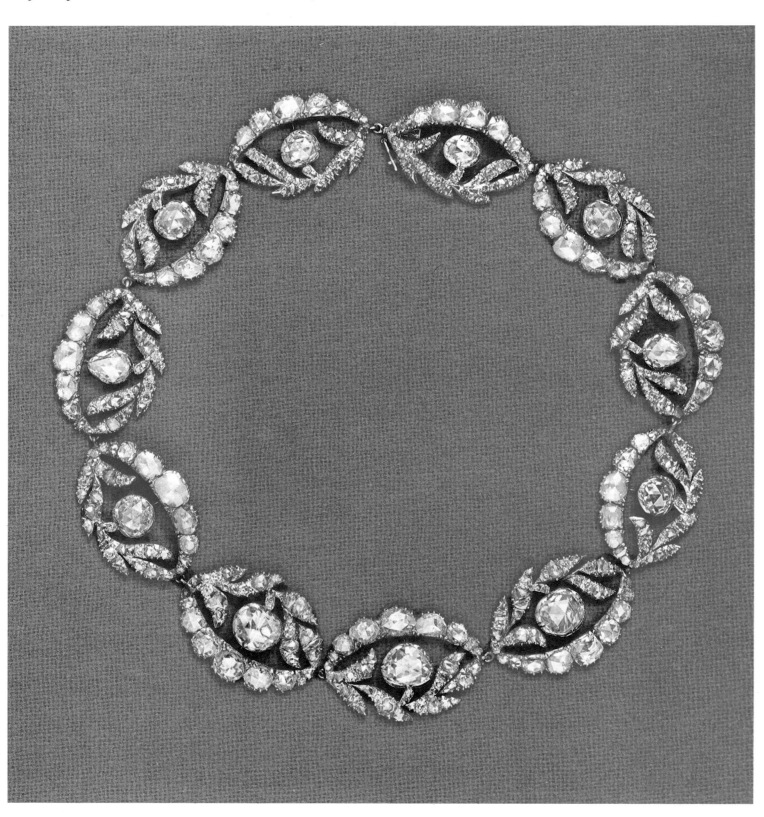

Châteaudun (not far from Orléans), in which the piece was given a background of one colour, fired, the design painted on the firing with a brush and then fired again. Another French technique was *émail en resille sur verre*, that is, enamelling on glass or crystal. The design was etched into a hard glass base, the etching was lined with very thin gold sheet and then filled with low melting point coloured enamel, a very difficult operation to carry out without cracking the glass. This style of enamelling was used for some wearing jewellery, but more so for small boxes, watch cases and so forth. The technique was practised in Britain with much skill.

The age of the diamond

The 18th century was the age of the diamond, in jewellery terms. Right from the start, and for the first half of the century, diamonds were used in every conceivable kind of jewel piece, to the almost total exclusion of all other gemstones. Pieces such as girandole ear-rings (a large stone with three or more stoned pendants hanging from it), crochets (brooch-like pieces mounted on a pin and worn on the chest), Brandenbourgs (jewelled clasps for bodice fronts, sometimes sported in different sizes in descending order), rings (including mourning rings), châtelaines (decorative plaques of jewels with accessories hanging on chains such as a watch, a watch key, a seal), Sévigné brooches (still fashionable), pendant necklaces, pendant crosses and crucifixes, floral sprays, aigrettes (sprays on stalks worn at the side of the head, the stalks sometimes mounted *en tremblant*, that is, on tiny springs so that even slight movement sent the whole jewel shimmering), were made in great quantity and with the finest skill in most European countries. The jewels of this century were notable for their lightness and delicacy, the settings skeletal to provide the minimum background and support for the dominating stone or stones.

Many jewels were set in silver, which was less obtrusive than the gold of earlier periods. So popular was the diamond that even in the earliest years of the century there was a flourishing market for substitutes, and among the best of these was the white paste of Georges Frédéric Strass (1701–73), the Viennese jeweller who settled in Paris in the 1730s and produced a splendid imitation by adding lead oxide to flint glass, in the manner of George Ravenscroft's invention of clear crystal glass (see pages 86, 87–8). Before Strass, jewellers had used rock crystals, known in Britain as Bristol diamonds because of the

A diamond ribbon brooch, with suspended pearl, of about 1760.

A lovely emerald drop brooch, of late-18th century design, recently sold at Christie's.

industries there that made them. A great deal of paste jewellery was made in the 18th century, some deliberately to deceive, some simply to meet demand.

The innovation that set off this mania for diamonds was the invention of the brilliant cut. This technique of diamond cutting was introduced by the Venetian lapidary, Vincenzio Peruzzi, in about 1700, and by it he was able to exploit to the full the glorious optical qualities of the diamond without seriously affecting its weight. He cut the stone in fifty-eight facets, all visible when set in open-claw settings. The light entered the stone and was reflected by the rear facets. Brilliant cuts generally rise to a point in the centre of the top side. The brilliant was a dramatic advance on the rose cut, and the technique was applied to other gemstones. Rose cuts, however, were not discontinued, for they were cheaper and so satisfied the demands of people of moderate means.

Opposite page: Fine 18th-century diamond and emerald necklace with pendant, pair of diamond and emerald drop ear-rings, a diamond and ruby brooch with pendant, and two diamond and emerald rings.

Left: Eighteenth-century paste jewellery, English or French: at the top, a white paste tiara set in silver; in the centre, a white, yellow and red paste brooch, also set in silver; at the bottom, a yellow paste brooch, set in gilt-metal.

A finely executed pair of bracelet clasps, in diamond and blue paste, set in gold. The pair was made in France in the late 18th century.

The designs of the jewellery of the 18th century did not slavishly follow the changing styles of that interesting and extravagant age. The advent of the Rococo which materially affected interior decoration, furniture, silver and some ceramics, had a minor influence upon jewellery, noticeable chiefly in asymmetrical designs in France of the 1740s and 1750s and by the re-appearance of other gemstones alongside the diamonds to produce splashes of colour. Rococo designs were especially popular in Spain, Italy and Russia. Among the pieces in Rococo style were *rivières* (chains of separately set stones as necklaces), *pavé* settings to many pieces (*pavé* means stones placed so close together that the surrounding metal is barely visible, a highly skilled technique), and *parures* (sets of matching pieces of necklace, ear pendants, bracelet and brooch).

Despite the enormous quantity of jewellery made in the 18th century, some of it listed in inventories, diaries and correspondence of the period (and, of course described in novels), comparatively little has survived in its original form, since it was re-cut and re-set in later generations. Most brilliant cuts were altered, and there are few originals to be found even in museums. Some rose cuts were also altered, but rose cuts have survived in greater quantities, probably because they were not always considered worth re-cutting. Some diamond floral sprays, a speciality of the later part of the century, have survived because they remained fashionable along the years while other styles were dropped.

Above: *An 18th-century pendant of rose-cut diamonds, enamel, seed pearls, ivory and hair. Human hair was often employed in jewellery, and pieces containing it were favourite gifts to loved ones.*

Cut steel jewellery

In the second half of the century, there was a vogue for jewellery made from cut steel. Steel had been used for small articles since the Middle Ages, chiselled or cut to very intricate patterns, but it was not until the late 17th century that cut steel began to be used as a material for a variety of jewellery items. Steel could be cut in facets to produce the sort of brilliant gleam one gets from marcasite, that is, iron pyrites, often used as a diamond substitute. The steel was soft and easy to facet, and many interesting and in some cases very attractive items have survived.

Opposite page: A most attractive Spanish necklace and earring set, of different coloured topazes and rose-cut diamonds. The set was made in the 18th century.

192

Cut steel jewellery was produced in Britain in a number of cottage industries in and around Woodstock, near Oxford, from about the middle of the century, and it was also produced at Salisbury. Horace Walpole (1717–97), an arbiter of taste, actually approved of some of the products! The Woodstock industries were superseded by the products from the factory in Birmingham set up in the 1760s by Matthew Boulton (1728–1809), in partnership with John Fothergill (d. 1782). Their business produced, among other things, jewellery and cut steel buckles, sword hilts and buttons. Shoebuckles were then worn widely throughout the land and in Europe by men, and were decorated in diamond or paste or made of silver or of cut steel faceted and polished to look like diamond. Boulton and Fothergill co-operated with the Wedgwood china firm to produce cut steel frameworks for Wedgwood 'jasper' stoneware which was finely polished to yield stones of great beauty, particularly for necklaces, bracelets and châtelaines. Some of these combined efforts are regarded as among the most beautiful steel jewellery ever made. There is a necklace, a lovely example, at the Lady Lever Museum at Port Sunlight in Cheshire.

Two interesting 18th-century English buckles, the left one used to hold a cravat in place.

Jewellery for a wider market

Jewellery fashions changed quite sharply as a result of the French Revolution of 1789–94. In France itself, jewellery almost disappeared after the first days of the upheaval following the fall of the Bastille (14 July 1789) and for several years it was no place to be seen wearing any jewellery – unless it was a mounted stone chip from the walls of the Bastille itself or an ear-ring in the form of a miniature guillotine! Vast quantities of royal and aristocratic jewellery was seized (though some was hidden on a barge near Brest), broken up, the gold and silver melted down and the stones sold off to help the bankrupt French treasury and to pay the troops of the Revolutionary armies. But in fact, even before the Revolution, jewellery was being worn less and less in western Europe, and much more of it was already being made of less costly materials, even at court and among the wealthy.

Once the Revolution was over, the jewellery began to reflect the tastes of the bourgeoisie that had triumphed over the aristocracy, and the new styles were different from those of *l'ancien régime*. Similar changes took place elsewhere in Europe and in Britain. Emphasis shifted from the production of jewellery made of costly stones in expensive settings, especially diamonds which, in France at all events, were a dirty word, and by using improvements in technique, jewels were fashioned with cheaper semiprecious stones in mechanically produced settings, that is, machine stamped rather than hand chiselled. The resulting jewellery looked expensive even if it was not, and it became accessible to a much wider public. There was a return to costly jewellery, including diamonds, in the time of Napoleon, especially after his coronation as Emperor in 1804, and his first wife Josephine spent huge sums on individual items, quite as much as Marie Antoinette, widely considered the supreme spender in her time, whose extravagances as much as anything else had contributed towards the determination of the National Assembly to put her to death in 1793. But below the circles surrounding the Emperor's court, the cheaper jewellery continued to prevail.

The Napoleonic era was marked by several jewellery vogues, among them a widespread enthusiasm for cameos in numerous guises – on tiaras, bracelets and necklaces, as individual brooches and on rings, portraying Roman emperors, Greek mythological heroes and heroines, pastoral scenes with cherubs, and pictures of celebrated or royal historical personages. Original cameo stones were employed where obtainable, but copies were also made in abundance, sometimes imitated by engraving on sea shells. Cameos were not new, but never before had they been worn in such profusion (belt, necklace, bracelet, tiara at one and the same time, complained a Paris women's magazine in 1805), nor by so many people. And to celebrate Napoleon's Egyptian campaign,

A group of Berlin ironwork jewellery: top and bottom, a bracelet and pendant cross of about 1870. The necklace in the middle is of ironwork cameos and mesh linked with gold settings, made about 1800.

scarabs had become fashionable, as well as rings etched with hieroglyphic designs.

Coral and amber beads began to appear as decoration for the superstructure of the new fashion of combs worn to hold the hair in place, and ear pendants and necklaces were decorated with these stones, sometimes strung in several rows. The tiara, invented in an earlier age, came into fashion at the turn of the century, and there was hardly a woman in court circles anywhere in Europe who did not wear one with formal dress at balls or receptions, dinners or public engagements. Some were made in elaborate openwork settings with diamonds, pearl drops, emerald briolettes, while others were of fine gilt metal bands, or pinchbeck (gold substitute), encrusted with cameos or imitation cameos or shells or semiprecious stones. Another new fashion, worn on both sides of the English Channel, was the long necklace, which coiled round the neck several times and ended with a large coil reaching to the waist. These were of pearl beads, or enamel plaques, or small stone clusters, linked by chains of gold or gilt or silver. A French variation, the *sautoir*, was draped over one shoulder, extended to the waist and ended with a locket or pendant or cluster of jewels.

A type of jewellery that emerged in the last years of Napoleon was Berlin ironwork. This was first seen in quantity in the first decade of the 19th century, characterized by fine pieces created from black enamelled thin wire woven into geometrical or naturalistic patterns. Medallions in necklaces of Berlin ironwork were particularly beautiful, like wrought iron in miniature. After the collapse of Napoleon's Russian campaign in 1813, the conquered peoples of central Europe began to stir, and in Germany there was a Prussian rising against the French. Expensive jewellery was called in to finance the war, and in its place, patriotic donors were given ironwork jewels, mostly from the Berlin workshops, much of it stamped with the legend 'I gave gold for iron' in German (*Gold gab ich für Eisen*). Berlin work continued to be made long after the downfall of Napoleon in 1815.

The end of the Napoleonic régime and the resulting economic depression in a Europe ravaged for years to finance Napoleon's military adventures were marked by a slump in the jewellery business, and it was not considered right in many circles to wear expensive jewellery in the face of so much distress. In Britain, the recession struck as hard as anywhere else, and austerity ruled for some years. But there were some interesting developments in jewellery. Emphasis moved back to the settings as the use of semi-precious stones replaced precious stones. Amethysts, pink topazes, aquamarines, turquoises, chrysolites, and many others became popular, some set in filigree gold work, or in a new technique, granulation, created by the depositing of numerous tiny gold grains on a prepared gold surface, yielding a matt surface to accentuate the less brilliant semi-precious stones. *Parures* of these stones mounted and linked with filigree or granulated or plain gold began to be made and sold in special *parure* cases, many of which have survived. Brooches began to appear in naturalistic patterns, such as butterflies, flowers, ears of corn, wild roses, in diamond, precious stone and the new semi-precious stones. Ear pendants became elongated but narrow, 2 to 3 ins (5 to 7 cm) long, bracelets began to be worn on a scale said never to have been enjoyed again since, and enamelling returned to fashion, especially for colouring jewellery in floral patterns. And mourning jewellery continued to be made.

The accessibility of jewellery opened up to a far wider public, made possible by the use of machinery for pressing out the metal framework or for cutting the stones, generated a variety of styles and colours too extensive to summarize here, and which more properly belong to a resumé of Victorian jewellery, beyond the scope of this book.

Prints

Prints have always been a favourite subject for collectors. It is possible to assemble a collection to suit the most modest of resources and to please more or less any taste. They can be framed and hung on the wall or they are easy to store in a folder. The great artists of the past regarded prints as a worthy medium of expression, and whilst a painting by one of these artists would probably be out of range of most people, a fine proof etching or engraving might not. Whilst not as unique as a painting or drawing, prints have their own variations depending on the edition and thus the strength of image. Collectors will gradually improve the quality of their print stock as their knowledge increases.

At its simplest, a print is an impression made by a block or plate which has a design made on it by one of a number of processes. Some familiarity with the different techniques of print-making is necessary for a full enjoyment of the subject.

The first kind of printing method used in Europe was the woodcut. A block of beech or pear wood was cut, leaving raised lines and surfaces which would print as the finished design. It is believed that playing cards were being printed in this manner as early as the 1370s, and it is assumed that fabrics were decorated with repeat woodblock patterns considerably before this. The oldest existing prints on paper, from the early 15th century, are called 'black books', and were produced in Germany. By the end of that century books such as the *Biblia Pauperum* were using woodcuts to illustrate the printed text. Some of the great exponents of the woodcut at this period include Albrecht Dürer (1471–1528), Lucas Cranach (1472–1553), Lucas Van Leyden (1494–1533) and Hans Holbein the Younger (*c.* 1497–1543). Of course genuine prints by these masters fetch huge prices when they are sold, but it is sometimes possible to purchase 15th- or 16th-century single pages from psalters or bibles, so that this period can be represented in a collection. Towards the end of the 16th century the woodcut was superseded by line engraving, and was only revived sporadically after that by artist-craftsmen like William Blake and William Morris.

Line engravings are printed from highly polished metal plates – usually copper, but sometimes steel, silver or pewter – on which a design has been incised with a sharp tool called a burin. This craft is first recorded in Europe in about 1450, but the first major artist in the medium was a man named Martin Shongauer (1430–91). The great Italian painter Andrea Mantegna is also credited with some fine engravings. The English came onto the scene in the 1540s, but this was mostly in the field of book illustration, and it was not until William Rogers' famous late 16th-century work entitled *Eliza Triumphans*, celebrating the victory over the Spanish Armada, that English engraving came into its own.

The average collector is unlikely to buy pre-17th-century prints, and even in the 17th century English engravings are rare. One name

Portrait of the 17th-century English philosopher Thomas Hobbes, by William Fairthorne, one of the supreme masters of engraved portraiture.

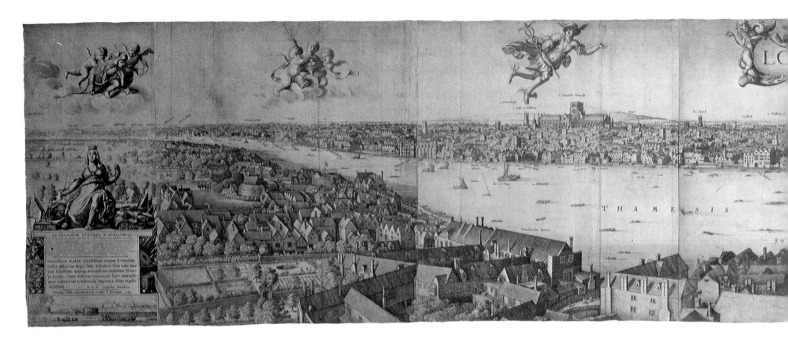

Above: *London, as engraved by Wenceslaus Hollar in 1647.*

stands out from the early years of that century, that of William Hole. He is well known for his maps but he did publish some good portraits, including one of Chapman in the 1616 edition of the latter's *Homer*. William Fairthorne (1616–91) was a master of the engraved portrait, and he cut plates after Van Dyck which retained the artistic power of the originals.

Right: *The copper-plate engraving 'Melancholia' by Albrecht Dürer, the foremost German artist of the 16th century, who was for a time court painter to Emperor Charles V.*

Diverse techniques

During the 17th century, etching became the most widespread technique for printmaking, and all the great artists practised it to some degree. Simply, the method involves coating a copper plate with a special kind of wax into which the artist cuts his picture. The plate is then immersed in acid and this bites into the metal where the wax has been removed. Great subtlety is possible in etching, as the plate can be cut again and again, giving many grades of shading.

Wenceslaus Hollar (1607–77) introduced the art of etching into England. Most people are familiar with his famous panoramic views of the Thames, but his total output was over 2,500 plates of such diverse subjects as religious scenes, portraits and townscapes. His etchings are of great interest for their topographical detail, and this was a feature that was to become more and more important in English print-making. Indeed it is true to say that by the 18th century the English were in the forefront in recording the landscape and its antiquities in an accurate and matter-of-fact way that is invaluable to modern historians. Many collectors who cannot afford the expensive productions of the artist/printmaker concentrate on the humbler works by copyists.

The development of the English print in the 17th century is traceable through the work of four major artists – Fairthorne and Hollar, already mentioned – and Francis Barlow (1626–1702) and Francis Place (1647–1728). Barlow was supreme in the painting of birds, animals and field sports. His 110 etchings illustrating *Aesop's Fables* are very important in the history of the art. Francis Place started as a talented amateur, but under Hollar's guidance produced some good topographical etchings from sketches made on his travels. From the late 17th century there was an increase in the number of topographical and travel books published, and England seems to be the greatest producer of such works. Dozens of amateur antiquarians had their researches published by subscription, with the result that numerous histories of small towns and antiquities have come down to us. These are usually illustrated with engravings of varying artistic quality and accuracy – some indeed are so primitive that they are almost laughable in their naïvity. Nevertheless, collectors of modest means have frequently been interested in the comparison of different views of a particular locality known to them. Sometimes these engravings are coloured (usually done in recent years) which makes them more attractive.

F. Boucher pinxit.　　　　　　　　　　　　　　　　　　　　　　J. Janinet sculp

Prints from books such as *Boswell's Antiquities of England and Wales* appear loose in booksellers' folders. These vary enormously in quality. Some of the best are by engravers like W. and J. Walker and Lowry, others, such as those by Thornton and Carey, are more primitive.

By the early 19th century steel engravings were more common than those on copper. Some beautiful views of cathedrals (drawn more accurately as a result of the new interest in medieval architecture) were engraved after drawings by Hablot K. Browne (1815–82) – 'Phiz' of Dickens fame. Other sets of views include well-known London scenes by Thomas Shepherd of 1828, and those of the Thames and the Medway after Tombleson. The truly romantic taste can be seen in the views of the coast of England and the Scottish Highlands taken from originals by W. H. Bartlett. Even J. M. W. Turner's work was engraved at this period – a considerable task considering this great artist's 'impressionistic' style of painting.

The 18th century

Until the early 18th century the French and Italians favoured highly stylized mannerist subjects or wildly romantic ones, but the work of Antoine Watteau (1684–1721) signalled a change in emphasis to a soft lightness of touch characteristic of the Rococo. Important names at this time were those of H. F. Gavelot (1699–1773), François Boucher (1703–70), Charles Eisen (1720–78), Charles N. Cochin (1715–90) and Jean Honoré Fragonard, (1732–1806). Their subjects were often of fantasy and the method sometimes employed was a mixture of engraving and etching on the same plate.

Venice was the centre of Italian printmaking. Both Tiepolo and Canaletto published etchings, but perhaps the most remarkable of Venetian etchers was Giovanni Battista Piranesi (1720–78). His views of the ruins of classical Rome have an awesome grandeur and melancholy made all the more poignant by the inclusion of tiny human and animal figures in 18th-century dress. His etchings were exremely popular, as the discovery of the remains of Pompeii and Herculaneum had given rise to an upsurge of interest in the archeological past. Since his time many copies have been made of his work.

Above: *'The Consultation', one of the illustrations by 'Phiz' (Hablot Browne) for Charles Dickens'* Nicholas Nickleby.

Opposite page: La Toilette de Venus. *Coloured engraving by François Janinet of the original by François Boucher.*

Opposite page: *One of the leading portrait engravers of the 18th century was George Vertue, who engraved or etched pictures of nearly every famous person, both male and female, of his time, as well as many notables of earlier days. This is an engraving from the Kneller painting of the philosopher John Locke.*

Below: *Engraving by William Hogarth, 1747, from his* Industry and Idleness *series. This is 'The Industrious 'Prentice grown rich & Sheriff of London'.*

Below: *For decades after Hogarth's death in 1764, copies were made of his famous engravings. This is one of Hogarth's 'Gin Lane' by H. Adlard.*

The most famous engraver of the 18th century in England was William Hogarth (1697–1764). He proved that printmaking could be both aesthetic and popular, and became rich after the first editions of his series, *The Rake's Progress* and *The Harlot's Progress*. First editions of these are very expensive, but competent copies abound up to the early 19th century. Hogarth also published a book called *The Analysis of Beauty*, delineating aspects of art in an allegorical manner, but these curiosities are not perhaps so much to the modern taste as *Marriage à la Mode* or his satirical engravings of electioneering.

As far as portrait prints are concerned, George Vertue (1684–1756) is probably the best known in England. His series on the kings of England and great figures of the past can be found frequently in antique and print shops, but most are late editions.

The INDUSTRIOUS 'PRENTICE grown rich & Sheriff of London.

Proverbs Ch: IV. Ver: 7, 8.
*With all thy getting get understanding,
Exalt her & she shall promote thee: she
shall bring thee to honour, when
thou dost Embrace her.*

Plate 8

JOHN LOCKE EH

Lock
Vol III.

G. KNELLER Eques PINXIT 1697

203

The Northumberland artist Thomas Bewick (1753–1828) re-introduced the art of wood engraving (as distinct from woodcut) whereby the picture was engraved into the end grain of a boxwood block. His exquisite prints of animals and birds have a naturalistic charm that has made them popular ever since. In fact the technique of wood engraving became the primary method for copying photographs for newspaper printing until the end of the 19th century.

Another process that became fashionable towards the end of the 18th century was that of mezzotinting, originally introduced in the mid-17th century. Basically this involves roughening the surface of a plate, then working over it to produce areas of varying smoothness. The effect is one of softness, like a watercolour. Aquatinting was a similar method except that the plate was covered with resin, which was worked on and then dipped in acid. Both these techniques suited the prevailing artistic tastes of the day represented by Thomas Gainsborough, Sir Joshua Reynolds and George Morland. William Ward (1766–1826) copied originals by these and other artists. He was particularly adept at

Opposite page:
An aquatint of the Great Hall at the Bank of England, by Thomas Rowlandson (1756-1827), of c. 1809.

Opposite page, below: *The celebrated Northumberland wood engraver, Thomas Bewick, specialized in nature subjects, notably animals. His* History of Quadrupeds *(1790) featured many charming engravings, including 'The Lancashire Ox'.*

Below: Hare Shooting, *coloured engraving by George Morland.*

the technique of stipple engraving, in which many dots and dashes were incised into the plate to suggest subtle gradations of shading. One of the most successful series of prints using this method was the *Cries of London* engraved after Francis Wheatley by Shiavonetti and Cardon. A Florentine artist called Francesco Bartolozzi (1728–1815) moved to London in 1764 and was soon made Engraver by Appointment to George III. His most notable stipple engravings were a set of portraits after Holbein. Interesting Bartolozzi prints can still be bought for less than £10.

It was the British who excelled in the field of mezzotinting at the end of the 18th century. One of the greatest names associated with the art is that of Valentine Green (1739–1813). He had a skill in the subtle gradation of tone that makes his work almost superior to the originals from which he copied (usually Reynolds). Most mezzotints are taken from portraits. The first English ones, by men like William Sherwin, Isaac Becket and John Smith in the 17th century had been from originals of Charles II and his court by Sir Peter Lely and Sir Godfrey Kneller. The mezzotint lost favour in the early 18th century, but was revived

Below: *Caricature by F. Bartolozzi, the 18th-century engraver, entitled 'Dr. Arne playing Rule, Britannia!'.*

Right: *Engraving, probably by Schiavonetti, of one of the series of paintings* Cries of London *by Francis Wheatley. This one is 'Round & Sound! 5d a Pound! Duke Cherries!'.*

Opposite page: *A lithograph of St Dunstan's in Fleet Street, London, by Thomas S. Boys (1803-1884), dated 1842.*

in the later years, when the great portrait painters gave artists new inspiration for working in this medium. It was the steel-engraving process invented at the end of the 18th century that dealt the final death blow to the mezzotint.

Of all subjects, by far the most numerous from the later 18th and early 19th centuries are sporting prints. Neary every country antique

James Gillray, Scottish-born caricaturist, engraved over 1500 caricatures, full of humour, and sharp satirical comment on the leading personalities of his day, and on social follies which often drew his most biting criticism. This is an etching entitled 'Metallic tractors'.

Opposite page: *'Dr Syntax Skating', by the English caricaturist, Thomas Rowlandson, from his illustrations to his* Tours of Dr Syntax.

Below: *The most famous sporting artist of the first half of the 19th century was H. W. Alken, who produced colour prints on all aspects of hunting, and other sports. This is one of his series on fox-hunting.*

shop or sale has at least one sporting print showing hunting, racing, shooting or boxing, taken from original paintings by artists like James Pollard (1797–1859), T. Blake or Henry T. Alken (1785–1851). Hundreds of sets of sporting prints were published, but some of the most interesting are *Shooting Discoveries*, *How to Qualify for a Meltonian*, *On the Road to Derby* and *The First Steeplechase on Record*. Coaching scenes are also of perennial popularity, and engravers like Thomas Sutherland (b. *c.* 1785) and T. H. A. Fielding (1781–1851) produced some fine prints after Pollard's paintings.

The Napoleonic Wars inspired both patriotic and satirical feeling which were celebrated in prints and paintings. The great naval battles like the Nile and Trafalgar, painted by such artists as Thomas Whitcombe (b. *c.* 1760) or Clarkson Stansfield were engraved by many craftsmen and sold in quantity. The satirical strain in English temperament reached its most vitriolic in the political cartoons of James Gillray (1757–1815) and Thomas Rowlandson (1756–1827). The latter specialized in etching the follies of society with no punches pulled, but he was equally at home in more gentle mood lampooning the foibles of his clerical creation, Dr Syntax. This came out in book form, describing Syntax's various tours, and went into many editions.

Left: *'Whooping Crane' from* The Birds of America *by J. J. Audubon, the great American ornithologist and artist.* The Birds of America, *produced over the years 1827-38, contained fine coloured figures of over a thousand birds.*

Bird prints

The 18th century was a time of scientific inquiry, especially in the sphere of natural history. This resulted in the publication of many beautiful books embellished (from about 1730) with coloured engravings of birds and plants. This type of book was produced up to the 1830s when lithography and chromolithography tended to replace the copperplate. Books with bird prints have always been in the greatest demand by collectors, and one would need considerable resources to purchase a complete volume by one of the better-known artists. Nevertheless, individual plates can be found much more reasonably, and the collector can specialize in prints of a certain species of bird, the work of one artist or one nationality.

The three countries most associated with this kind of print are Britain, France and Germany, though the name of the American ornithologist J. J. Audubon (d. 1851) stands above most for his great work *The Birds of America*, published between 1827 and 1838. Altogether there are 435 aquatints, the first ten of which were engraved by W. A. Lizard and the rest by Robert Havell and his son Robert Havell junior. Even if these were within the scope of the average collector (in January 1984 a volume of Audubon's *Birds* fetched a record £1 million at auction in London) these prints are hard to come by outside the United States.

In France in 1802 Jean Baptiste Audebert published *Les Oiseaux Dorés ou à Reflets Metalliques*. This had 190 engravings printed in colours by colouring the plate rather than hand-colouring afterwards. The French excelled in this sort of innovation in colour printing, exemplified by the well-known early 19th-century flower plates of Redouté. One of the great German authors of the mid-18th century was Johann Frisch, famous for his *Vorstellung der Vogel in Deutschland*. This contained 255 folio-sized engravings, but they are now very rare, despite two reprintings.

Perhaps the most complete series of bird books from one author are those by John Gould, who issued plates of over 3,000 different birds between 1831 and 1888. These, which were lithographs, dealt with the birds of temperate and tropical regions of the world. He was assisted in this work by his wife, H. C. Richter and Edward Lear.

Opposite page: *Redouté rose prints are collected widely. They were produced by various members of the Redouté family, the best known probably being Pierre-Joseph Redouté, who executed this 'Rosa Damascena' in his volume I of* Les Roses, *1817.*

210

Rosa Damascena.　　　　　　*Rosier de Cels.*

P. J. Redouté pinx.　　　Imprimerie de Rémond.　　　Charlin sculp.

Technical advances

Apart from the commercial uses to which wood engraving was put, lithography as a process temporarily took over from copper engraving in the 19th century. Lithography, which was invented about 1796 by Aloys Senefelder, involves drawing on smooth stone with a special greasy pencil or ink, which then accepts the greasy printing ink and rejects water. It proved to be remarkably robust in large editions, enabled an almost photographic clarity and was of particular attraction to watercolourists like Richard Parkes Bonnington (1802–28). With the backing of the French government he published the lavish *Voyages Picturesque et Romantiques dans L'Ancienne France* in 1822. Samuel Prout, J. D. Harding and Thomas Shotten Boys also contributed lithographs. The latter is now famous for his *London as it is* (1842) and *Entrance to the Strand at Charing Cross*. A final perfecting of the lithographic process took place when Charles Hullmandel (1789–1850) developed a means of printing colours instead of hand-tinting a print. This made lithography the most popular illustrative form in the late 19th century, especially on the continent, where it was exploited with great skill and imagination by such artists as Toulouse-Lautrec, Degas and Delacroix.

Here we should mention one of the great innovators in the field of colour printing in the 19th century – George Baxter (1804–67). His development of printing techniques that could produce colour cheaply in quantity yet excellent quality was literally to bring colour into the lives of many – all those too poor to afford hand-tinted prints. Baxter's work reflects the preoccupations of the Victorian era – missionary exploits, the royal family, children, sentimental love, and romantic scenes abroad. Many of his smaller prints were used to embellish the multifarious little boxes that Victorian ladies would use for pins, buttons etc. Baxter's processes were eventually 'stolen' by other printers, adapted and developed, and Baxter himself died poor, unable to cope with this harsh business world. His prints enjoyed a revival in the 1920s (when many fakes were made) and are enjoying popularity again today in common with all things Victorian. Serious collectors should, however, make a careful study of Baxter's techniques, his subjects and his stamped mark, to avoid the pitfall of reproductions and forgeries.

Below: *A view of the North Midland railway line, showing alternative transport of the 1840s – packhorse and canal boat. This is a lithograph by S. Russell.*

Opposite page: *Baxter prints are collected widely today. George Baxter introduced new techniques enabling colour prints to be produced cheaply. This is a print of the painting* Hollyhocks *by V. Bartholomew.*

The last decades of the 19th century and the first of this saw a revival of many of the old printing skills, partly due to the interest shown in them by artists of the so-called 'Arts and Crafts Movement'. Many amateurs 'had a go' at etching, which is probably the most accessible of the processes, and junk shops are full of these rather gloomy products. Nevertheless, there were some supreme artists working in the field of print-making at this time, and they may be at present considerably undervalued by the majority of dealers.

The opening up of Japan in the mid-19th century led to a craze for anything from that country, and the Japanese woodcut (which was virtually the only method used there) was avidly collected and copied by Western enthusiasts. The brilliantly coloured Japanese prints of the 18th century are now mostly in the hands of the great museums or private collections, but a modest but attractive collection can be put together by not being too fussy about chronology or completeness. Whatever the grade of prints one decides to specialize in, condition must be a prime consideration. This, of course, must be weighed against rarity and the stature of the artist.

Engraving of the Battle of New Orleans and the Death of Major General Packenham, January 1815.

Overleaf: *Hand-coloured mezzotint portrait of Benedict Arnold, the notorious American general who defected to the British side during the War of Independence. This portrait was by the English engraver Thomas Hart, 1776.*

American prints

America produced a great variety of prints, especially in the 19th century. The earliest examples of American subjects were done by Europeans, but by the end of the 17th century locally produced prints were being made. John Foster was the first truly American printmaker whose name is known, although there are a number of anonymous prints by amateurs. These early prints are usually fairly crude and are rare in the British Isles. It was not until the early 18th century that individual prints began to be produced in quantity. William Burgis published views of New York (1719) and Boston (1722), but even these were engraved in London. Only a few engravers were working in America in the 18th century, and these were mostly employed illustrating Bibles and periodicals. After the war of independence the influx of professional printers changed things yet again. The first years of the 19th century saw a proliferation of very attractive aquatint views which are eminently collectable today. Robert Havell Jr, having completed the engravings of Audubon's *Birds of America*, did some good aquatints of New York, Hartford, Connecticut and a view of Niagara Falls in the 1840s. In 1846 Henry Papprill engraved Catherwood's view of New York from Governor's Island and in 1849 his bird's-eye view of New York from St Paul's steeple.

The Americans also produced many interesting historical scenes of battles from the War of Independence and the War of 1812–14. Amos Doolittle engraved some important plates depicting battles, *The Battles of Lexington and Concord*, in 1775, and in the same year Bernard Romany engraved his *Exact View of the Battle of Charlestown* (Bunker Hill).

As far as portraits are concerned a large number were produced from the late 18th century onwards. Charles Wilson Peale (1741–1827) made some rare mezzotints of Benjamin Franklin, Lafayette, William Pitt and George Washington. George Washington's portrait was obviously popular, and other engravers, including Edward Savage (1761–1817) and Cornelius Tiebout (*c.* 1777–*c.* 1830), made likenesses of him; a total of 880 different portraits of Washington are in fact recorded.

Lithography became popular in America soon after its introduction in Europe. Businessmen soon appreciated the commercial possibilities of this process, and consequently a large amount of interesting historical material is available to collectors. There are portraits of all sorts of settlers as well as of the North American Indians after the artists J. O. Lewis and George Catlin (1796–1872). Others include romantic scenes, the farmstead, city and suburbia. As in England, portraits of soldiers in regimental dress were popular at this time, and artists include A. Hoffy and F. J. Fritsch. Similarly, sporting prints were liked in the United States – a particularly American type being those of the famous trotting races and the horses involved. Another field for the collector is that of maritime prints, which became more common as America's navy built up after the War of Independence. Edward Savage, Francis Kearney (b. *c.* 1780), Benjamin Tanner (1775–1848), Tiebout and Abel Bowen (1790–1850) all contributed memorable plates of naval actions. Accurate 'portraits' of ships were also fashionable – the frigate *Constitution* being the most often depicted. Lithographs of the 'state' class of frigates appeared in the 1830s, published by Childs and Inman.

Of the many other aspects of American life delineated by the printmakers, the railroad provides perhaps the richest field for the enthusiast. Lithographs of locomotives, viaducts and disasters were made from the late 1830s. Endicott and Swett published *The Carrolton Viaduct* in 1831, a typical civil engineering print of the time, whilst large and very colourful lithographs of individual locomotives were issued by S. W. Chandler of Boston some twenty years later.

COLONEL ARNOLD.

Who Commanded the Provincial Troops sent against QUEBEC, through the Wilderness of Canada, and was Wounded in Storming that City, under General Montgomery.

Maps

The vast majority of maps fall into the category of printed matter, although collectors can spend large amounts of money on rare manuscript maps which, if they come on to the market at all, usually appear only in specialized sales. Most book and print dealers carry a selection of antique maps, as many of these were published first in books and atlases which may have been broken up for some reason or another. They are now very popular decorative objects, with the added appeal that they are a view of a particular part of the world as one of our ancestors might have seen it. In recent years the interest in early maps has increased faster than in many other branches of collecting. This perhaps reflects the current enthusiasm for local history, archaeology and the history of early travel.

To study the development of cartography in the ancient world is beyond the scope of this book. Many maritime and wayfaring peoples have put together charts to assist them in their trading and hunting journeys, but the name that stands out above all others in the early days of geography is that of Ptolemy, who lived in the second century AD. His *Geographia* dominated the Christian and Muslim world for 1500 years. During the Middle Ages, map-making changed little – some would say its accuracy increasingly gave way to religious allegorical imagery. The art of producing charts for trading voyages was preserved by the Arabs, and to a lesser extent by the Portuguese, Catalans and Italians.

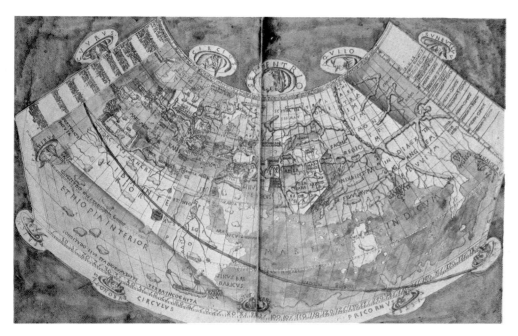

Terra Australia Incognita, *a map based on a description by the 2nd century AD geographer Ptolemy.*

Italy's favourable geographical position combined with a tradition of navigation and skilled craftsmanship made her a natural centre for the map-making industry at an early date. In the realm of printed maps Italy has the distinction of being the first to print Ptolemy's *Geographia* in Bologna in 1477. This and later printings in Rome and Florence display beautiful-quality copper engraving. By the late 16th century other great atlases had been issued, including Bartolemeo Dalli Sonetti's *Isdario* (on islands) of 1547, and Livio Sanuto's *Geografia* of 1588 which was the most important work on Africa up to that date. In spite of the number of these atlases published, very few appear on the market today. Individual maps can be found and are always worth possessing for their singular virtues of sobriety and accuracy. However, Italian supremacy was to be short-lived. By the end of the 16th century the important trade routes had moved from the Mediterranean to the Atlantic seaboard, and this was to give the ascendancy to cartographers from the north west European countries such as Britain and the Low Countries. Some would class the Dutch and Belgian map-makers as the best in the history of the science, and indeed they seem to dominate the period from about 1570–1670. Abraham Ortel, or Ortelius as he is better known, born in 1527, was one of the best of these. Having already published maps of the world, Egypt and Asia, Ortelius issued his famous *Theatrum Orbis Terrarum* in 1570. This was the first uniformly sized systematic collection of maps of the countries of the world taken from contemporary sources since Ptolemy's original work. The *Theatrum* was immediately popular and was reprinted many times in a number of languages until the early 17th century.

Map of the World by Abraham Ortel (Ortelius), published in 1571.

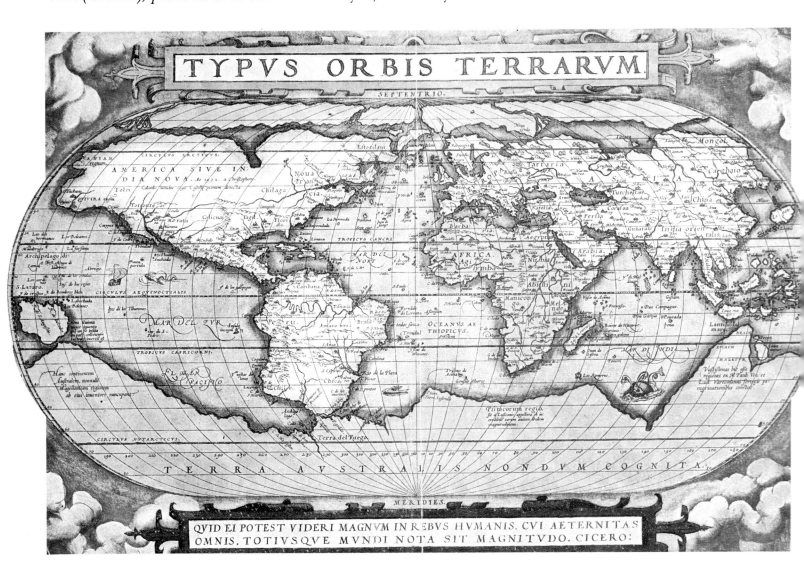

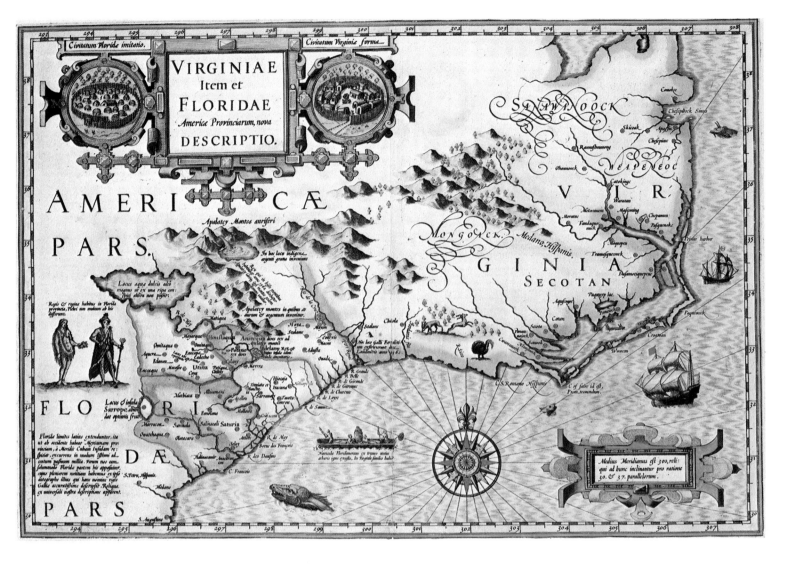

Map of Virginia and Florida, taken from the Mercator-Hondius Atlas, *early 17th century.*

Gerhardus Mercator's name is known to most of us through his projection of the globe (1568). (It was he in fact who first used the word 'atlas' to describe a collection of maps.) In 1583 he started his best-known work called simply the *Atlas* (only a handful of his earlier maps exist), and this was divided into three sections – France, Belgium and Germany, with fifty-one maps. In 1590 the second part added Italy and Greece (23 maps), and in 1595, a year after he died, came 36 more plates. All these maps are beautifully engraved (some are coloured) and have fine lettering. Mercator's maps can be bought individually in Britain, but after 1595 the *Atlas* went into no fewer than forty-six editions with variations of format and in different languages (French, Latin, English, German and Flemish), so the date could be anything from 1602 to 1641. The true pleasure of finding these old maps lies partly in constantly broadening one's knowledge of the different editions and comparing them.

Mercator's publishing business eventually fell into the hands of Jodocus Hondius (1563–1612), who continued to issue the atlas from time to time. Jan Jansson joined Hondius's son in 1633, giving Mercator's work nearly a century of continued impetus.

In England at this time two of the household names in Elizabethan map-making had been active publishing the much-loved county maps which were to become typical of the next two centuries. The first of these cartographers was Christopher Saxton, who was born about 1542. Under Queen Elizabeth's authority he surveyed the English counties, and between 1574 and 1579 produced his striking county maps. They are to be found plain or hand-coloured, and are among the most sought-

219

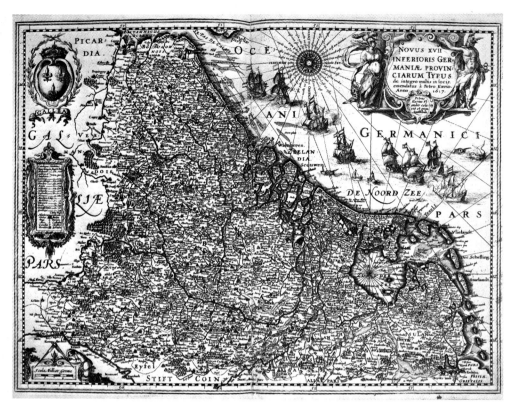

Map of the Province of the United Netherlands, by Pieter van der Keere, 1617.

Copper-plate map of Northampton and adjacent counties in original hand colours. Engraved by Christopher Saxton, 1576, and published in London, 1579.

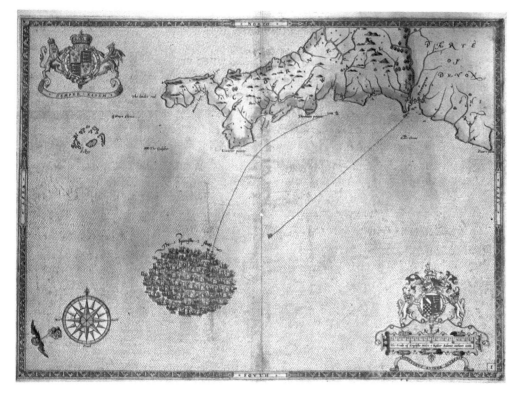

after in the British Isles, for good reason. Not only is the standard of engraving superb, but the maps are surprisingly accurate, and there is just the right amount of pictorial decorative detail. Originals from the first edition are rare, but they were reproduced a few years later in smaller format as part of Camden's *Britannia* (1607). One of the contributors to these later editions was John Warden (1548–1625), who is perhaps second in stature to Saxton at this period. Unfortunately, however, he did not have Saxton's patronage, and he was unable to complete his own surveys of the English counties. When considering the small versions of Saxton's county maps in which the text is still in Latin, it is as well to remember that the maps of Hampshire, Surrey, Sussex, Kent, Herefordshire and Middlesex were probably by John Norden (1548–1625). Norden included some roads in his maps.

Robert Adams' contemporary map of the Devonshire and Cornwall coasts, showing the Spanish Fleet at the time of the Spanish Armada, 1588.

John Speed (1542–1629) is still the most popular English cartographer, and many reproductions of his maps have been made this century. The book in which Speed's maps appeared was called *Theatre of The Empire of Great Britain* and it was published in 1611. A small number of maps were sold before this; they bear the date 1610 and have no printing on the reverse. Much of the information from Saxton's and Norden's surveys was used, but Speed was an eminent antiquary in his own right and added some features of his own. He introduces some information on antiquities and heraldry, decorating the corners with views and street plans of the principal town. Speed's maps ran to a number of editions, some of the later ones being the rarest. However, as the engraved plates were used they became worn or damaged, and consequently later editions have a weaker, less dark appearance. There were nine main editions of Speed's county maps published following the first printings of the maps separately (these have no text on the back). The 1611 and 1614 issues were published by Sudbury and Humble, as was the 1616 edition, the difference being that the latter had a Latin text. The 1627–31 maps were published by George Humble, but continue to bear the imprint of Sudbury and Humble. In 1646 William Humble published a set and from 1650–62 Roger Rea produced some with and some without text and a corrected date (from 1610). The 1676 edition (there are a large number of these) was by Chiswell and Bassett, and the 1713 and 1770 maps were by Henry Overton and Dicey respectively. Another clue to dating these maps is the initial letter to the text on the reverse. The first edition has an elaborate design of cornucopia, masks and naturalistic foliage surrounded by a line and dot frame. The later editions became simpler, with stylized leaf arabesques.

Two other fine cartographers of the pre-Restoration period in England are J. Bleau and Jan Jansson. Though their maps have less of the charm of a Saxton or a Speed, they are beautifully produced plates.

The last major English map-maker of the 17th century was Robert Mordern. He was a prolific, if a less polished craftsman than Bleau or Jansson, and his county maps appeared in the 1695 edition of Camden's *Britannia*. Most of them are fairly plain with a cartouche round the main title.

Robert Morden's Map of Herefordshire, published in Camden's Britannia. Copper engraving, 1695.

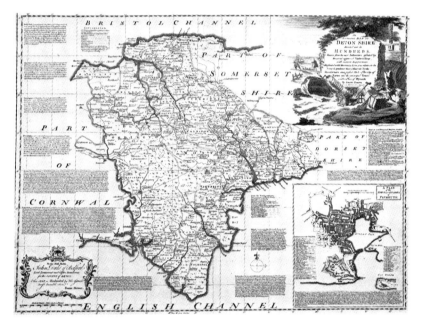

Copperplate hand-coloured map of Devonshire by Emanuel Bowen, published in London in 1777, by Bowles, Tinney and Sayer.

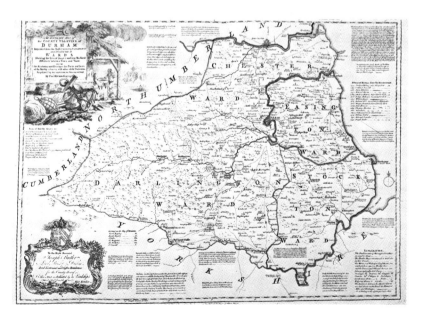

Copperplate map of Durham in original outline colour. By Thomas Kitchin, 1777.

France was not one of the principal map-making countries, and it was Ortelius who printed the first series of maps of the French provinces in his *Theatrum*. Mercator followed in 1585 with his *Galliae Tabulae*. Many of the earlier maps by native Frenchmen seem to have perished or to be represented by one one or two rare copies. The nearest to Saxton's great atlas was Maurice Borjuereau's *Le Théâtre François* of 1595, but this too is limited to only about a dozen known copies. A cartographer called Nicholas Sanson really began the school of French geographical science, which from the late 17th century to the end of the 18th century was to take over from the Dutch in its influence. Maps by the De L'Isle family dominated the early 18th century, and later such great names as Jean Baptiste Boinguignon and the family Robert de Vaugondys. The latter produced an *Atlas Universal* in 1757, which had 108 charmingly decorated maps, in themselves the products of painstaking surveys. By the end of the 18th century the French Revolution had disrupted much of the artistic and scientific life of the country, and England was gaining ascendancy as the naval power – great mapmaking is usually linked with the maritime prowess of a nation.

Some people collect marine charts, which are of interest perhaps more for their technical than their aesthetic qualities. An Elizabethan, Robert Adams, issued a series of charts illustrating the engagements between the English fleet and the Spanish Armada, but it was not really until the later 17th century, and Captain Greenville Collins, that sea charts in England came anything near those of the Low Countries for accuracy. His series *Britain's Coasting Pilot* (1693) was so standard a work that it was re-issued constantly throughout the 18th century.

Maps of the world (other than those medieval fantasies) were being printed from the 16th century, and there is a very well-known one based on Drake's voyages by Hondius. Exploration and colonization led to a quantity of maps from the European cartographers, and early ones are not often met with. There were various maps of the New

A 'Map of the World' by the French mapmaker Delamarche, geographer to the Crown, c. 1780.

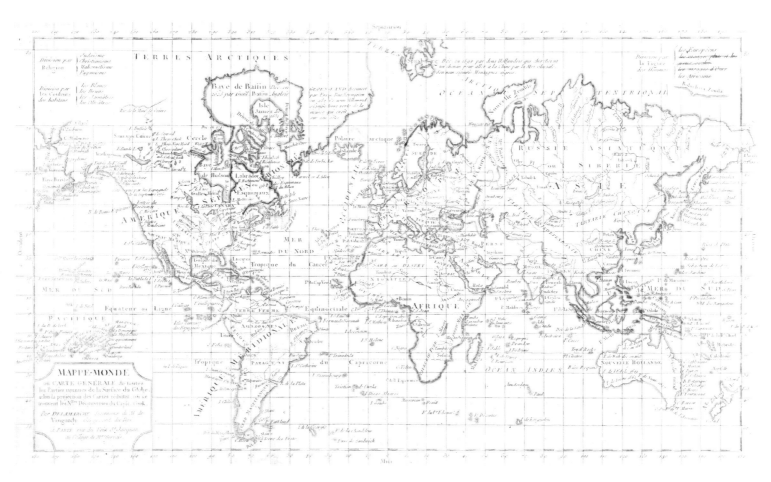

World including Captain John Smith's *Virginia* engraved by William Hole in 1612, and in 1627 John Speed published his *Prospect of the Most Famous Parts of the World* which is the first printed general atlas by an Englishman. This (and a miniature edition) was re-issued at intervals throughout the 17th century.

Of all the countries mapped in early atlases, America is perhaps the best researched today. Many were produced in the first part of the 16th century, but these are mostly so rare as to be out of the range of the ordinary collector. More accessible are the maps from atlases by Ortelius and Mercator, which went into many editions. Englishmen like Frobisher, Drake, Humphrey Gilbert and Robert Thorne contributed a great deal to the surveying of the Americas. This led to many maps of the continent in the 17th century, the Scotsman Ogilby's *America* being a notable example of British work.

The 18th century saw an even greater mass of material published, mainly in England and France, indeed, the War of Independence, in which both countries were involved, stimulated a need for accurate maps and charts. Herman Moll's maps of North and South America show some attractive vignettes of Indians, Niagara, fishing etc. Two editions of this are known, 1710–15 and 1730. Henry Popple's map of 1733 was hitherto the most detailed, but it was out of date when William

Early-18th-century map showing French possessions in North America.

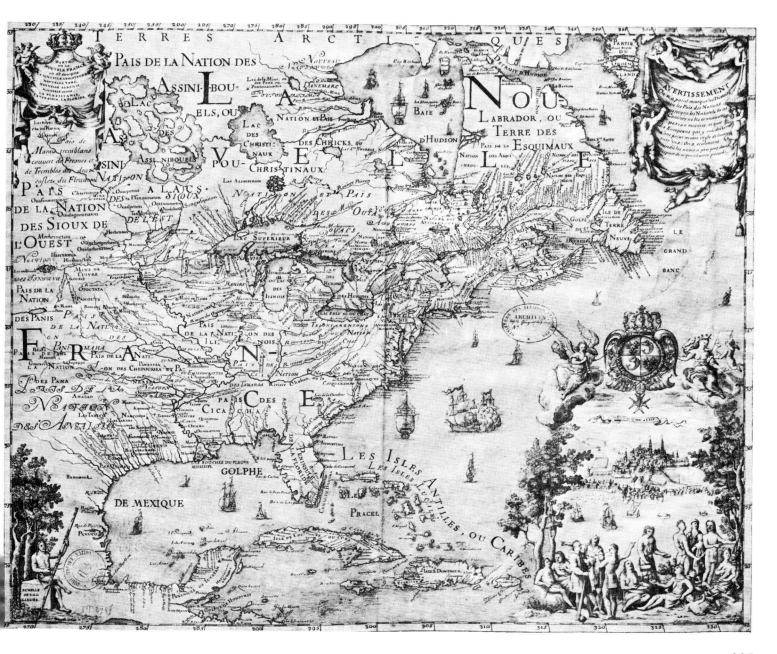

Faden published the *North American Atlas* in 1777. He also produced some fine large-scale plans of military operations in the War. The last Europeans to make atlases of America were Carey and Lea (1832); after that date, the study of American geography became largely the province of native cartographers.

John Ogilby (1600–76), already mentioned in connection with his map of America, is perhaps best known for his famous road maps, which were the last achievement of a very varied life. In 1675 he published his *Geographical and Historical Description of the Principal Roads*, which had a hundred engraved plates showing the roads in the form of long strips. Incidentally, Ogilby was the first to adopt the standard scale of the statute mile (1760 yards) in his maps. The atlas was re-issued in 1698 and, with reduced-size maps and extra country maps, was published by Owen and Bowen in 1720 and thereafter many times during the 18th century.

Eighteenth- and 19th-century maps are the most common in antique shops, probably due to the large number of published topographical and historical books, which were embellished with maps. Two of the great names of the 18th century were Emanuel Bowen and Thomas Kitchen. Bowen's maps are extremely decorative, and have the added interest of descriptive notes and vignettes. Kitchen's maps also have a look of 18th-century elegance combined with accuracy. Less ornamented are the later maps by John Carey, who was perhaps the greatest cartographer of the period.

Early in the 19th century the best county maps were produced by Charles and James Greenwood and Thomas Moule. These return to the decorative style, with detailed architectural views, heraldry and costume figures.

The 19th century saw a proliferation of maps, but one important landmark was the establishment of the Ordnance Survey in 1791. The full set of 200 sheets with index was completed in 1858.

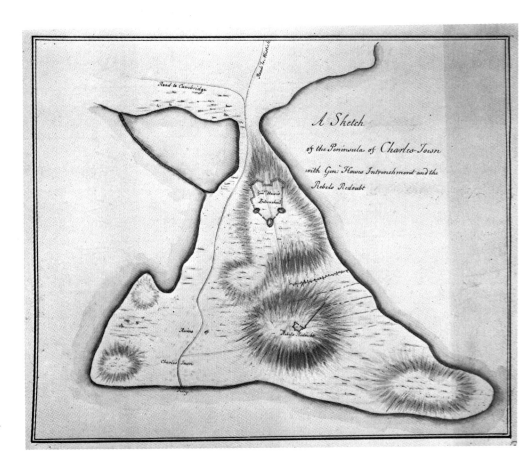

Plan of the peninsula of Charlestown, showing General Howe's entrenchments. A military map used during the American War of Independence.

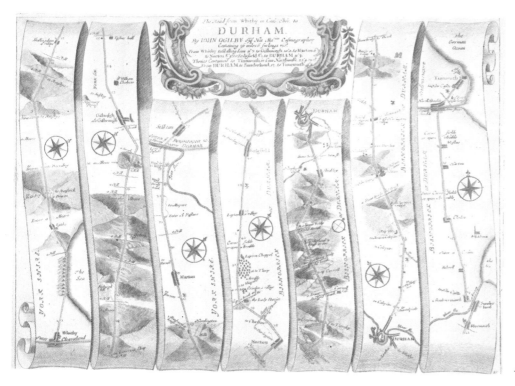

The Road from Whitby to Durham, a hand-coloured map from John Ogilby's road atlas of Britain, published in 1675.

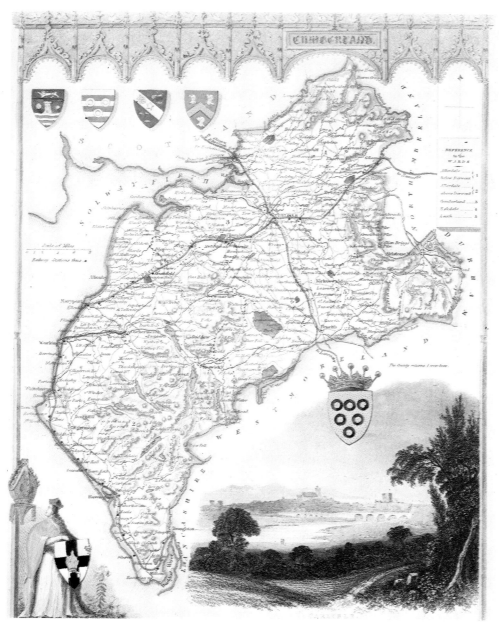

Steel-plate, hand-coloured map of Cumberland, by Thomas Moule, published in London in 1840, showing the early railway routes.

227

Scientific Instruments

Scientific instruments make a fascinating field for collecting. They are not found widely in antique shops, which means that you will have to search for dealers who specialize in them, and you could start at the famous one in London's Jermyn Street. Instruments do come up for sale regularly at auctions, however, and if you are collecting it is worth watching the catalogues of all your nearest auction firms and for sales at private houses.

In the 17th and 18th centuries, many instruments were made, most with the greatest skill and care, and they were often profusely decorated, especially on the flat surfaces. The variety of instruments made is an extensive one, and collecting can range from the simplest 19th-century rolling parallel rule which today fetches as little as £20 (more if it is in its own box) to the complex surgeon's instrument set for £700 or so, a microscope of the late 18th century made by one of the principal optical instrument makers like Adams or Dollond or a Dutch quadrant of the 17th century, either of which might cost £3000 or more. There are so many different instruments that we can only cover a small but representative selection here, starting with some surveying and navigational items.

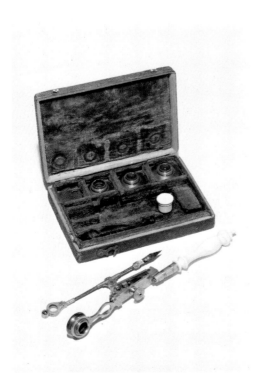

A late-18th-century scientific drawing set and case.

Measuring instruments

In the ancient world, the main instruments for measurement available to land surveyors and builders were the *groma*, for right-angle setting, and the plumbline for straight vertical lines. The *groma* was a cross-staff which had plumblines hung from the four ends, and enabled surveyors to mark out right angles. (If there was even a gentle breeze, the angle might well be over or under 90°, which is often taken to explain why rectilinear structures, like forts and marching camps in Roman Britain, have a slightly parallellogram or rhomboid plan). Measurement of distances was done by cord with regularly spaced knots, or by using the surveyor's pole, called the *decempeda* in Latin. This was 10 Roman feet long (a measure fairly close to our 12 in or 30 cm).

In the Middle Ages, measuring rods and lines were used; perhaps the *groma* may have been re-discovered, but medieval builders in Europe had similar difficulties over right angles until the rediscovery of Euclidean geometry in the early 12th century.

The navigational instruments used in the Middle Ages were the astrolabe, the quadrant and the magnetic compass. The astrolabe reached Britain from Europe in the early 12th century. It was an instrument for measuring the altitude of stars and planets above the horizon. It could also be used to calculate the time of day. In the late 14th century, Chaucer is said to have given an astrolabe to his son when the

A splendid astrolabe by Mabribi.

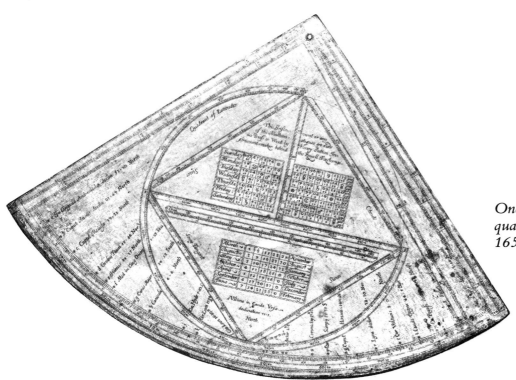

One side of a rare double-sided oak quadrant, by Henry Sutton, London, 1658.

latter was at Oxford, and with it went a manual on how to use it. The astrolabe consisted of a circular flat plate and a rotating rule, with sights mounted on the plate. There were variations in design, some of which took the form of open spheres in place of plates. As a measuring instrument the astrolabe was not very accurate, but it was the only instrument available. Most of them were made of brass or bronze, some of iron, and many were very beautifully engraved, the figures and distance marks most carefully etched. Medieval astrolabes are extremely rare, almost entirely confined to museums, but 17th century versions have come up for sale in recent years, one of them in 1983 fetching over £10,000. The astrolabe was superseded in the 17th century by newer instruments such as the circumferentor and its associated instruments like the graphometer, sextant and octant, and it is these instruments that can be collected, though unless they are late 18th or 19th century, they are very expensive.

The circumferentor was invented in the early 1500s in Germany and was an instrument for measuring vertical and horizontal angles. It consisted of a flat ring of metal, usually brass, marked off in the degrees of a circle. In the centre of a cross inside the ring was a pivot on which rotated an alidade (shaped indicator with sights) whose outer end had a pointer that matched up with the scale on the outer ring. In the centre pivot part was inserted a compass. Most circumferentors had four sights, set at 90° from each other, on the ring. Circumferentors were often very finely ornamented with scratch decoration on the more spacious parts. As measuring instruments they were not very accurate in the first decades, and could indeed be as much as one sixth out. This was to some extent obviated in the early 17th century by the introduction of the Vernier scale, an auxiliary scale device fitted on the pointer end of the alidade enabling finer adjustment and producing smaller intervals on the scale. The scale was invented by Pierre Vernier (1580–1637), a French mathematician, and it was to become a standard component of most surveying and other measuring instrumentation – indeed, it is still a component of many instruments today.

The circumferentor was the first of a succession of similar instruments, and continued to be made right into the 19th century even though it had been superseded by other, more accurate instruments. 18th- and 19th-century circumferentors do appear in shops and sales, and the 18th-century models are likely to cost over £1000. The successors included the graphometer (invented in France in the late 16th century), the sextant (early 17th century) and the octant (mid-17th

An early-19th-century seaman's quadrant.

Below, right: *A late-16th-century Italian compass set in an ivory case.*

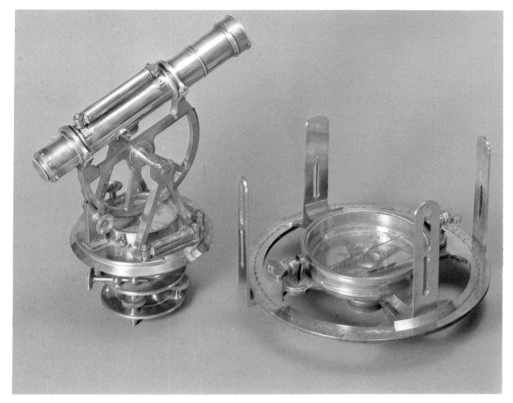

An 18th-century mechanical orrery set by W. & S. Jones.

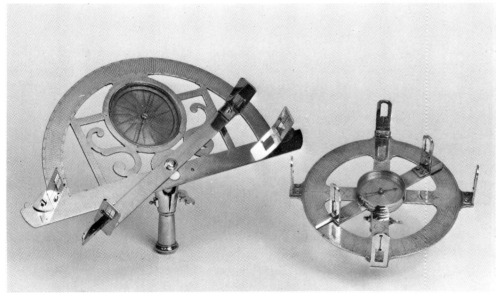

Late-18th-century French brass graphometer, with fixed sign vanes.

Left: Early-19th-century altazimuth theodolite, by Berge, London. Right: late-18th-century circumferentor by T. Heath.

century). And to this list we should add the quadrant, invented probably in ancient times and re-emerging in medieval Europe as a navigational instrument, but not being used for surveying until the 16th century.

The graphometer is in effect a half circumferentor: its construction was a semi-circle instead of a circle, otherwise it was very much the same though it had two, not four, sights. It was a popular instrument in France, and had reached Britain before the end of the 17th century. Graphometers were also made in North America.

The sextant emerged in the 1620s, and strictly speaking was an instrument with an angle of 60° (six of which make a circle). It was for measuring the altitude of stars and planets and was also used for navigation, but there were variations which had application in land surveying. The sextant had an alidade with a Vernier scale, which traversed the calibrated arc of the frame, and it had a small telescope mounted on one arm through which to look at the images. The nautical sextant was used ocassionally for astronomical work, and there was a smaller and slightly simpler version for land use, the box sextant, so-called because it was portable in its own case. The term sextant is often though incorrectly used for all nautical angle-measuring instruments. Numerous firms made excellent models both in Britain and in North America. 18th-century sextants can cost over £1000 or so, but the later 19th-century ones, almost as well-made and certainly more accurate, cost only about £200, probably because so many were made and there has been a high survival rate.

In 1731, John Hadley (1682–1744), the English mathematician, invented the reflecting octant. The octant, originated in the previous century, had a traverse of one-eighth of a circle, i.e. 45°, and as with sextants and quadrants, it was necessary for observers wishing to measure angles to look in two directions at once. Hadley's invention got over this by the use of mirrors.

In the late 16th century, meanwhile, the first theodolites began to appear. The theodolite is an instrument for measuring horizontal and vertical angles, generally for land surveying and map-making, and it came in to meet the demands of the recently introduced technique of triangulation, that is, measurement or mapping an area by means of dividing it into triangles, operating from a fixed base of precise length. The theodolite was – and in many respects still is – the key instrument in land surveying. It consisted of a telescope mounted on an apparatus of two graduated circles, one horizontal, one vertical, the axes of the telescope passing through the centres of the circles. Theodolites did not change enormously over the years, though they did acquire refinements and were also fitted with mounted spirit levels, Vernier scale and so forth, and were fixed to tripod stands or had bases with adjustable feet. They often appear in sales, and good 19th-century ones cost several hundreds of pounds, particularly if made by well-known makers like Troughton & Simms, George Adams (who supplied many to customers in North America).

These instruments were fine works of craftsmanship, as were many others that we can only mention, such as orreries (instruments that demonstrate the solar system by means of globes supported on wires), compasses, armillary spheres (skeletal spheres which tell the time), globes, pedometers (instruments carried on one's person which measure the number of paces one walks), and of course telescopes. One very interesting piece of equipment for surveying and measuring was the waywiser, hardly an instrument in the same sense as the foregoing, but a geared wheel, or pair of wheels side by side, which was pushed along the countryside or town and which had a gauge for measuring the distance travelled. These occasionally come up for sale, and fetch up to about £300, depending on condition.

A good example of an early-19th-century waywiser, by Charles Baker.

Time-telling instruments

The first apparatus for telling the time was the sundial, and the earliest were invented in the Near East in the 4th millennium BC. An Egyptian sundial of the 8th century BC has survived. Vitruvius Pollio, the great Roman engineer-architect writing just before the reign of Augustus, devotes several paragraphs to various modes of sundial and how they worked. A sundial gives the times from the shadow cast on the surface of a dial graduated in hours or fractions of hours by an object on which the sun's rays fall. This object is called the *gnomon*. Corrections have to be made for the difference between sun's time and clock time, and this difference varies every day, and also for the difference in longitude between the situation of a sundial and the standard time meridian of a given locality. Early sundials were divided into daylight hours only, which of course varied from day to day. Thus, sundial time was not very accurate, but apart from water clocks, it was all the ancients had for many centuries.

By the 17th century AD, mechanical clocks had been well established for several hundred years, but nonetheless sundials – or dials, as we henceforth call them – were still being made. They came in several forms, including horizontal dials, vertical dials facing north, south, east or west, vertical dials not facing the cardinal points, inclined dials, and equinoctial dials (sometimes also known as equatorial dials because the flat face was set at right angles to the axis of the earth). Many dials were portable, a kind of 17th-century pocket watch, as it were, and they were equipped with magnetic compass and were made in a variety of patterns.

One pocket dial was the diptych type. This consisted of two equal dimension flat rectangular blocks of ivory, or some other material, hinged together. The upper half was engraved with the cardinal points and perhaps a windrose, with a brass pointer. The lower half had an inset compass and a dial (or two) marking the hours. Connecting the halves was a string or cord which, when you opened them, stretched taut and acted as a *gnomon* to throw the shadow on to the dial. Diptych dials were made in most Western European countries, particularly in Germany and Britain. They, too, were affected by differences in latitude, and some could be adjusted, by reference to a set of figures relating to various latitudes. Diptych dials sometimes come up for auction, but appear to cost over £1000, probably because few have survived.

One of the best known makers of dials was Michael Butterfield, instrument maker to King Louis XIV of France, and a bit of a mystery man: English name, but was he English or French or German? He settled in Paris, made hundreds of dials, and died in about 1732. His dials are collectors' items, but they have been sought for so long that many forgeries exist, and not a few pass under the hammer as genuine. His dials were generally (though not of course always) mounted on an octagonal base plate and made of silver, or less frequently brass. They normally carried hour scales for 43, 46, 49 and 52 degrees latitude and could be adjusted by moving the *gnomon* to 40 degrees at one end and 60 degrees at the other end of the scale, thus covering any position in France, and most places in central Europe and a part of Britain. Some of them had a list of towns engraved on the back. The triangular *gnomon* was often – and characteristically – in the shape of a bird. Most of his dials were fitted with a compass, and were small enough to be held in one hand. It should be noted that not all the octagons were symmetrical, that is, some were rectangular with the edges cut off. Butterfield dials have fetched as little as £300 to £400 in recent years, despite their age, but there is the problem of establishing whether they are genuine or false.

This is a particularly good example of a late-17th-century French Butterfield dial, signed Butterfield, the silver octagonal base inset with a compass and engraved with four hour scales for latitudes 43°, 46°, 49° and 52°. The gnomon is supported by a bird.

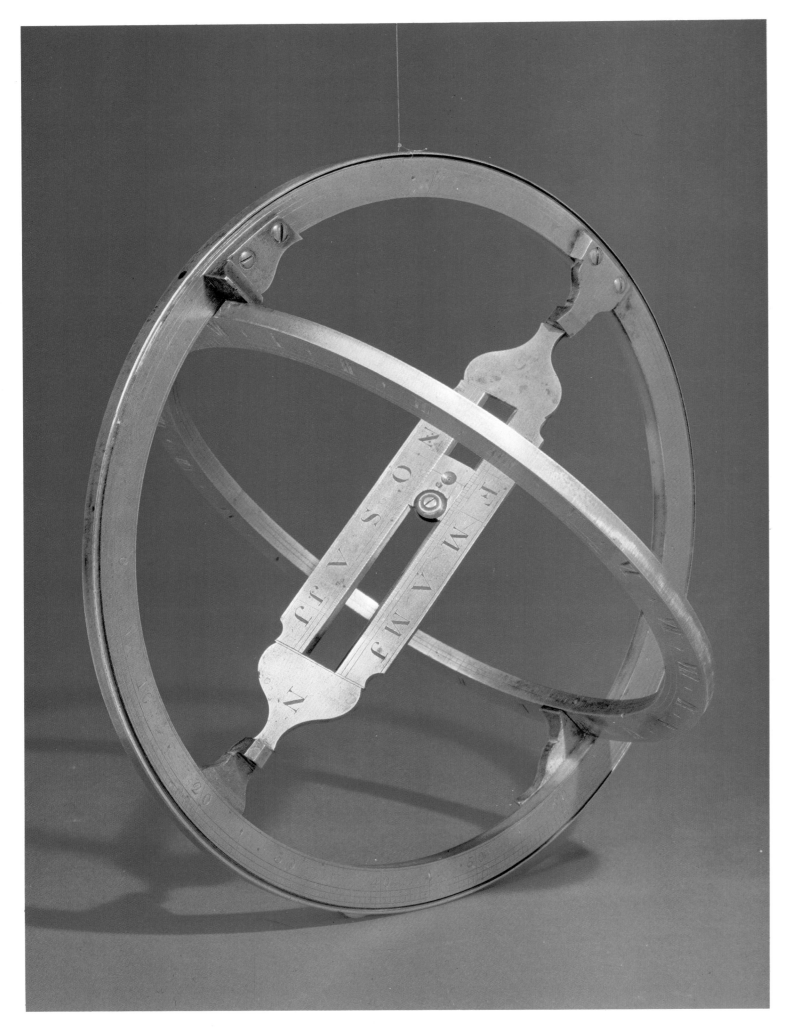

A late-18th-century equinoctial ring dial.

These flat dials and variations of them were made by other instrument makers in Europe in the 17th and 18th centuries, and makers to watch out for are Johann Willibrand (1720s), Edmund Culpeper (early 18th century), Johann Martin (1642–1720). One type of dial was the equinoctial, and this was basically a ring with Roman hour numerals round a flat surface, which hinged at one side of a base plate dished to incorporate a compass, with a folding *gnomon* on one side. The hour scale was set parallel to the plane of the equator.

Telescopes

One of the most ubiquitous instruments, which is still an easy one to collect, is the telescope. It was invented by Lippershey in 1608, who discovered that a double convex lens as the object glass and a double concave lens as the eyepiece, located a certain distance apart, could magnify distant objects. He experimented with a simple tube. This was a refracting telescope. The idea was taken up by the incomparable Galileo in Italy, who made his own telescope, a considerable advance on Lippershey's, used it for studying the heavens, and made several momentous discoveries. Galileo called his instrument a *perspicillum* or spyglass, and it magnified up to about thirty times. Other people began to make telescopes, but all of them were affected by what is called chromatic aberration, that is, the images seen were coloured and blurred at the edges, due to light dispersion. Galileo and contemporaries continued to work on improving these instruments, but the aberration could not be overcome, until in the 1670s Isaac Newton (1642–1727) discovered the nature of the spectrum and constructed a telescope in which he used a curved mirror in place of one of the lenses, which eliminated the coloured blurring. Yet the reflecting telescope, as it was called, had its disadvantages, the chief one being that most of the light was lost through the inefficiency of the mirrors. Meanwhile, refracting telescopes had been getting better as new techniques of lens grinding and positioning were introduced, and when the idea of using a different type of glass for each of the lenses was tried out, the aberration almost disappeared. Effectively, this means you could today have a quite satisfactory telescope made on Galileo's model!

Opposite page:
An 18th-century Butterfield type dial.

Right: *Eighteenth-century English brass reflecting telescope on folding tripod support, the 3½ in. (9 cm.) diameter barrel having a detachable eyepiece.*

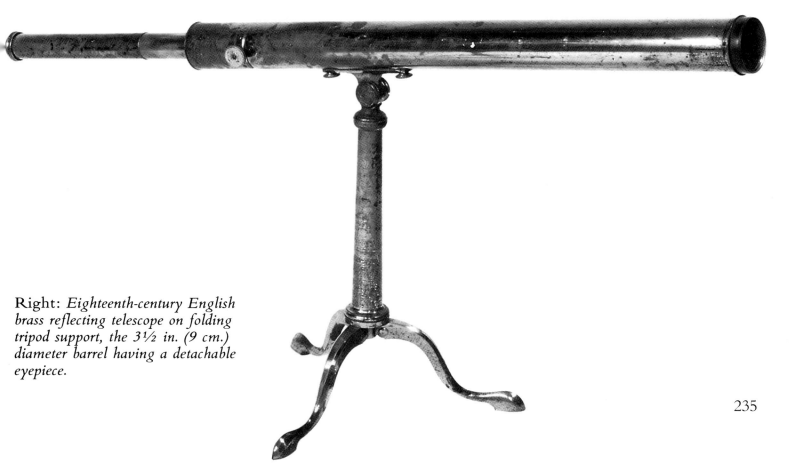

235

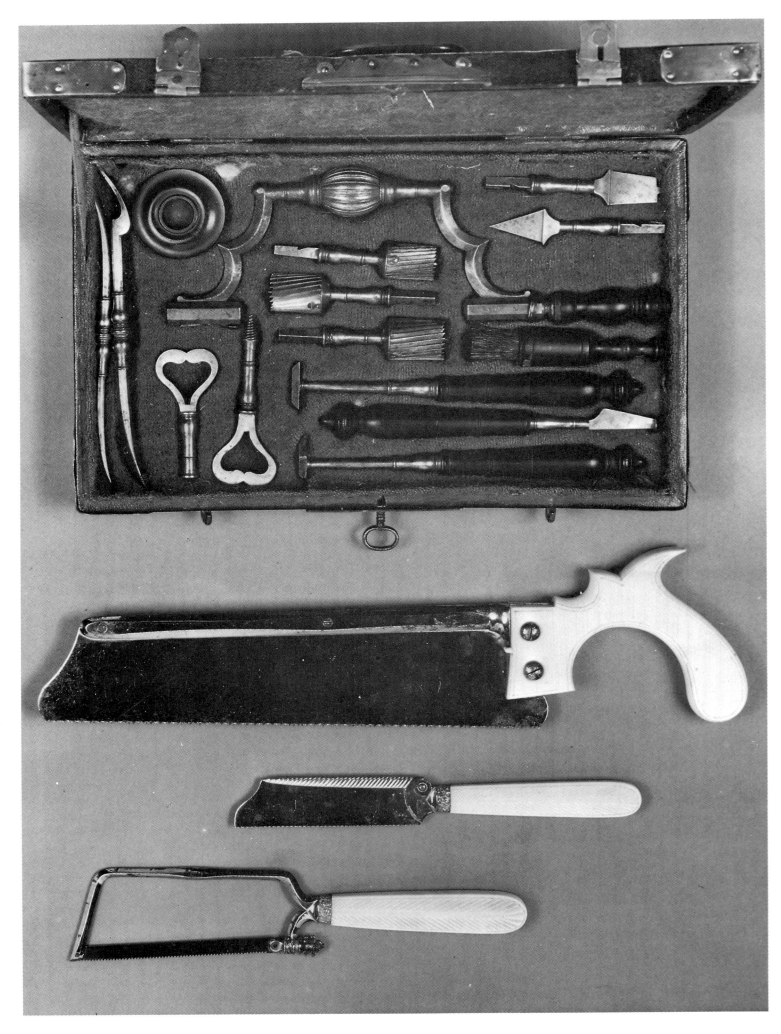

236

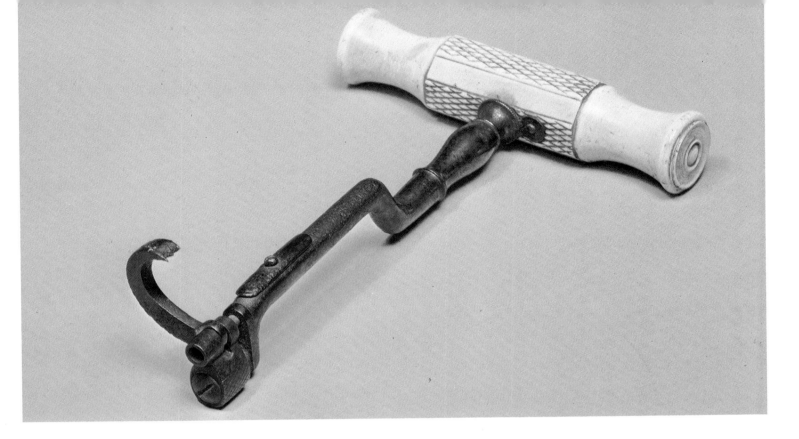

A late-18th-century tooth extractor of iron, with bone handle.

Opposite page:
An interesting early-19th-century set of trepanning instruments by Leesuer.

Telescopes were not limited to astronomical use. Very soon their military and nautical value was appreciated, and from the mid 17th century onwards telescopes of many sizes were being made by a variety of specializing firms. The shorter 2 ft to 3-ft (91-cm) type, much like Galileo's, were single tube. But before the end of the 17th century longer versions were produced, in which short lengths of different diameter tubing were devised to slide one into the next, in three, four or five, which has given an additional meaning to the word 'telescope'. Among the many makers of the late 17th and the 18th centuries, whose instruments you can still find to buy, are John Marshall (1663–1725), James Mann and sons, Edward Scarlett and his son Samuel (late 18th and early 19th century), Benjamin Martin (1704–82), Jesse Ramsden (late 18th century to late 1830s), Charles Tulley (who made several reflecting telescopes as well as refracting telescopes and who bought Benjamin Martin's business) and the Dollond firm. Brass refracting telescopes of the 18th century, some with their stands, fetch several hundreds of pounds and are understandably more interesting if they have their original fitted boxes, with spare eye pieces and so forth. Simpler naval telescopes of the 19th century can generally be found for much less than £100. Negretti and Zambra was and still is a well known firm for telescopes and other instruments.

Surgical instruments

It may seem ghoulish to some to collect surgical instruments, but they are evidence of attempts by men to help other men, and so in this author's opinion are preferable to armour and weapons. Ancient and medieval instruments for surgery were crude and on the whole ineffective. Stone Age 'doctors' used to cut holes in the heads of people with head injuries, and perhaps to relieve migraines, using sharp flintstones. This was called trepanning (or trephining), and amazingly the technique has continued to be practised here and there ever since. Special trepanning sets were still being made in Britain in the 18th and 19th centuries for surgeons to cut holes in patients' skulls – but for sound medical reasons rather than to allow devils to get out! A trepanning set made by William Hutchinson & Son, of the 19th century, was sold recently for £500.

A late-18th-century shagreen cased set of five dentistry knives; set of carved ivory dentures; pair of steel extracting pincers (c. 1820); and two early-19th-century wood handled steel dental extractors.

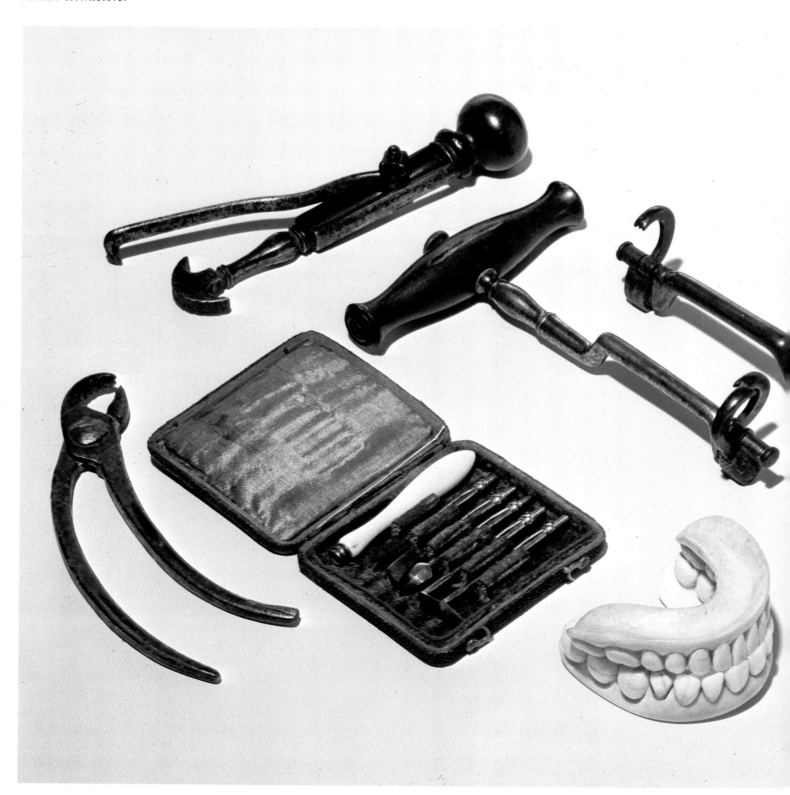

Above: *Two domestic medicine chests: left, a 19th-century chest holding 12 bottles, the lower drawer containing glass pestle and mortar, pill canisters, set of balances and a set of weights; and right, a Regency rosewood brass-fitted chest that has a 14-division bottle tray.*

Surgical instruments as we know them began to be devised in the late Middle Ages, and one of the earliest summaries of contemporary instruments appears in the works of Ambroise Paré (1510–90), probably the greatest surgeon of the 16th century and court surgeon to four kings of France. Paré invented various instruments, including the first artery forceps (in the 1570s). He described many others (some of which were also originated by him). Obstetric forceps for assisting at difficult childbirths were invented by Peter Chamberlen, a Huguenot doctor who emigrated to England and introduced them in the early 17th century, though the family kept the inventor's name secret for over a century. William Smellie (1697–1763) made several improvements, including pairs out of wood to eliminate the disturbing noise made by metal ones. He also made metal ones which he covered with a leather skin, for the same reason.

Sir Thomas Spencer Wells (1818–97) invented the special artery forceps which are still in use today. These had narrow grooved blades, and 19th-century examples can still be bought by collectors, though you would want to have proof of their date. Auguste Nélaton (1807–73), a French physician, invented the porcelain-tipped probe specially to locate bullets in bullet wounds. The first time he used the probe was on the great Italian patriot leader, Garibaldi. Hermann von Helmholtz (1821–94), invented the ophthalmoscope for examining the eye's retina, in 1851, and 19th-century ophthalmoscopes do appear for sale.

One of the most widely used instruments in medicine is the stethoscope. The idea was originated by René Théophile Hyacinthe Laennec (1781–1826), a Breton doctor who worked for a time at the Necker Hospital in Paris. He perfected a stethoscope in about 1818, which he described as 'a cylinder of wood an inch and a half in diameter and a foot long, perforated by a bore three lines wide, and hollowed out into funnel shape at one of its extremities.' The more familiar stethoscope most of us have had used on our chests at some time or other began to appear in the later 19th century, but based entirely upon Laennec's ideas.

Many surgical instruments prior to the 1860s were finely decorated and embossed on handles, blades and other parts, but the surgeons who used them did not appreciate that this ornamenting was in fact a germ trap. Even if the blades or working edges were plunged into warm water and washed after use, the handles generally were not. After the

Opposite page: A fine-quality mid-19th-century surgeon's amputation kit by Weiss, London, contained in a brass-bound mahogany case lined in green plush velvet. It fetched £680 in a London sale in 1982.

Right: *An early-19th-century pine and ivory mounted stethoscope, the cap turned in the form of an acorn finial, contained in its original leather case. It fetched £240 at a London sale in 1982.*

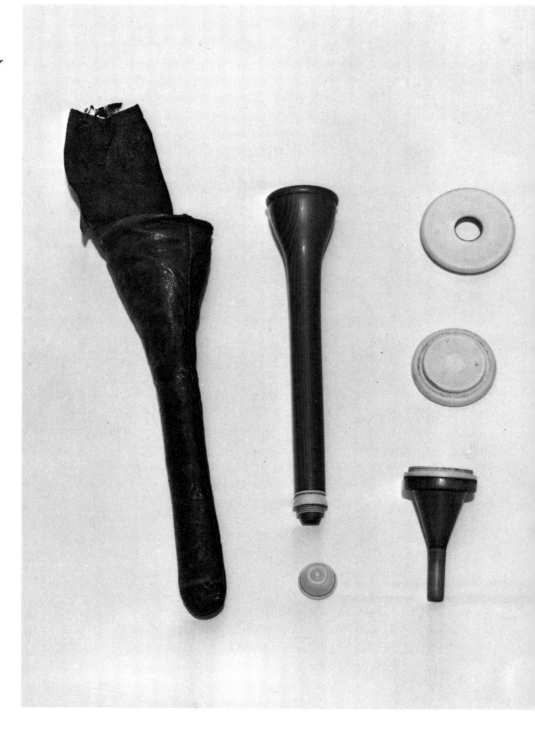

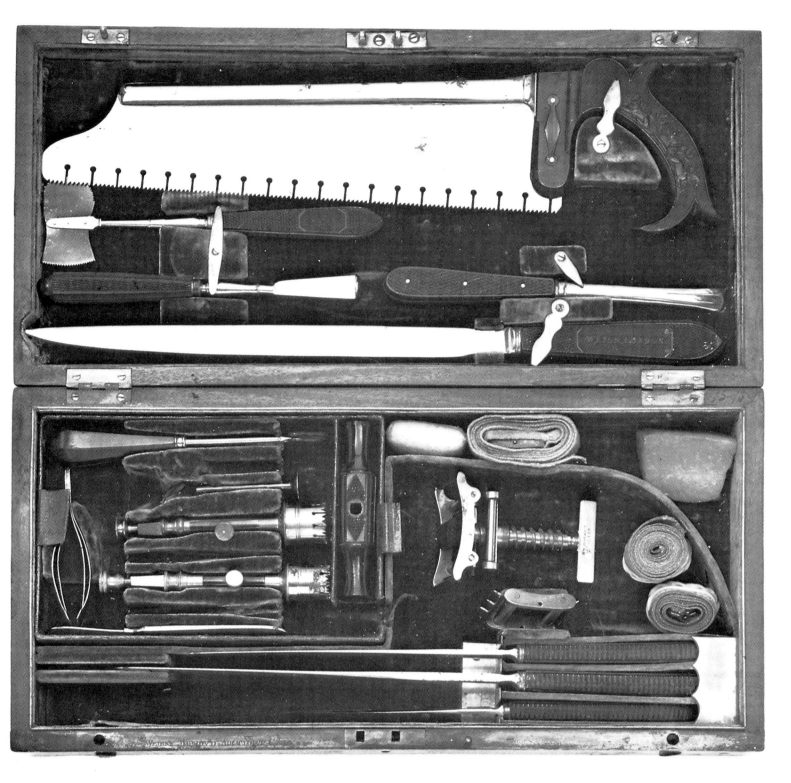

dramatic introduction in 1867/8 of antiseptic techniques by Joseph, Lord Lister (1827–1912), perhaps the greatest medical man of all time, handles began to be scrubbed and sterilized after every use. Makers of instruments began henceforth to reduce substantially the decorative treatment of their products. You can see this change in surgeon's general purpose instrument sets by comparing those of the early decades of the 19th century and those after Lister, both types appearing from time to time in sales or to be found in antique shops specializing in medical antiques. A general-purpose set would usually contain, among other things, an amputation saw, sets of artery forceps (one way of roughly dating a set is whether it contains Spencer Wells artery forceps), choice of scalpels and knives, pair of bone cutters, needles, catgut, retractors and clamps, and 19th-century sets fetch anything from about £350 for simple ones to about £800 or so for the more comprehensive variety.

Musical Instruments

Musical instruments go back to the earliest times of civilization, the first being musical pipes and simple stringed instruments like lyres. As long ago as the 3rd century BC a primitive type of organ was developed, consisting of an arrangement of pan-pipes blown by means of leather bags and bellows. By the 9th century AD, organs were being used in cathedrals in Western Europe, and Old Sarum (the forerunner of Salisbury) and Winchester both had theirs by the 10th century. By the 13th century a key-system organ was widely in use in larger ecclesiastical buildings throughout Europe, and by the mid-14th century the chromatic keyboard had been invented. Churches usually had their own orchestras (more generally known as bands) instead of organs for musical accompaniment, and these were made up of local instrument-players, playing viols, recorders, guitars, rebecks (or rebecs), psalteries, shawms, and timbres. Sometimes, bands played in larger churches or cathedrals, in the minstrels' gallery, instead of or even along with the organ. There is a 14th-century sculpture in the minstrels' gallery at Exeter Cathedral and it shows a band of players with their instruments. Organs became standard equipment for churches from the later 18th century onwards.

The viol was a stringed instrument not unlike a double-bass though smaller, and was held downwards and played with the hand under the bow, or held between the knees. It had six strings, and there were at least three kinds, treble, alto and bass. It appeared in the 14th century and was still popular in the 17th, having superseded the much older instrument, the rebeck, a bowed instrument that had three strings. The rebeck was more like a violin to which it was ancestor. The recorder probably emerged in the 15th century as a development of the reedless musical pipe with finger holes, known as the flute (but not to be confused with the somewhat more sophisticated cross-flute introduced in the late 18th century). Henry VIII not only played the recorder, he also composed music for it. The guitar has a rather longer history. It was a six-stringed instrument from the Near East, and was brought to Western Europe and thence to Britain in the 12th and 13th centuries by returning Crusaders. However, it took a long time to catch on as a popular instrument in Britain. Charles II is said to have brought one back from Europe when he returned to take up his throne in 1660, though Pepys did not think much of it. The guitar only became popular in Britain in the later 18th century.

Another earlier instrument of the medieval church band was the 14th-century psaltery, a triangular-shaped stringed instrument that was plucked, not struck. This was a kind of forerunner of the harpsichord. The shawm, also medieval, was rather similar to an oboe, and the sackbut, also originating in the 14th century, was an early form of trombone. The lute, which was common from the 14th right to the

Above: *A miniature by an unknown artist, showing Queen Elizabeth I playing a lute, a popular instrument at the time.*

Opposite page: *Two French musical instruments: on the left, a 17th-century guitar, made in Paris; and on the right, an early-19th-century lyre-guitar designed as a drawing-room instrument.*

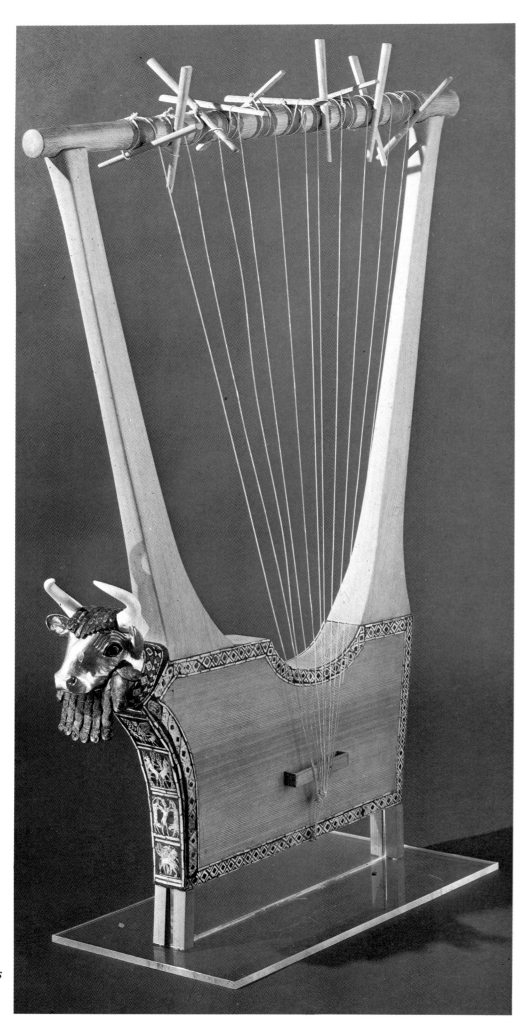

This music maker of over 4000 years ago is a reconstruction of a bull-head lyre from the Sumerian city of Ur.

244

17th century, was like a guitar, pear-shaped and played by plucking with a plectrum. Contemporary with these, but possibly of earlier beginnings, was the dulcimer, sometimes referred to as a primitive piano. This had its strings stretched across a flat, box frame, and was played by striking the wires with hammers, a little like the 20th-century xylophone. The dulcimer had a long run of popularity.

Most bands also had timbrel players, whose instrument was a small drum, a little like a tambourine. The Exeter sculpture also shows a set of bag-pipes, but this instrument was never very popular in England. Samuel Pepys called it 'mighty barbarous' though as everyone knows it caught on with vigour in Scotland. There were also various horns and trumpets, single-keyed only up to the 17th century, but after that improved by the introduction of detached crooks for changing the keys, and in the 19th century further developed by the introduction of valves, or stops.

Bands were not restricted to churches, though since so much of medieval life was centred on religion, more music was perhaps made inside the church than outside. Minstrels and mummers also used bands or individual instrument-players for accompaniment in their performances.

Two theorbos, the larger one at left by M. Rauche, of the mid-18th-century, and the smaller by C. Choco, of Venice, 17th-century. The theorbo was a lute-like instrument, with double neck to accommodate additional bass strings.

Examples of these instruments can be found in museums and private collections, but they do not turn up at sales, and in any case they are extremely rare. This is partly due to their having perished through age, and partly to their destruction during Puritan days in the 17th century, though to a lesser extent than is generally credited. We should not think, for example, that Oliver Cromwell prohibited the playing of musical instruments – far from it, for it was he who encouraged the spread of violin playing in England and who had the organ of Magdalen College in Oxford moved to his residence at Hampton Court! What the Puritans did not approve of was music in church; outside, it was quite different – they were all for domestic music. Another cause of the rarity of these old instruments is that they were quite simply replaced by more modern ones.

Early keyboard instruments

Over and above these orchestral instruments were the keyboards and the organ developments. Keyboards came into fashion in Britain in the 16th century, and the popularity was tremendously increased by the compositions and performances of a fine school of keyboard music

Above: *A spinet by the English maker, John Player, dated towards the end of the 17th century.*

Right: *Virginals made by Adam Leversidge, London, 1670.*

headed by William Byrd (1540–1623), Orlando Gibbons (1583–1625) and John Bull (*c.* 1562–1628). The instruments included virginals, early harpsichords (not quite the same thing), harps (which went back to Celtic times before the Romans) and spinets. The virginal was an oblong box with a keyboard, which could be placed on a table or was mounted on a frame with four legs. Its strings were plucked. There was usually only one string for each note. Virginals were usually beautifully decorated, and the cases were mainly of oak. Some virginals of the 17th century can be found apart from those in museums and country-house collections, but they are very expensive. They were made throughout the 16th and 17th centuries, but by the end of the latter they were being overtaken by spinets and harpsichords.

The spinet, like the virginal, is a keyboard instrument with one string for each note, played by plucking, but its shape is different from the virginal, not rectangular but trapezoid or wedge-shaped, a bit like a harp on its side. The spinet first appeared in Britain in the mid 17th century and seems to have ousted the virginal fairly quickly, remaining a popular instrument right into the late 18th century. Spinets varied in size, some being as much as about 7 ft (2 m) across. Seventeenth-century spinets are generally in an oak case, sometimes mounted on a stand, and the 18th-century models were made of walnut or mahogany. Eighteenth-century spinets very occasionally appear in salerooms, but they are not cheap, especially if they are in good working order. Care should be taken not to confuse a spinet with the more rectangular instrument of the 19th century often called a spinet but which is an earlier type of piano. Spinets, like virginals, were essentially domestic instruments and were bought by or for performers in private houses rather than in public places of entertainment, though that is not to say that some public spinet recitals were not given. There is a fine spinet made by the 17th-century craftsman John Player, sometime in the 1680s, in the Victoria and Albert Museum, London.

The harpsichord looks something like a grand piano, but it is not of course the same thing at all. The earliest British harpsichords appear to have been made in the 15th century, but there are hardly any examples left of that century, or indeed of harpsichords before the late 17th century. One of the oldest is the splendid two-manual oak-cased instrument made by Thomas Hitchcock in the 1690s, now in the Victoria and Albert Museum. It has decorative wrought iron strap hinges for its two lids, and it is likely that many harpsichords of those times were likewise decorated. Some of the best British harpsichords, however, were made in the 18th century, particularly those by instrument makers like Kirkman and Shudi. A Kirkman harpsichord in working order could fetch as much as £20,000 today.

The harpsichord was made with two manuals and also with one manual, and it is impossible to say which was the more popular. We do know a little more about the two-manual variety because of the chance survival of so many of them from the 18th century. By about the fourth decade of the century, harpsichords were being made in fairly large size, with the two manuals, and fitted with hand-operated damper stops and two pedals. There were three strings for each note. In 1769, Burkhardt (Berkat) Shudi (1702–73) patented the 'Venetian Swell' pedal, a device that operated a louvred inner lid over the strings that could be raised or lowered to produce *crescendo* or *diminuendo*. Harpsichords continued to be made up to the end of the century, though musicologists note that from the 1770s to about 1800 there is a significant decline in the number of times the harpsichord is mentioned in musical literature. This is put down to the arrival and very rapid 'catching on' of the piano, invented in Italy in about 1700 but not made in England until the 1760s.

A rare harpsichord by Shudi and Broadwood, of 1770.

The lovely decoration on the back of
this late 17th-century English-made
violin incorporates the Royal Arms
of the House of Stuart, and the violin
is believed to have belonged to
Charles II or his brother James II.

The violin

Another instrument that began to appear in Britain chiefly as a popular
dance instrument at the end of the 16th century was the violin. This
had been developed in Italy at the end of the 15th century. The violin
was a four-stringed instrument with a tone more powerful than the
viol, though some specialists say not so nice. The violin was of thicker
wood and stronger construction. It soon became popular, and in 1654
John Playford (1623- c. 1686) published a treatise on music in which,
in a chapter on treble-violins, he described the violin as a 'cheerful . . .
instrument, much practised of late . . .' It is worth noting the date of
this book – 1654! For a time, viols and violins featured together in
orchestras and dance 'bands' but eventually the violin edged the viol
out. There is no certain date for this, but a clue lies in the fact that in the
first commercial concerts in Britain, organized during the Protectorate
(1653–58) of Cromwell and at his instigation, in 1654, violins were
noted as playing the major string rôle in the orchestras. Soon after
Charles II returned to his throne (1660), he set up a special band of
twenty-four violin players. And the one great English composer of the
second half of the century, Henry Purcell (1659–95), composed violin
sonatas and other works.

The Italian violins of the 16th, 17th and early 18th centuries were –
and still are – probably the finest ever made, particularly those from
the now world-famous makers at Cremona, the Amati family (c. 1540–

Below: *A bass viol attributed to
J. Tiekle of Hamburg, made at the
end of the 17th century.*

Right: *A viola d'amore by Jean
Nicholas Lambert.*

251

A violin by Antonio Stradivari (1644-1737), of c. 1699. It is in the foreground of a group of instruments displayed at the Victoria & Albert Museum.

c. 1684), the Guarneri family, especially Giuseppe Guarneri (1698–1744), and Antonio Stradivari (1644–1737).

In the 18th century, the English violin makers were producing extremely fine instruments. None of them were as famous as the Cremonese masters, but instruments by Hudson, Lockey Hill, the Banks family and William Forster and Sons fetch over £1000 today, and sometimes nearer to £2000 – a good sum, but not much when compared with the six figures that an Amati or Stradivari can command. These British makers followed the Cremonese styles on the whole, but they often preferred to make their own bows or commission other native firms. One leading bow maker was John Dodd (1752–1839) who invented the 'hatchet' head type with very slight, gentle curve to the bow. These were often silver or ivory mounted, and had inlay of pearl, and still fetch £400 to £700 or so.

The piano

We have seen that the first pianos were made in Britain in the 1760s. The manufacture of pianos was given a dramatic boost by the arrival in England of several German piano makers who were driven out of their homeland by the ravages and the uncertainties of the Seven Years War in Europe (1756–63), in which Prussia and other German states were battlegrounds for other contending armies. Among the craftsmen were men from the celebrated factory of Gottfried Silbermann in Dresden. The first instruments in England were called pianofortes, and

English grand pianoforte of about 1775, made by Americus Backers, who introduced the 'English' pianoforte action after 1770. Backers worked with Broadwood.

they were basically square plan, about 4 to 5 ft (1.2 to 1.5 m) long, 20 to 24 ins (50 to 60 cm) wide, and 5 to 6 ins (12 to 15 cm) deep. The strings were struck by hammers controlled by dampers. The mechanism was housed in a mahogany case, sometimes decorated with boxwood stringing inlay, though very luxurious models were made from satin-wood, decorated with cross-banding and marquetry. The maker inscribed his name on a nameboard above the keys. The piano had two strings to each note. The first models had no pedals but were fitted with damper stops. The whole piano was provided with a special stand on square tapering legs, with a shelf half way down the stand, and this was known as a French stand. Alternatively, the piano rested upon a simple trestle. These early pianos are often wrongly called harpsichords in some quarters. They were made in considerable numbers right to the end of the 18th century. The oldest surviving early British piano is of 1766, and it was by Johannes Zumpe, one of the German exile craftsmen, who worked in Hanover Square, off Oxford Street, in London. He was one of the first piano makers in England. There is one of his models, of 1767, in the Victoria and Albert Museum.

It is difficult to appreciate the effect of the introduction of the piano to the British musical scene. As an instrument it 'caught on' more quickly and more widely than any other musical instrument before it – and perhaps after it as well, up to the present century. The first public recital on a piano in England was given in London by Johann Christian Bach, one of the eleven sons of Johann Sebastian Bach (1685–1750) the greatest musical genius of all time. Johann Christian bought his piano from Zumpe for £50. Zumpe's pianos in fact formed the basis for most models of square piano built from the 1760s to the end of the century.

By the 1770s the piano had become a serious rival to the harpsichord,

A square piano of about 1795, by Longman and Broderip.

which declined in popularity as we mentioned earlier (but there has been a revival of their manufacture in the present century, spearheaded at the end of the 1890s by Arnold Dolmetsch). Square pianos were a considerable test of the makers' skills, and for a long time, most improvements to pianos and grand pianos were tried out on these early models first.

There were of course other piano makers, and Zumpe did not have a monopoly. One such was John Broadwood (1732–1812) from Berwickshire in Scotland, who walked all the way from his home to London to found his workshop. In 1770 he formed a partnership with Shudi, the harpsichord maker, and they produced square pianos as well as harpsichords. At much the same time, Broadwood began to experiment with the grand piano idea (he was not the inventor), and along with the piano maker Robert Stodard (fl. *c.* 1770–96) he produced a marketable instrument sometime in the later 1770s. The grand piano looked much like the harpsichord externally. It had three strings to each note, two pedals (one for soft and one for sustaining notes), and by about 1800 the keyboard had five and a half octaves.

In the early years of the 19th century, Isaac Hawkins in America introduced an upright piano, and this had a major impact upon the piano market. Uprights became popular because they were cheaper, they took up less room and they were quite satisfactory instruments for amateurs wanting to enjoy themselves at home, and even for professionals to practise on (also at home). But square pianos and grand pianos continued to be made, and a number of improvements were developed: frames were strengthened, first with metal bracing, and somewhat later by being made of metal.

Woodwind instruments

In the 18th century there were some interesting developments in both woodwind and brass instruments. The recorder, often known as the English flute, which enjoyed immense popularity for so long, finally began to decline and give way to a new concept, the cross-flute, which we know today. This had been invented in Germany, and it produced a better tone. In the 1760s the new flute started to be made in England, and English makers introduced their own modifications. Early in the 19th century, Theodore Boehm (1794–1881), a German flautist and goldsmith, was shown a new variety of flute made by a British flautist, Charles Nicholson, in which the finger holes were larger and differently spaced, producing better sounds and greater flexibility. Boehm designed a flute based on this model, and it had enlarged holes widely spaced, but some of these were covered with padded stops operated by levers, enabling the player quite easily to control all the holes and produce very fine sounds, and it revolutionized flute-making. Early transverse flutes can very occasionally be found in sales, with or without their original cases, or at dealers who specialize in musicalia, but you will have to pay £500 or more for an 18th-century one, which will generally have ivory mounts and silver keys.

A new instrument of the 18th century was the clarinet. This was invented by J. C. Denner in the first years of the century, but it was a long time in developing into a manageable instrument, since makers had difficulties with the single reed mouthpiece arrangement. The earliest clarinets were produced in England in the 1760s, and one maker was Cremer & Simpson. The clarinet came in four sections, had five keys of brass, or less often, of silver, and produced a full and mellow tone.

Another delightful woodwind instrument which is now very hard to find is the serpent. Its name aptly describes its shape, like an 'S' with an extra loop, the bottom end wider than the top. Invented in the late 16th century in France, it was played with a cup-shaped mouthpiece more familiar in brass instruments. The serpent first appeared in England in the 18th century, but there are very few left from that time. Rather more of the earlier 19th century have survived, and they generally have six finger holes edged with ivory and anything from one to twelve keys operated by levers. The mouthpieces were of ivory and slotted into a right-angled crook of brass that started the top loop of the 'S' which thereafter continued in wood bound with leather for the rest of the length.

Horns and trumpets

One family of musical instruments that enjoyed an exciting period of experiment and development in the 18th century was the horn family. The original idea of blowing down the narrow end of the head horn of a dead animal to produce a calling sound goes back to the earliest days of civilization, though the horn did not become an actual musical instrument until comparatively late. By the 18th century at least two types of musical horn were becoming prominent features of an orchestra, the 'French' horn and the trumpet, and there was also room for the sackbut (the forerunner of the trombone) and the cor anglais. The French horn was circular and coiled in shape, with its bell end a foot or more across. The overall length was about 11 ft (3.30 m), which had been found to be the right length to achieve a reasonable range of sounds. It could be adapted to meet the right key for the composition to be played by inserting an interchangeable crook, or bent length of tube.

In the mid-18th century a German horn player, Anton Joseph Hampel (1710–71) introduced the idea of modifying the pitch of the sounds from his French horn to produce full harmonic scales of notes by the simple expedient of putting one hand up the horn's bell and holding it in various positions while blowing. This technique greatly enriched the range of performance for players and encouraged composers to introduce greater roles for the horn in orchestral works. What particularly pleased music lovers (and still does today, though a special mute can now be inserted to take the place of the hand) was the contrast between the open and unimpeded sonority of the horn when blown without muting and the quite different and dreamy notes produced by inserting the hand up the bell. These French horns of the 18th century are still obtainable, but you would have to pay over £1000 for one without big dents. In the early 19th century, the introduction of valves operated by stops greatly increased and enriched the whole scope of the horn as an instrument, and it also made it easier to play.

Trumpets, meanwhile, which also had interchangeable crooks, had in the 17th century been fitted with a simplified slide, not unlike a trombone, to widen the range of notes and expand the number of keys. Curiously, the adaptation appears to have gone out of favour for a time in the 18th century, but by the end it had returned. Like the horn, the trumpet was improved in the early 19th century by the introduction of finger-stop-operated valves.

A handsome French horn, by Marcel Auguste Raoux, Paris, 1826. This once belonged to the virtuoso Giovanni Puzzi, and is said to have been given to him by Louis XVIII or Charles X.

Treen

The word 'treen' literally means anything made of trees, but its actual application is limited traditionally to small useful household items made of wood. It is a term that has been in use since at least the 16th century, and appears in many inventories of domestic chattels.

The commonest small wooden objects in early houses would probably have been bowls, spoons and other vessels connected with the kitchen. But even by 1577, when John Harrison published his *Description of England*, the use of wooden utensils was declining. He writes of 'the exchange of vessel, as of treene platters into pewter, and wooden spoons into silver or tin. For so common were all sortes of treene stuffe in old time that a man should hardly find foure peeces of pewter (of which peradventure a salt) in a good farmer's house . . .' Nevertheless, this sort of treen, made right into the 19th century, is fairly easy to find in antique shops, particularly those which specialize in country furniture.

It is difficult to define the precise area of collecting covered by the word treen, and each individual has his or her own particular view. On the whole it is safe to say that wood should be the main material used, and that the object should be no larger than, say, a spinning wheel. Furthermore, cabinet-work, however small, is not usually classed as

Domestic tableware in wood: a trencher, a bowl cut from a log, and a platter.

A fine English wassail bowl of the mid-17th-century, turned from lignum vitae wood. It consists of a bowl, cover with three finials, central cup for holding spices and three turned cups.

Two English wooden tea caddies shaped like melons. End of 18th century.

A 19th-century Welsh wooden lace bobbin winder.

treen. The craftsmen most responsible for treen are the turner and the carver. Treen is nearly always utilitarian rather than purely decorative but the two elements are often nicely combined when an interesting wood is employed.

The kitchen is one of the places where treen was – and indeed is – most found. Wood in its various forms provided suitable raw material for all sorts of vessels, spoons, graters and other mechanisms. Even today most kitchens have the odd wooden spoon, pepper mill or wooden mortar and pestle.

Apart from the rich, who ate off silver and pewter, the majority used wooden platters from the earliest medieval times. These took a square form in the Middle Ages, but by the 16th century had assumed their more familiar circular shape and were about 9 in (22.5 cm) in diameter. They were designed to be wiped clean with bread after the first course and then turned over. Not many early platters can be found, and when they are they do not often come in sets. Before buying, one should examine the surface for knife marks and other signs of wear. Anything that has had the sort of heavy use kitchen treen would have had in a few centuries must show the many pits, dents and scratches of that use. One of the great attractions of treen is the mellow rounded appearance of the wood and the depth of colour caused by years of friction polishing, which cannot be artificially imitated.

Utensils connected with food, either its preparation or consumption, had to be made of a close-grained and reasonably waterproof timber that was easily cleaned. The humbler items would have been of sycamore or beech, but anything that might be on public view could be made in a variety of woods with more attractive patterning. Fruitwood was always a popular choice, being readily available in most country districts and eminently suitable for turning into cups, bowls, salts, castors, etc. Pear and cherry are the turners' favourites, the former creamy in colour and the latter of a pale pinkish hue. They are somewhat subject to worm and decay, and do not take heavy use, but are ideal for goblets or condiment sets. Apple comes in smaller sizes, is yellowish and heavy. Its hardness makes it ideal for small moving parts and fine turning.

In the 17th century, *lignum vitae* began to be imported from the tropics, and this very hard and dramatically figured wood became

A harvest barrel.

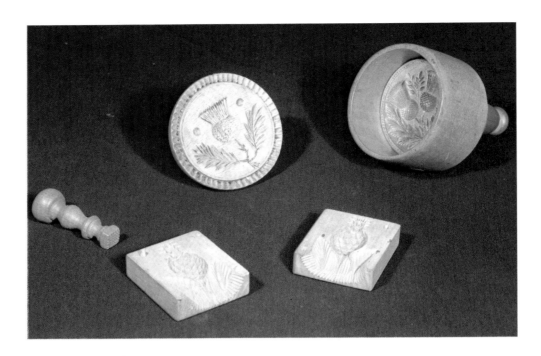

Wooden pastry jigger and three butter moulds.

popular for expensive cups or wassail bowls. Some of these are embellished with silver rims, which contrast very well with the alternating dark chocolate and yellow of the timber.

Spoons of all sizes have survived in surprising numbers, considering their tendency to be lost or discarded when old. English spoons usually have straight turned handles and are quite plain apart, sometimes, from initials of individual owners. In times past spoons were personal items and were replaced in a rack when not in use. Forks were rarely made of wood, but knives – the all-purpose tools of the 16th and 17th centuries – were frequently beautified with carved handles.

As in furniture, the Welsh produced their own charming styles, the best known being the love-spoon. Many of these were finely carved out of a single piece of wood and given to sweethearts. They are literally a labour of love.

Other small interesting kitchen utensils found in antique shops include lemon squeezers, apple corers, rolling pins, nutmeg graters and various grinders. The latter were introduced in the late 17th century, and have a metal grinder at the base. Nutmeg graters were made of coquilla nuts, whose top unscrewed to reveal the grater, which itself is removed so that the powdered nutmeg could be shaken out. These were often quite small and might be carried in a pocket and used to spice wine or punch.

One important branch of treen ought to be mentioned here, and

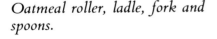

Oatmeal roller, ladle, fork and spoons.

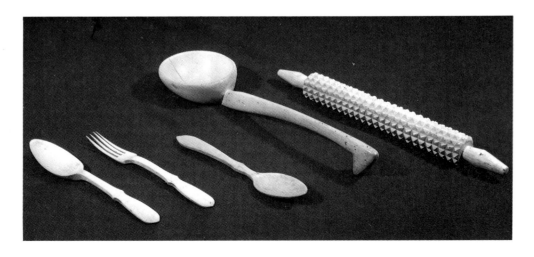

*Some 18th- and 19th-century treen:
top, sycamore wood cream skimmer;
left, larchwood pap boat; right,
Scottish drinking vessel (bicker), of
sycamore and alder staves, with
willow banding; bottom, caddy spoon.*

*English Noah's Ark, with numerous
figures, in carved and painted wood,
made about 1860. The ark is about
10 in. (25 cm.) high.*

that is coopered ware. Apart from small barrels and kegs, many buckets and pails were made in this way as an alternative to using metal. Smaller vessels were coopered in the north of England and Scotland, and whether this was due to a shortage of substantial amounts of solid timber for turning is not known. However, the small drinking cups or 'quaiches' from Scotland are most charming and collectable. They are usually made with alternate staves of, say, box or holly, next to *lignum vitae* or laburnum. The staves were bound together not with iron bands but with willow hoops. This method of making beakers is both ancient and very practical, indeed their durability is amply proved by the recovery of perfect examples from the wreck of the *Mary Rose* in 1982.

Many of the trades and skills associated with agriculture provide scope for the collector. Butter pats, moulds with regional differences of motif, churns and cream bowls are now sought after, along with wooden agricultural implements and malt shovels. Even relics of the early Industrial Revolution, such as shuttles and wooden planes, are collected, but many of these things belong more properly to the field known as bygones, as they are often the product more of mass-production processes.

Pre-Victorian toys were nearly always wooden and frequently homemade. Dolls were often made out of a single billet of wood, carved in at two points to form a waist and a neck, and then given a wig and arms attached with leather. Wooden animals were made in the same way, and small horses of this type were mounted on trolleys to be pulled along. Tops varied in sophistication from the plain turned examples to those with ivory spindles and holes drilled in them to make them hum.

The turner was responsible for some beautiful toys such as cup and ball – familiar today – which was made in different sizes for adults and children.

Games can make interesting subjects for a collection. Chess and draughts come in all degrees of elaboration of turning and carving, and are really a subject in themselves. Cribbage, which is a card game, has wooden scoreboards. Some of these are carved and curved (Yorkshire and Westmorland) but most are straight.

Lace-making was carried on as a domestic pastime as well as, until the late 19th century, a cottage industry in such areas as Devon, Nottingham and the Waveney Valley of Suffolk. Lace bobbins were made in many woods, mostly the close grained sorts like fruitwood, box or sycamore. These are turned, but some – perhaps special gifts – are carved as well. There are also regional variations. Nottinghamshire bobbins tended to have wires with coloured beads on them to act as a counterbalance while in use, whereas the fine lace work of Honiton, Devon, required the bobbin to be pulled through, thus necessitating a

Opposite page: *Jigsaw puzzle of about 1839/40, illustrating Prince Albert of Saxe-Coburg, who became Prince Consort only in 1857, though his marriage to Queen Victoria was in 1840.*

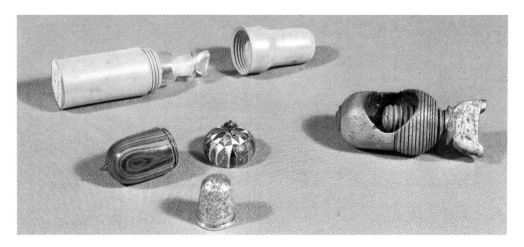

Left: *Early-19th-century treen: top left, boxwood bottle container; bottom left, thimble container with thimble; right, screw-down nutcracker, perhaps of mulberry wood.*

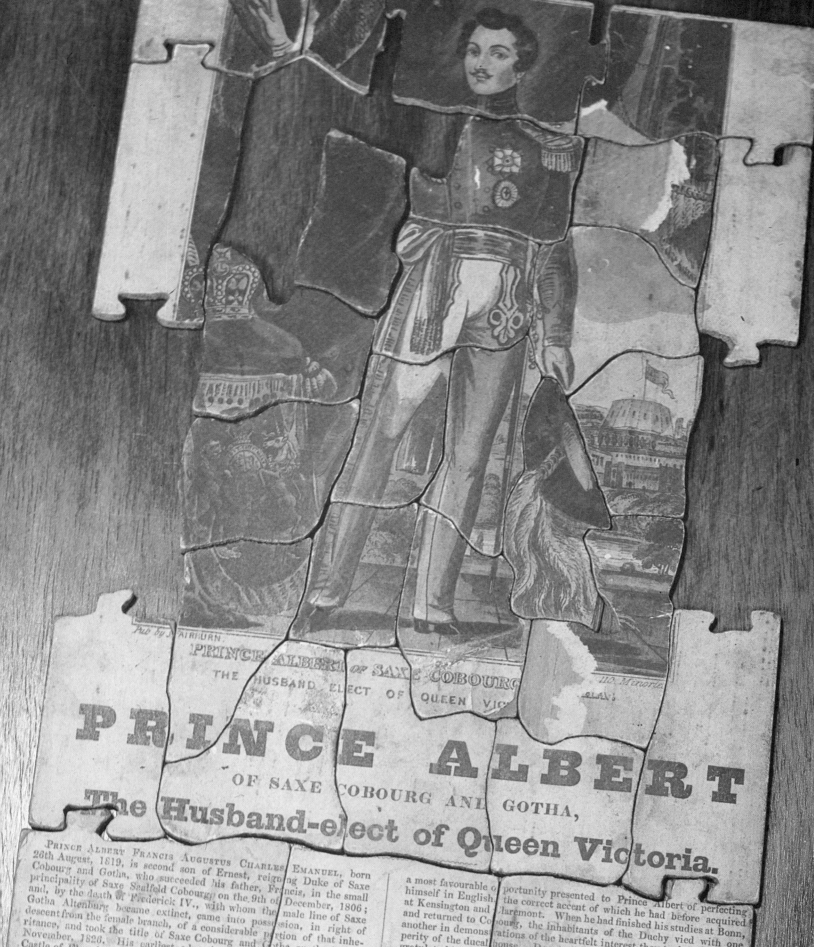

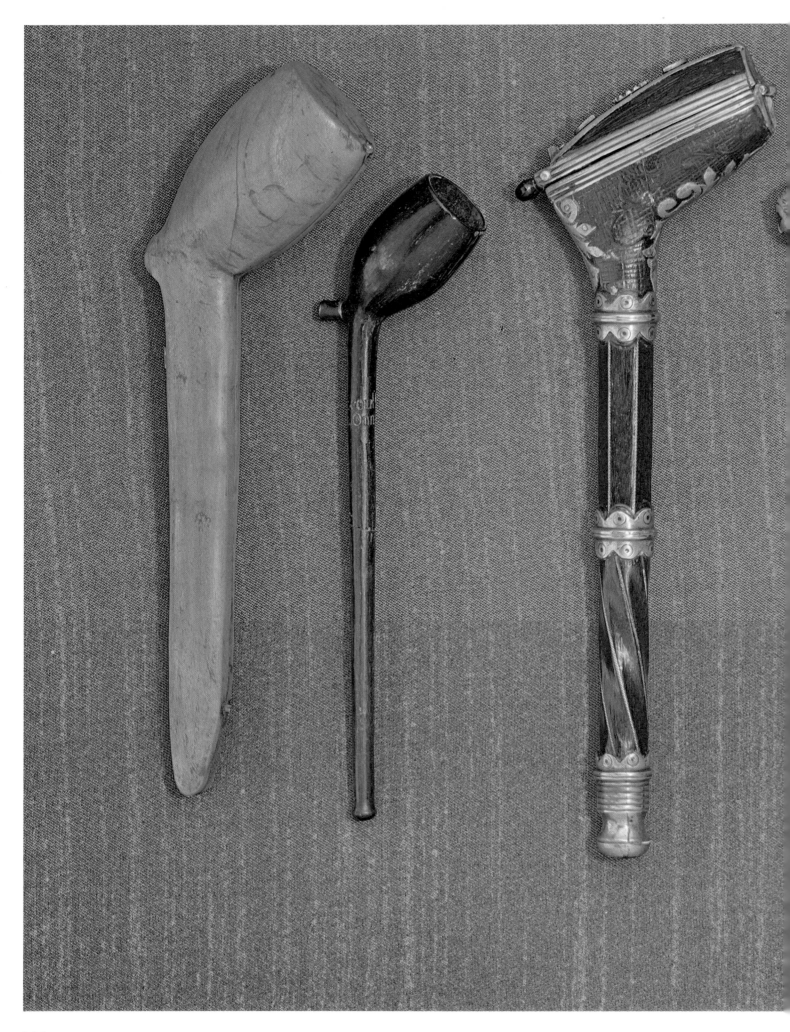

266

A group of 18th-century pipe cases. From left to right: Dutch, boxwood; Austrian, boxwood; Dutch, ebony; English, clay.

267

slim and pointed shape. The cotton thread was wound onto the bobbins by means of a winder, which might be screwed to a table with a wooden turnscrew.

The habit of smoking and taking snuff led to the proliferation of many small objects connected with the ritual of cleaning pipes, chopping and storing tobacco and snuff. Pipes were always made of clay until the 19th century and these had to be protected in pipe cases, which are now not at all common. More usually found are the simple racks on which the long churchwardens' pipes were laid horizontally. Tobacco and snuff boxes were made in many materials, but the aim was always to keep the contents fresh and, in the case of tobacco, to prevent it drying out too much. Close-grained hardwoods were best for this. Sometimes found but always expensive are the little snuff boxes shaped like boots with lifting lids over the heel. Another type of rare piece is the carved tobacco tamper, made perhaps of boxwood, which has acquired a beautiful rich colour as a result of being handled and used in contact with tobacco smoke.

A fascinating collection of treen, including double-end egg-cup, pepper pot, nut-cracker, long-handled castanets, and wooden case for holding a medicine bottle.

A 19th-century German copy of an earlier Black Forest toy, a dancing pair, with musician. The handle at the right turns the table on which the dancers stand.

Miscellaneous

Tunbridge ware

This is the name of a peculiarly English form of woodware first made in the last quarter of the 17th century by craftsmen in and around the district of Tunbridge Wells and its neighbour town Tonbridge, in Kent. In the earlier part of the century Tunbridge Wells had become a fashionable watering place, and in the 1680s wood craftsmen began to make, for quick sale to people with time to kill and money to burn, small articles such as boxes, small tables, miniature chests, candlestands, etc., decorating them with what is often called wood mosaic. The neighbourhood was blessed with a great variety of trees, such as furze, yew, holly and cherry, in addition to the more widespread oak, walnut and fruitwoods, and there is evidence, too, that imported woods were also used. The remarkable traveller Celia Fiennes, who made many journeys on horseback through the small towns and countryside of England, noted in her diary for 1697 that at Tunbridge Wells there were 'shopps full of . . . all sorts of curious wooden ware which this place is noted for, the delicate, neate and thin ware of wood . . .'

One of the first makers was a craftsman called Jordan, another was a craftsman called Wise, and there is also a tradition that the originator of the ware was William Burrows, of Gibraltar Cottage.

The usual method of making these geometrical or simpler floral-patterned articles was roughly as follows. Thin strips of different colours and grains were glued together in bundles, and when the glue had set,

Below left: Selection of 19th-century Tunbridgeware small boxes. One box lid bears a wood mosaic picture of Queen Victoria.

Below: Late-18th-century Tunbridgeware box, with highly ornamental wood mosaic.

Above right: *Regency Tunbridgeware teapoy on stand.*

Above: *Small Tunbridgeware workbox, with wood mosaic decoration. 19th century.*

the bundles were sliced transversely to produce very thin wafers of patterned wood, which were applied as veneers to a range of small objects. The technique was a relatively simple way of making very attractive patterns and pictures, and the use of imported woods further enriched the overall colouring. A demand for this ware was generated very quickly, far beyond the environs of the two sleepy Kentish towns, and London dealers gave it the name of Tunbridge ware. By the 19th century, it had become one of the best-known forms of English wood decoration. Its popularity led to its being imitated in several other parts of the country, and there is still quite a lot of the ware about. It is easily recognizable from its mosaic appearance, in squares, diamonds, circles, rectangles, and less usual shapes of several fascinating natural colours.

Tunbridge ware was still being made in the early part of the present century, and one of the last firms to produce fine-quality pieces was Boyce, Brown and Kemp. Some of their products are hard to differentiate from the original ware. They provide a fruitful field for collecting. Much Tunbridge ware of the 19th century comes up for sale at auctions and is not always expensive. Work boxes with floral patterns or geometric designs on the lids made in the later 19th century can be obtained for less than £50, but you will have to pay much more for those interesting pieces of earlier date which carry landscape pictures of famous buildings, such as Windsor Castle, Tonbridge Castle, or Malvern Abbey.

Card cases

Anyone who was anybody in the late 18th century and through the 19th century carried visiting cards (indeed the custom continued into the first half of the present century), and naturally these cards needed to be kept clean and flat. Card cases, usually in the form of small, flat rectangular or square boxes with hinged lid on one narrow side, were almost always the subject of considerable decorative skill. Hundreds of thousands – perhaps millions – must have been made over the years, in a great variety of materials, gold, silver, mother-of-pearl, papier-mâché, leather, wood, bronze, brass, beadwork, porcelain, ivory, enamel, tortoiseshell, even glass. This is a field in which you can still build up an interesting collection quite easily and at not too great expense.

Silver and silver-plate card cases are often to be found in antique shops, and many are most beautifully decorated, some quite out of proportion to the importance of the article! Perhaps the most attractive of the silver cases is the filigree type (ornamental openwork of intricate design), with richly chased decoration round a raised view of, say, a famous cathedral or mansion. These are expensive, over £100. Nathaniel Mills of Birmingham was a noted maker of silver card cases (as well as of many other articles) in the mid-19th century. One of his card cases with a relief picture of St Paul's Cathedral fetched over £250 at a 1983 auction.

Much cheaper are mother-of-pearl cases, with the surface decorated in a pattern of lozenze-shaped pieces of veneer, and leather cases, whose top half slides over the bottom half and may be decorated with petit-point embroidery or a tooled design with gilt.

Samplers

Surprisingly, quite a lot of antique needlework has survived in various forms and conditions, some even reaching back to the 17th century (and in one or two museums, even earlier). A type of needlework which is ideal for collecting is the sampler, and you could hardly start in a better way than with an example handed down from an ancestor (many families have one or two samplers of the 19th century at least). The sampler is an embroidered panel which, in the 16th and 17th centuries, was a kind of reference panel for types of stitch, pattern specimens and

An early-19th-century Tunbridgeware jewel cabinet, with a wood mosaic picture of Bayham Abbey on the top.

271

Opposite page: *An attractive American sampler, by Lucy Symonds, of Boxford, Massachusetts, 1796.*

occasional figures, human and animal. A piece of linen was stretched across a square or rectangular frame and a variety of lacework motifs was stitched to make up the 'chart'. The usual patterns were geometric shapes, occasional architectural shapes, sometimes patterns resembling inlay patterns found on contemporary furniture. By the end of the 17th century, the production of a sampler had become much more a children's exercise in needlework, and coloured wools and silks were used. Children were set to embroider a wise saying or motto, or a verse from the Bible or the Book of Common Prayer, and to fill up the space above and below with a full alphabet, in capitals and in small letters, adding perhaps numbers 1 to 10, and if room, signing off with their name and age. In many cases, the length of the wording to be embroidered was miscalculated, and it turns upwards at the end of the line.

But samplers were not always children's exercises: adult students of needlework also made them for practice. They were made in England and Wales, less often in Scotland, and they were also widely done in America from the 18th century onwards. There is a fine American sampler of 1774 in the American Museum at Claverton Manor, near Bath. Seventeenth-century samplers are hard to find today, and are expensive, but late 18th-century and 19th-century specimens come up for sale frequently at auctions, often in frames with glass covering, and can be expected to make anything from £30 to £100, according to age, condition, colour, originality and size. One interesting sampler made in 1721 fetched £300 in a sale in 1983.

Right: *A sampler by Esther Copp, aged 11, executed in America in 1765, before the War of Independence.*

Below: *English alphabet sampler of the year 1847.*

Tea caddies

Tea drinking began in Britain in the mid-17th century, the habit having come across from Holland. The diarist Samuel Pepys recorded his first cup of tea in the entry for 28th September 1660. 'I did send for a cup of tea (a China drink) of which I never had drank before.' It was in his time an expensive commodity, anything between £6 and £10 per lb in the money of the day, and thus vastly more costly in relative terms than today. It remained expensive for many years, dropping only slowly to between 10/- and £1 per lb throughout much of the 18th century. It was drunk almost exclusively by the upper class, and because it was so expensive, that class considered it necessary to hide it from their servants! They kept it in containers in locked cupboards.

The earliest containers for tea, or caddies, were made of porcelain in China, and consisted of jars, round, oval, vase-like, barrel-shaped, octagonal, oblong with rounded shoulders, and supplied with cap or lid. The name they were given, 'caddies', came from the Malaysian measure of weight – of about 1.2 lbs – the *kati*. At first, the measure was corrupted in English to 'catty', though we are not sure when the term was first used.

The porcelain caddies were decorated with a variety of motifs – in blue and white, in polychrome, in celadon – and the range is both wide and beautiful. Then caddies began to appear in silver, in much the same shapes, and these fetch large sums today if they date to George I (1714–27) or George II (1727–60). They also appeared in pewter and in pottery in the later Georgian period, and are less costly to buy today. Caddies also appeared in other materials such as wood (with the interior lined and the box having a tight-fitting lid). Wooden caddies were finely decorated on the exterior with boxwood or satinwood inlay or with

An interesting Prattware china tea caddy of the end of the 18th century. The decoration is a caricature of contemporary ladies' fashions.

274

An unusual Regency tea caddy, decorated with rolled paper work.

Late George IV rosewood teapoy of about 1830. The photograph shows the interior, with the teapot. Note the glass tea-mixing bowls in centre.

marquetry of various patterns, many caddies having marquetry shell motifs. Sometimes these wooden caddies had two compartments, for two different brands of tea, and some had three compartments, the middle one providing space for a cut-glass bowl in which to blend the two teas. The bowl could also be used for sugar, which was first taken with tea sometime in the middle of the 18th century.

Some types of wooden tea caddy were mounted upon a single pillar stand with tripod or quadrupod base. These pieces, which are often called teapoys, were introduced at the end of the 18th century, and were made in walnut, mahogany, rosewood, and less often in papier-mâché. They can be found for as little as £200 to £250. Less common are tea caddies mounted on a frame consisting of four legs linked low down with stretchers on all sides, or by a brass-edged gallery.

Above: *A tea caddy of the late 19th century, hand-painted with flowers and decorated with mother-of-pearl inlay.*

Right: *Late 18th-century oval tea caddy, painted with landscape pictures, with figures, buildings and trees.*

Right: *Late 18th-century tea caddy veneered in scarlet tortoiseshell, with brass keyhole and handle.*

Far Right: *George III octagonal sycamore tea caddy, chequer strung and inlaid with satinwood and tulipwood decoration, dated 1789.*

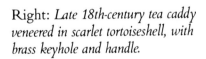

Buttons

Twenty years ago, few people would have bothered to collect buttons, fewer still would have thought they had much value. But in 1961 an interesting collection of buttons with painted scenes covered with clear glass was sold at Sotheby's in about 200 lots for a total of £6,600. Before long, a shop specializing in antique buttons was opened in central London, and soon after that interest began to spread to the USA, where a National Button Society was formed, publishing a monthly bulletin. Then came the books on buttons, and the craze for collecting was on.

Buttons are among the oldest artefacts of civilized men and women: they were known as far back as ancient Egypt, and examples can be seen in the major collections of Egyptian domestic artefacts, such as at the British Museum in London and the Louvre in Paris.

Buttons were devised to fasten or to decorate clothing. Many were prominently displayed for others to see, and so no amount of skill was

Above: *Some 18th-century and early 19th-century buttons:* top left, *brass sporting button (1830s);* top centre, *one of a set painted in watercolour on parchment, c. 1770;* top right, *livery button in silver, European, c. 1800;* bottom left, *gilt metal, bone and cat-gut, of the mid-18th century;* bottom centre, *silver and purple foil, with silver lace, of c. 1760;* bottom right, *silver button converted to brooch, c. 1800.*

Above: *French mid-19th-century enamelled and gilt button, in mid-18th-century style.*

Three attractive early-19th-century enamel and diamante buttons.

This is a French button illustrating the Storming of the Bastille in Paris, on 14th July 1789, the event which signalled the outbreak of the French Revolution.

Collection of 18th and 19th-century buttons.

spared in the design. A vast quantity of buttons has been made over the centuries, even before mass-production methods were introduced, and an almost limitless variety of materials was used; among them precious and base metals, enamel, porcelain, pottery, glass, mother-of-pearl, bone, ivory, wood, painted silk, papier-mâché, tortoiseshell, leather, seashell, semi-precious stone, cameo and fabric. Obviously there are many areas for making interesting collections; for example many hunts had waistcoat and top-coat buttons of brass or rolled gold bearing the crest of the particular hunt.

Buttons were (and still are in some quarters) sometimes employed to indicate rank or position, to identify military regiments, government departments, railway and shipping lines, private companies, famous or noble family households (often called crested livery buttons) and of course for numerous commemorative purposes. American collectors are particularly interested in buttons that record the story of the republic since the War of Independence (1774–83), such as those celebrating Lafayette's arrival in America, Paul Revere's ride, the early railroads, or regiments which fought against the British in the War of 1812–14. At the beginning of the present century, advertising agencies started to use buttons to promote clients' products. Most were made of celluloid and carried pictures and slogans exhorting people to buy the goods.

Pricing buttons is very difficult, but few buttons of the 18th century have fetched less than £2 in sale rooms.

Chessmen

If you play chess at all, you will surely enjoy setting out to collect chessman. The game has been played in Europe since the Middle Ages, even longer in the Middle East, and longest of all in China. Today, sets are made in plastic, wood, metal and other material, but in the past they were fashioned in a wide range of materials, often in the most original and sometimes beautiful styles, in gold, silver, porcelain, ivory (frequently), ebony and other woods, bone, cast iron, even jasperware (by the Wedgwood factory). So popular is the field for collecting that there are now many shops in Britain specially devoted to chess sets. One of the best known is in the narrow alley called Lansdowne Place, near Berkeley Square in London, and there is another chess shop in the small town of Mildenhall in Suffolk! And so many sets have been made over the centuries in Europe alone that hardly a sale of any importance does not have several sets for auction.

Chess sets prior to the 19th century are rare, and if complete they are expensive. Much sought after but costly are porcelain pieces, perhaps in Meissen – there is a famous Meissen set of chessmen in Turkish costume, with the chessboard also made of porcelain. Some chessmen were made to commemorate notable military victories, in which one 'king' was the victorious commander (such as Napoleon). Sets were made representing the main opposing sides in famous wars, such as those between Crusaders and Saracens, Indians and East India Company forces, or Cavaliers and Roundheads. But a collection can be made at prices within the average income capacity if you stick to 19th-century European, Chinese or Indian chessmen. In England, the Hon. Howard Staunton, the first Englishman to win the world chess championship,

An unusual silver and silver-gilt chess set, on circular bases, the kings and queens in Austrian or Turkish dress. This set is of late 18th-century make.

in 1847, designed chess sets in boxwood, which were in natural colour for one side and dyed red or black for the other. His sets were made by the London firm of Jacques and Sons. One of these fetched £500 in a 1983 sale, but you don't need to pay this high price if you look around. Indian or Chinese sets in ivory, of the mid to late 19th century, can be bought for a little over £100, and you might find them for less. Some Chinese sets have figures representing members of the Chinese imperial family, with mandarins, army commanders and – for the pawns – soldiers with swords or lances.

English 19th-century ivory chess set, in white and brown.

A Far Eastern ivory chess set, with red and white pieces, possibly from Macao. This set was made in the later 19th century.

Fitted boxes

In the 18th and 19th centuries people used wooden fitted boxes for numerous everyday articles and purposes. They were useful at home, even more so if you were going away for holiday or long business trip or for more extended visiting. They were employed to accommodate the essential tools, containers or apparatus required for one or other of a vast range of activities. Many were specially compartmented for the various articles to fit in tightly so that the box could be carried about in a bumpy coach or at sea, and these were particularly useful for bottles with liquids. Boxes were made of mahogany or rosewood, less often of oak or walnut or fruitwood, and usually had brass handles, mounts and bands inset flush with the woodwork, to protect the corners and edges and to give general reinforcement. They were often fitted with escutcheon or similar shaped lockplates, and a panel for the owner's name or initials, and the inside of the lid was frequently upholstered in velvet, smooth or crinkled, to keep stoppers in bottles, lids on jars and generally to prevent other things moving about in transit. There is often a long, thin rod of brass or other metal running down inside the casing and ending in a receiving hole in the casing of a drawer at the bottom or at the side. This acts as a lock when the whole box is locked. Opening the drawer is done by lifting the rod. Many boxes had secret compartments opened and shut by a variety of contrivances.

One type of fitted box was the household medicine chest or dispenser. This contained several bottles, jars, and a drawer or drawers

A typical mid-19th-century English writing box. This one is of walnut decorated in key pattern. These boxes frequently come up for sale at auctions.

Pearwood workbox with looking-glass lining in the lid (right), and (left) a writing box opened out, ready for use. Mid-19th century.

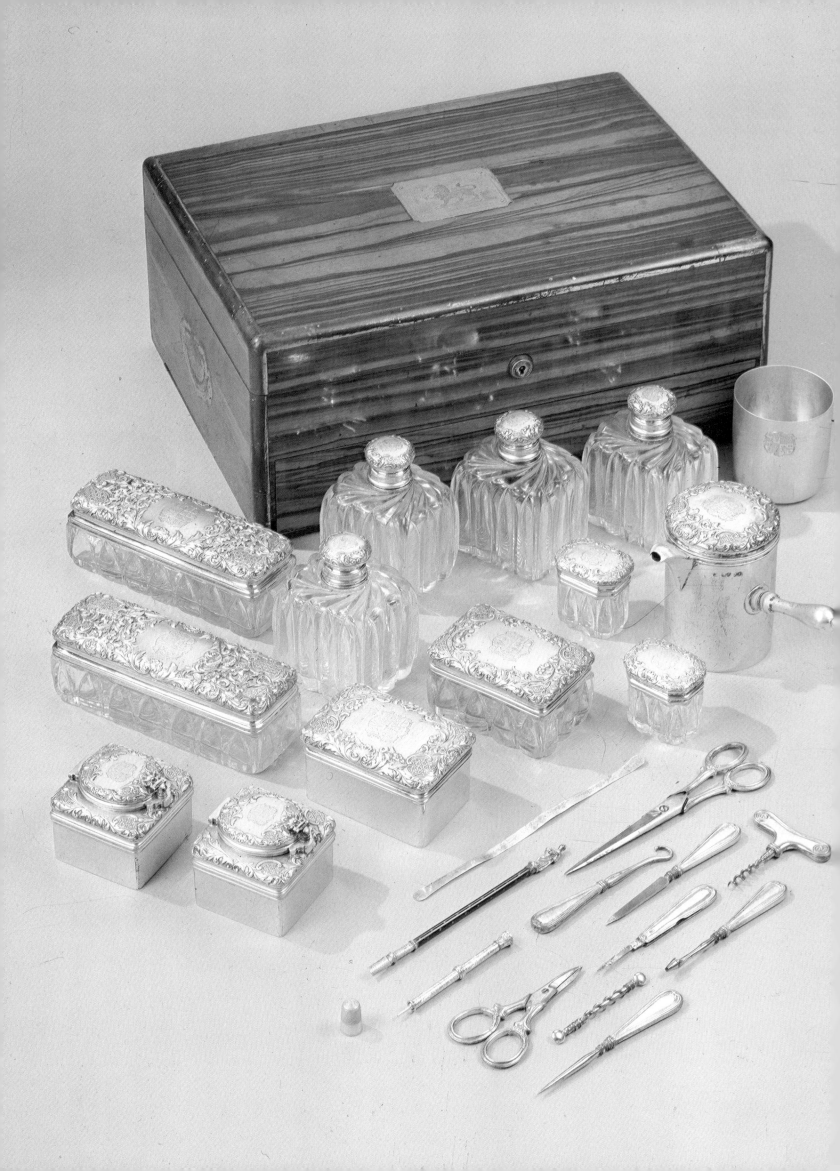

with various bits of simple apparatus such as scales and weights to
weigh out powders, small pestle and mortar for grinding salts, forceps,
spatula, knife or two, and so on. Doctors had more sophisticated medicine chests, often known as apothecary's boxes, and surgeons had
instrument sets in specially fitted boxes.

Other boxes were made for various uses, including writing boxes,
toilet boxes, sewing boxes, artists' boxes (Queen Victoria gave one as
a present to William Evans, the well-known watercolour painter, who
was art master at Eton and had given her art lessons), drinking boxes,
knife boxes (particularly those designed but not made by Sheraton),
perfume boxes, stationery boxes and jewel boxes. Writing boxes, also
known in some quarters as *escritoires*, were made from the late 18th
century right to the end of the 19th. These were, until recently,
numerous in Britain, frequently appearing in sales and also to be found
in nearly every antique shop, generally for small sums for the 19th-
century ones. Usually rectangular, anything from about 15 to 22 in (38

to 56 cm) long, with brass mounts, with a writing slope (in many examples the bottom and top half come together in an incline and not horizontally), compartments for inkwells, sand bottles (early blotting techniques), seals and sealing wax, pens, etc., and with one long drawer along the bottom reached from one or other side and a series of secret compartments under the ink bottle and pen-rack section. These boxes now fetch anything from £50 to £200 according to quality, variety of inside fitting and age, but the 18th-century and early Regency ones are more expensive.

Toilet boxes go back to the 18th century, and some were inlaid with brass and mother-of-pearl, the toilet bottles having silver screw caps or glass stoppers (these boxes are generally more expensive). Artists' boxes are rare, but they contain rows of solid watercolour paints, nicely labelled, with space for brushes, one or two mixing dishes, and room

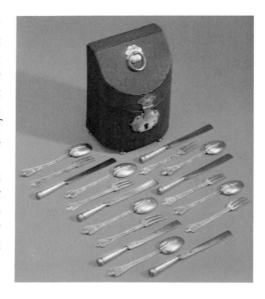

Opposite page: *The William and Mary case opened, showing the spoons, forks and knives in their slots.*

Below: *Early-19th-century carving knife and fork, with steel blade and fork-end, and ivory handles.*

Above: *A rare and very fine William and Mary silver-gilt canteen of spoons, forks and knives, dated about 1690, laid out beside the closed case.*

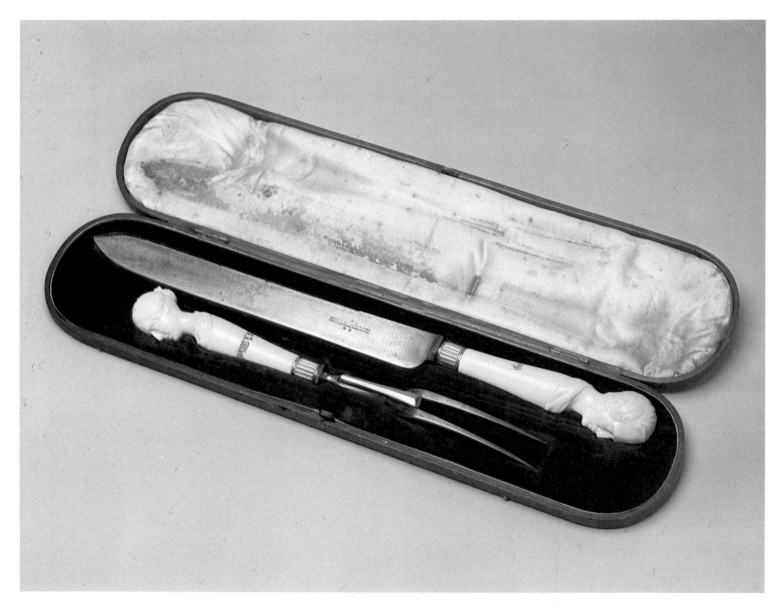

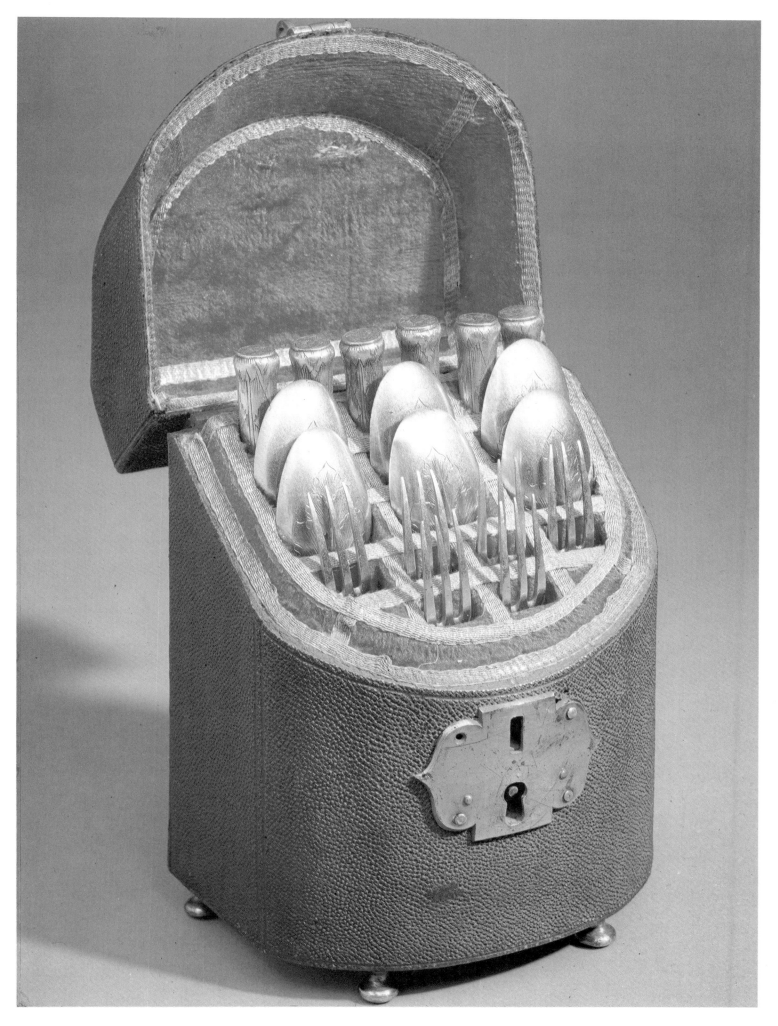

Above: *A good 19th-century mahogany and ebony strung domestic medicine chest.*

Right: *Another type of 19th-century medicine chest, which opens horizontally, with bottles in racks in both doors.*

in the lid for a palette or two. Drinking boxes contained fine cut-glass mini-decanters and sets of glasses whose stems fitted into velvet-edged slots for steady holding. These were liqueur cases or spirit cases. A great deal of skill went into designing and making all these boxes, even when they were being produced in quantity in the second half of the 19th century. They present a delightful area for collecting, though they take up a lot of room, twice their closed area – because, of course, they have to be opened up!

Barometers

A country whose natives worry so much about the weather should be rich in artefacts connected with weather forecasting. And so it is, particularly in barometers. The barometer was invented in the early 1640s in Italy by Evangelista Torricelli (1608–47), a physicist who was also amanuensis for the great Galileo in the latter's last years. There is a copy of his first 'Torricellian tube' – a stick-type barometer – in the Science Museum, London. Some decades later, the English scientist, Robert Hooke (1635–1703) devised a marine barometer in the form of a wheel as opposed to a stick, and until the introduction of the aneroid barometer in the 1840s, most barometers were of one or other type.

The stick barometer consisted of a thin glass tube about a yard long, sealed at the top end, and with the bottom end inserted into a bowl of mercury. The air is removed from the inverted tube, and this makes the mercury rise up the tube once the open end is pushed into the bowl. Once the mercury has found a level, it remains there, and only rises or falls according to the atmospheric pressure outside the tube. Behind the tube in the location of the mercury level a flat plate is positioned, on which is recorded a series of figures and phrases indicating low (unsettled weather) pressure, and high (settled weather) pressure, 26 to 31. This simple apparatus was enclosed in a thin rectangular box which over the years was the subject of a considerable variety of styles of adornment. Many were provided with an architectural top, a broken pediment, straight or swan neck, a fretwork frieze or a simple capital. The mercury bowl was enclosed in a circular or square box at the bottom end, and this was decorated with a polished dome or a flat brass or wooden vase-shaped plaque or shell inlay work. The tube case itself was also decorated with marquetry or whatever other decorative treatment was in vogue. Barometer cases were on the whole narrower after the turn of the 19th century than before, and the mercury tube began to be covered most or all the way to the top section that contained the pressure register, where the mercury level was.

Hooke's wheel barometer was the forerunner of what we call the banjo barometer – obvious from its shape. Wheel barometers had dial face and hands, and appear to have been more widely made than stick barometers for about two centuries. In the earliest years, some banjo barometers were designed by the greatest clockmakers of the time, such as Tompion, Knibb and the Fromanteels. Barometers by these masters are rare and fetch extremely high prices, but there were numerous excellent instruments made by lesser- or hardly-known craftsmen, and they can be bought for £100 to £300, even if they are of the 18th century. Many of them have a thermometer in the top half of the instrument, and some makers also fitted a clock in a second, smaller swelling of the top half. One or two found room also for a hygrometer for the humidity of the atmosphere, and a spirit level to ensure that the barometer was hung correctly.

The casing of banjo barometers received as much attention as the works themselves, and an interesting variety of decorative treatments are found, such as intricate brass inlay, mother-of-pearl inlay, architectural pediments, crossband veneer, ivory fittings, shell motif inlays and so forth. Names of makers to look for include Hallifax of Barnsley, Bird of London, Dollond of London, Rizzi of Leeds, Vassalli of Scarborough, Cary of London, Dring of West Chester, Pennsylvania, USA, James Green of Baltimore.

When buying a barometer in a sale or from an antique dealer, make sure that it works. Barometers are expensive to repair and there are not many craftsmen who can do this properly.

A group of English barometers: left, carved mahogany, of the mid-18th century; centre, carved mahogany, with shell motifs and brass plate with thermometer; right, a John Halifax barometer of burr-yew-wood, c. 1720.

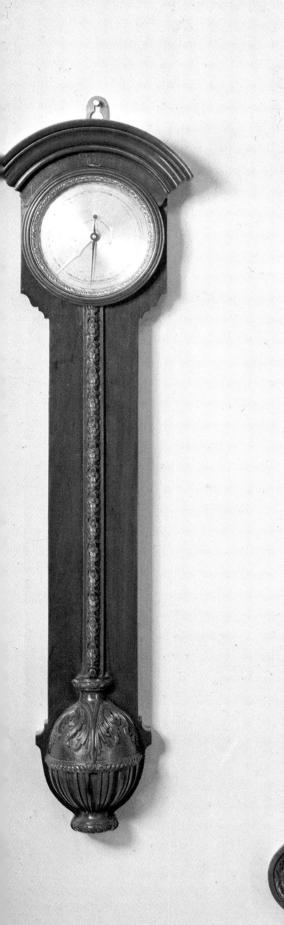
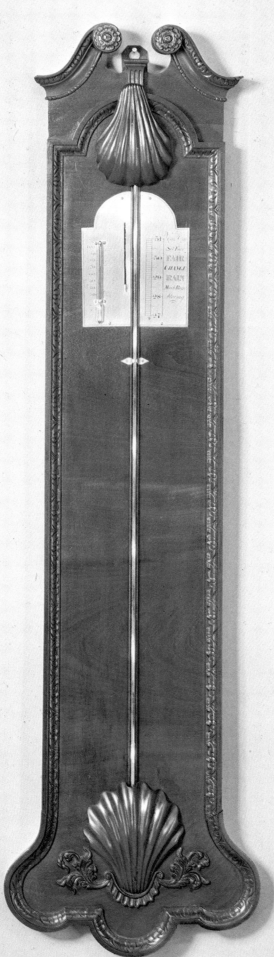

Early examples of papier-mâché: a bread basket and a tea caddy, both of the late 18th century.

Papier-mâché

Papier-mâché, literally translated, means 'chewed paper'. It was the French who introduced to Europe the technique of making articles out of this material, but the skill originated in the Far East. Indeed, objects more than 2000 years old have been discovered, which says much for the durability of the material. The Chinese used papier-mâché for war helmets, and later on, the Japanese and the Persians used it for a variety of decorative and functional purposes. The finish on these eastern objects was usually a form of lacquer, similar to that used on wood or metal, and this finish was continued when papier-mâché arrived in Europe.

Among the earliest uses for papier-mâché in Europe, in the 17th century, was for theatrical props and exotic scenery. Later, it came to be used for domestic articles such as boxes and trays. A Mrs Delany notes its manufacture in London, in 1755, which no doubt suggests the production of domestic wares at this early date. Its success says something about the perennial desire for vivid colours to brighten up the all-too-often gloomy interiors of English homes. A great deal of the papier-mâché still in existence retains its original vibrant paintwork and glossy lustre, as it is protected by a heat-hardened coat of varnish.

The Birmingham japanner, Henry Clay (d. 1812), revolutionized the craft in the 1770s, and this led to its establishment as one of the popular media in the furnishing and decorative arts. Clay was the most renowned maker of his period, and his products are much sought after today. In 1772 he took out a patent for a new form of paperware which was made by glueing together sheets of unsized porous paper, which was then shaped in a mould and left to harden. The result was a very tough material which could be planed and shaped like wood, and then coated with layers of paint, followed by varnish. Strictly speaking, this material was not papier-mâché, but what the French termed *carton pierre* – in reference to its stone-like hardness. Clay never ventured much beyond the manufacture of flat objects such as trays and panels, but even these were extremely time-consuming to make. Apart from the

An interesting English nest of four small tables, made of papier-mâché, the decorative panels hand-painted. Mid-19th century.

A rectangular straight-edge papier-mâché tray in maroon decorated in various metal colours, by Clay.

291

Above: *A Victorian papier-mâché desk set.*

Opposite page: *A pair of mid-19th-century papier-mâché câchepot pots, with lily-of-the-valley paintings on both sides.*

initial glueing-up, there was much rubbing down and finally a burnishing of the varnish, often done by women with their bare hands. The labour-intensive nature of this work is demonstrated by the fact that when Clay retired in 1802 he was employing about 600 craftspeople.

Notable artists sometimes worked alongside the artisans in the industry, and the subjects depicted on Clay's pieces range from coaching scenes through to landscapes, hunting groups and finally exotic birds. In the early 1800s, borders became popular, at first in gilt and after 1815 often in bronze. Views of country houses by John Nash, for example, were always in demand in the Regency period, and these were copied on trays by Beattie Lucas. Later in the 19th century, artists like Landseer often had their work plagiarized, until Parliament passed a Registration of Designs Act to prevent this. Earlier works, however, continued to be copied.

Clay became wealthy through his products, and his standing was much enhanced by commissions from George III's wife, Queen Charlotte. Clay made the queen a sedan chair of papier-mâché. He was appointed japanner in ordinary to the king and to the Prince of Wales. It is rare to find a stamped example of Clay's work, and collectors will pay highly for them. In February 1984 an unusual red japanned tray stamped on the reverse with Clay's name fetched almost £2000 in a country sale.

Left: *Papier-mâché sewing table/workbox, of about 1860.*

Anything made of sheets of porous paper was subject for a while to a paper duty, but a craftsman called Richard Brindley avoided this by introducing a method of using rag pulp, which he patented in 1836. He made large, thick panels of this substance, which could be worked like wood, but without the limitations of wood, which are dictated by grain. These were used to cut out the shaped legs and frets so characteristic of much Victorian furniture of the time, but despite the versatility (and cheapness) of Brindley's material, the smooth lustre of Clay's articles was never equalled.

Most papier-mâché to be found in antique shops and in sale-rooms is of the 19th century, and this usually of the period after 1830. Jennens and Betteridge are the best-known manufacturers of this period, and they had workshops in Birmingham which had become the principal centre for the craft. They were responsible for much of the papier-mâché of the first half of the 19th century in Britain, and most of their products are either stamped or (between 1864 and 1870) they have a metal tag attached. Other firms in the Midlands included Waltons, McCallum and Hodson, and Alsager and Neville, but these made a more limited range than Jennens and Betteridge, concentrating on souvenirs, tea caddies and trays. They also supplied 'blanks' to other retailers for them to decorate as keepsakes and gifts, and the best known of the shops to sell these wares was Spiers of Oxford, who decorated them with views of the city, the colleges and steeples, and surrounding

A pair of Victorian papier-mâché fans.

294

Papier-mâché occasional table, stamped Jennens & Bettridge, the top inset with mother-of-pearl, and painted and gilt painted. Mid-19th century.

areas. As with the fashonable lacquer of the early 18th century, papier-mâché backgrounds came in a variety of colours, black being the most usual, with red and green second. Decoration was often a mixture of stylized gilt arabesques with naturalistic flowers or scenes, sometimes heightened by the use of mother-of-pearl inlays. Many of the designs appear in pattern books, like Frederick Knight's *Fancy Ornaments*, published in 1834. But even in the mid-19th century there was a reaction against this form of decoration.

As early as 1812, a Clerkenwell japanner called Thomas Hubball began to experiment with a technique of constructing pictures, using metallic powders in as many as eighteen different shades. In the 1820s,

A Jennens & Bettridge shaped-edge tray of papier-mâché.

imitations of oriental lacquer were fashionable, as a result of the work of one of Jennens and Betteridge's craftsmen, Joseph Booth. He was eventually able to copy oriental methods of low-relief modelling, which he overlaid with pure gold and silver leaf. Metallic powders continued in favour, in conjunction with oil painting, which was heightened by their use. Typical subjects for this kind of treatment are moonlight scenes or dark landscapes with silver-edged storm clouds.

The material most associated with papier-mâché is of course mother-of-pearl, or more accurately, pearl shell, for contrary to popular belief the shell most often employed was the pink aurora and another form of greenish shell. The Chinese had used shell along with ivory and precious stones in their lacquer work, and papier-mâché, with its japanned surface, was the ideal medium for its use. The paper-thin sheets of pearl were cut and laid on the papier-mâché and the lacquer groundwork built up round it. The two were then cut back together to form a uniform smooth surface. The shell was sometimes etched with acid to heighten the detail. A wash of translucent colour would produce different effects such as that of moonlight. In the middle of the 19th century, glass panels were introduced on some pieces. Such treatments are not to everybody's taste, and many prefer the more restrained articles from this period, especially the attractive blue convolvulus designs of George Neville (one of Jennens and Betteridge's artists). Latterly, the standards of much of this paintwork declined, and cheaper wares were produced by the employment of less skilled child artists!

There were two main types of manufacturing process involved in papier-mâché. One was pasting sheets of paper on moulds, and the other was using paper pulp that was pressed between dies. By the 1820s, Jennens and Betteridge were employing the second method to produce

296

An unusual papier-mâché cabinet on stand, made by Jennens & Bettridge.

furniture such as chairs and tables, where previously it had only been used in a limited way for panels and trays. Despite the ambitious nature of the designs, papier-mâché was not really equal to the strains imposed on large furniture. Chair legs were frequently broken, with the result that wood was eventually substituted and papier-mâché reserved for the moulded seat and back.

The popularity of papier-mâché, however, was such that wooden furniture was made in imitation, with similar japanned ornament. At its height, the craze led to incongruities such as the piano cases made of papier-mâché, which had the slight drawback of having no resonant qualities whatsoever. Attempts were made to offset the structural disadvantages of papier-mâché by various methods of overlaying a core of wood or metal. A patent for this was taken out in 1842, but in due course the vogue for japanned furniture declined and the taste was more and more for the authentic artefacts of the newly accessible Japanese-made products.

Musical boxes

The musical box is a lovely artefact to possess, and since many were no bigger than about 2 ft by 1 ft (60 by 30 cm) by about 6 to 8 in (15 × 20 cm) high, it is quite practicable to collect them. They come up for auction regularly and they can be found in many antique shops. A considerable number must have been produced in the two centuries since their invention, quite a few in the first half of the 19th century.

The cylinder musical box mechanism was invented in 1796 in Geneva by Antoine Favre, a watchmaker – indeed, most of the early musical mechanisms of this kind were made by watchmakers. The principle on which the early mechanisms worked was a revolving barrel or cylinder of brass set with projecting pins that plucked a metal 'comb' of tuned-to-scale teeth (made up of sets of three or four teeth). The tips of the teeth vibrated to make the sounds. The cylinder was activated by clockwork. Early mechanisms were made as novelties fitted to other articles such as snuff boxes, jewel cases, clocks and watches, and they generally only played one tune. Then, mechanisms were cased in boxes specifically to produce music for home entertainment, probably from about 1810. A great deal of experimenting was needed to get the musical reproduction better than just an obvious mechanical 'clink-clink' and to extend the capacity of the box to produce more than one tune. Early owners must soon have bored their families and friends stiff with the repetition of a single melody – which they may not have liked the first time! Useful improvements to musical boxes were made when the

A Swiss gold and enamel musical snuff-box mounted with a watch, by Piquet and Meylan, c. 1810. Its actual size is 2¾ inches across.

comb was produced out of one piece of metal and with a greater number of teeth, and also when small quills were fitted to act as dampers to soften the metallic noise. In the 1820s watchmakers introduced the idea of staggering the metal pins in order to extend the range of melodies, up to a dozen or even twenty different ones in some cases.

By the 1830s, musical boxes were becoming popular all round Europe, and the simpler versions were not an expensive luxury any more. Yet each one had to be made by hand. Boxes began to vary enormously in size, some reaching over a yard long, and this was partly to accommodate developments in the mechanism. In 1838, Nicole-Frères of Geneva produced boxes with two combs, giving a piano-like

A charming ladies' nécessaire and musical box combined, in the form of a miniature grand piano, the cover inlaid in ebony and ivory, the interior with fitted tray holding silver objects. About 1840.

reproduction of the melody and plenty of scope for chordal and arpeggio sounds. This firm was later on to produce three, four and even five combs in one box. And in the 1850s, there emerged another important development, the interchangeable cylinder, sometimes called the 're-change musical box', which enabled owners to put new cylinders into the box set with fresh varieties of tunes.

The first musical boxes were in relatively simple cases, of mahogany or oak, plain but polished. An introduction of the 1830s was a lift-up lid inside the box, which was a wooden frame containing a large glass panel through which one could see the mechanism at work. Controlling the mechanism was by levers at one side and the clockwork motor was key-wound. Then cases began to be decorated with inlays, marquetry, brasswork, and eventually all sorts of wood, common and rare, were employed for the case. In the 1851 Great Exhibition in London, a startling variety of boxes was displayed, cased in innumerable woods.

It is difficult to be precise about what sort of melodies the cylinders were designed to play. The earliest appear to have been popular tunes from operas, then these were followed with folk songs and ballades, occasionally a national anthem or patriotic song, and by the 1850s, some cylinders contained a range of waltzes.

Prices vary for these lovely boxes, but an 1830 key-wound Swiss made cylinder box which would play three overtures fetched over £1000 in 1983: a box that played twelve short airs fetched half that amount. And it should be possible to find a good working model of, say, the mid 19th century for under £200.

A fine early-19th-century Swedish-made musical box, now at Waddesdon Manor, near Tring.

Dictionary of Craftsmen

Adam, Robert (1728-92). Scottish architect and designer, one of four sons of a celebrated architect, William Adam. Designed buildings to achieve the most harmonious relationship between exterior and all parts of interior, including furniture and carpets. His elegant decorative style drew upon various sources, including English Palladian, French and Italian Renaissance and antique motifs.

Affleck, Thomas (d. 1795). Scottish cabinet-maker from Aberdeen who was apprenticed in London, and in 1763 chosen by John Penn to emigrate to Philadelphia to become resident cabinet-maker. Became the foremost cabinet-maker in Pennsylvania, responsible for adapting **Chippendale**'s designs to suit American tastes; supplied furniture to many leading Americans, notably Benjamin Franklin.

Amati family. Instrument makers, working in Cremona, Italy. Andrea Amati (*c.* 1511-1580), credited with introducing the violin, viola and cello as they are known today, employed two sons, Antonio (*c.* 1540s-1620s) and Girolamo (1561-30). Girolamo bought his brother out but continued to employ him; many instruments made by them were labelled as being by the Amati brothers. Girolamo, who invented the contralto viola, was succeeded by his son Nicolo (1596-1684), often said to be the greatest craftsman of the family. For some years Nicolo was almost the only top-class violin maker working in Italy, because of the effects of a national plague which he survived; two of his leading apprentices were **Andrea Guarneri** and **Antonio Stradivari**. Nicolo was followed by his son, whose skills, however, were not on the same level.

Banks family. English violin makers, based initially at Salisbury. Benjamin (1727-95) learned to make violins and cellos in London, often in the manner of Amati instruments; he opened a business in Salisbury and it flourished for many years. Two sons, James and Henry, continued the firm up to 1811 and then moved it to Liverpool.

Bateman, Hester (1709-94). Mrs Bateman was wife of a leading goldsmith and silversmith, was widowed in 1760 and took over the firm, running it well, and also crafting some of the silver articles herself, notably flatware and tableware. She registered her mark, HB, in script, between 1774-6; in the late 1780s she handed the business on to her sons.

Beilby, William (1740-1819) **and Mary** (1749-97). English glassmakers, decorators and enamellers. William Beilby specialized in enamelling flint-glass vessels, and worked with his sister Mary at Newcastle-upon-Tyne from *c.* 1776. He signed his best pieces and also stamped them with a butterfly. After 1776, he and his sister moved to Scotland. Mary Beilby, born at Durham, moved with her family to Newcastle in about 1760; learned glassmaking and decorating under her brother and made and decorated many pieces herself. She was an invalid for much of her life.

Berthoud, Ferdinand (1727-1807). Paris clockmaker, of Swiss birth; he made clocks, watches and chronometers; wrote several important works on horology, and constructed his first chronometer in 1761; examples of his work can be found at the National Maritime Museum at Greenwich and at the Wallace Collection.

Billingsley, William (1760-1828). Porcelain decorator, artist and potter, born at Derby, who developed a very white, translucent porcelain. He worked at Derby, left in 1796 to work at Pinxton, and in 1799 moved again, to Mansfield; from 1808 was employed at Worcester, but in 1813 set up his own business at Nantgarw in South Wales. Here he made very beautiful articles, but through a process so costly that it resulted in items being sold at loss. Billingsley drifted in and out of manufacturing in South Wales, and in 1819 sold out altogether to **John Rose** of Coalport. He died in great poverty.

Bloor, Robert (d. 1846). Porcelain maker who bought the Derby Business in 1811 and made bone china until 1826, when he is reputed to have been afflicted with mental illness. This was one of the glorious periods of Derby porcelain.

Boehm, Theobald (1794-1881). German flautist; developed his own four-key flute, and set up a factory in Munich. On a visit to London in 1831, he met the British flautist Nicholson who had invented a flute with large finger holes; Boehm developed the idea and in 1832 his factory began to make the Boehm flute, forerunner of modern flutes; he was often accused of appropriating the innovative ideas of others. Also an expert in iron-founding, Boehm advised on steel processes at the famous Bavarian ironworks.

Böttger, Johann Friedrich (1682-1719). Began career as alchemist, and in 1708 discovered the secret of porcelain making, using kaolin from sources near Meissen. He was the first European to make porcelain and, sponsored by Augustus of Saxony, he helped to found the Royal Saxon Meissen Porcelain Manufactory in 1710. He produced some superb articles, but was not successful in running the factory, took to drink and died young.

Boulle, André-Charles (1642-1732). French cabinet-maker, architect, painter, engraver and metal sculptor; recommended by Colbert to Louis XIV who made him cabinet-maker royal (*ébéniste du roi*) in 1672. He designed and supervised a great variety and quantity of fine individual pieces and suites of furniture for royal palaces, notably for Versailles; established his own workshop, where he employed craftsmen in many skills; introduced to French furniture (though he did not invent it) the special brass and tortoiseshell marquetry decoration of flat surfaces on such pieces as cabinets and commodes known now as Boulle marquetry; and pioneered the use of brass or gilt-bronze mounts to protect corners, feet and other vulnerable parts of furniture and to enhance their structural beauty. Few pieces have survived that can be ascribed to him as maker, but among them is a pair of commodes now at Versailles, and he left behind engravings and drawings that testify to his artistic ingenuity. He retired from work in 1715.

Breguet, Abraham Louis (1747-1823). One of the most celebrated French clockmakers whose watches display perfect workmanship and elegant design (there are many forgeries of his work). Breguet improved the lever escapement and made self-winding watches; examples are in the British Museum, London.

Broadwood, John (1732-1812). British harpsicord- and piano-maker, born in Scotland, became joiner and cabinet-maker; worked with **Shudi** from 1761 to latter's death; married Shudi's daughter in 1769 and became business partner in 1770; after Shudi's death in 1773, Broadwood continued partnership with Shudi's son, then ran the firm alone. Broadwood's early square pianos were in the manner of Zumpe's, but he greatly advanced the designs, improving dampers and replacing handstops with pedals. After about 1783 he turned to grand pianos, making many in cases of harpsicord shape, and achieving better tone after consulting acoustic experts. His workshop and products greatly impressed Haydn on a visit in 1794. A grandson continued the business, and the firm exists today.

Carlin, Martin (d.1785). French cabinet-maker who specialized in lacquer work decoration and use of Sèvres porcelain plaque adornment, for which he is best known. He worked for Oeben for a time, and was greatly influenced by him; he married the sister of Roger Vandercruse (La Croix), Oeben's brother-in-law, who signed his pieces R V L C. Carlin used bronze décor, particularly swags of tasselled drapery, and carried out commissions for Marie Antoinette and other royal personages. A pair of *bonheurs du jour*, with Sèvres plaque decoration, by Carlin fetched 82,000 guineas at Christie's in 1967, then a record for any item of furniture. When Oeben died he owed Carlin 500 francs, and left him some fine pieces of furniture in settlement.

Chamberlain, Robert (d. 1798). Decorator of porcelain at Worcester, but in 1783 left the firm and set up in opposition. From about 1792 he started to make hard-paste porcelain and specialized in the decoration of larger articles with flowers applied by cutting and shaping petals from very thin paste. His business prospered in his lifetime, but after his death its fortunes fluctuated, and in the mid-19th-century it was absorbed by the Worcester firm.

Channon, John (1711-83). Chairmaker, born in Exeter. Served an apprenticeship to his relative Otho Channon; went to London in 1737 and set up a cabinet-making business in St Martin's Lane. His work has a continental look about it, characterized by brass inlays and mounts. The Baroque, and often Germanic, nature of those pieces known to be by him may be explained by the fact that he is thought to have collaborated for a time with the German craftsman Abraham Roentgen, father of **David Roentgen**.

Chippendale, Thomas (1717/18-79). The most famous name in British cabinet-making, presumed to be the son of 'John Chippindale of Otley, joyner'. Our knowledge of the first thirty years of Chippendale's life is to say the least vague: possible early connections with the Lascelles family at Harewood House, Nr Otley helped get him commissions later in his lifetime; he was in London in 1748, because we know he married in May of that year; in 1749, he was established at an address in Conduit Court, Long Acre (near St Martin's Lane), but more is known once he moved to fresh premises in St Martin's Lane (1754). In that year he produced the *Gentleman and Cabinet-Makers' Director,* the first pattern book of its kind in Britain, which established his reputation for posterity. This signalled the change in taste from basically Dutch styles to French, although the romantic fashion for the Chinese and the 'Gothic' outweighs French designs in his subsequent furniture. Despite his fame, little is known of his business activities and he is scarcely mentioned by his contemporaries; he certainly made furniture for Nostell Priory near Wakefield and Kenwood in London; one of his eleven children, also called Thomas, continued the cabinet-making firm, and furniture by the younger Chippendale exists from the beginning of the 19th century.

Clement, William (d. 1695). Master of the Clockmakers' Company; he was the first to use the anchor escapement in clocks, and also the first to use spring steel for pendulum suspension.

Cookworthy, William (1705-80). Porcelain manufacturer, born in Devonshire. He was originally a doctor, but in 1758 discovered china clay in Cornwall and experimented with making porcelain. In 1768 he patented a hard-paste porcelain, known as Plymouth Ware, the first to be produced in England. He made animal figures, decorative shells and other excellent articles, moved the business to Bristol in 1770, and finally sold out in 1774.

Cressent, Charles (1685-1768). French cabinet-maker, born at Amiens, son of a sculptor and grandson of a cabinet-maker, from whom he learned his trade; attracted the attention of the Regent Orléans in 1718-19 and received many commissions from him and later his son, but he does not appear to have worked for the Crown. Cressent was the leading cabinet-maker of the Régence period of 18th-century French taste, which represented a turn-away from the formal Baroque of Louis XIV. He made his own gilt-bronze mounts, many of which were very beautifully executed, but this habit got him into trouble several times with the guild of *fondeurs* in Paris for usurping their functions, and he was fined. A good many pieces have survived that can be ascribed to him.

Cristofori, Bartolommeo (1655-1731). Inventor of the piano; Italian, born in Padua. He became keyboard instrument maker; started work on piano design towards end

of 17th century and completed first piano, for Medici family in Florence, in *c.* 1700. The first written description of his piano appeared in 1711. One of his surviving models, made in *c.* 1720, is in the Metropolitan Museum of Art, New York; it has four and a half octaves.

Davenport, John (1765-1848). Took over a pottery business at Longport in 1793 and ran it for nearly forty years. He made bone china, creamware and stoneware; and from about 1815 specialized in producing Japanese styles; introduced stencilled lustreware in 1806.

De Lamerie, Paul (1688-1751). The greatest goldsmith and silversmith in Britain for the first half of the 18th century, a second-generation Huguenot, born of French parents at Liège. He came to England at the beginning of the 18th century; registered his mark (No.1) as LA with surmounting crown, in 1712; in 1732, he registered mark No.2, PL, also with surmounting crown, for pieces made of the improved sterling silver. De Lamerie exerted a supreme influence over gold- and silversmithing, which threw up a score of first-class practitioners; he used to deliver his products with a short list of instructions on how to care for them.

Doulton, John (1793-1873). Founded a pottery in Vauxhall in London and transferred it to Lamberth soon afterwards. He made salt-glazed ware and produced interesting spirit flasks known as Reform flasks in 1831-33, bearing pictures of principal figures in the struggle to get the Great Reform Bill (1832) passed. His son Henry started the Doulton sideline of drainpipes for new sewage systems in Britain, a line that was to develop.

Duesbury, William (1725-86). Potter and financier. Began as potter in London, then moved to Derby to become manager of the porcelain works there; in 1770 bought the old Chelsea factory in London (from then on porcelain made there was known as Chelsea-Derby, until 1784 when the London works were closed and many of the moulds destroyed). During this period it is thought that Duesbury also bought the Bow porcelain business, and he directed the Derby works up to his death.

East, Edward (1602-95). An original member of the London Clock-makers' Company, which was granted a charter in 1632. East was clockmaker to both Charles I and Charles II. His work is distinctive for simplicity combined with good proportions.

Ellicott, John (1706-1772). London clockmaker; F. R. S., for a time clockmaker to the king. He published learned articles and also an equation of time table. His sons and grandsons were also clockmakers.

Frodsham family. Clock and watchmakers. The first of the name was William (b. 1728), who became a specialist in chronometers. He established a London business which was continued by his sons William and Charles and a grandson, John; one of John's sons, Charles, was a prolific maker of good lever watches, and founded the firm Arnold & Frodsham in 1843.

Fromanteel family (fl. *c*. 1625-1725). London clockmakers of Dutch descent. In 1658 Ahasuerus Fromanteel advertised clocks with the newly developed pendulum, but none of these survive; later examples of his work can be seen, often in ebonized 'architectural' cases with slide-up hoods. His sons Abraham, Daniel and Ahasuerus also made both watches and clocks.

Gaudreaux, Antoine Robert (*c*. 1680-1751). French cabinet maker; worked for Louis XV from about 1726 to his death in 1751, and was for part of the time principal

cabinet-maker royal (*ébéniste du roi*). Little is recorded of his career; his known pieces are distinctive for their ample, curved forms and single-colour marquetry decoration. One of the best pieces to have survived is his commode of 1738-9 now in the Wallace Collection, London, whose gilt-bronze mounts are executed by the bronze sculptor Jacques Caffieri; this is one of the most glorious articles of furniture ever made anywhere and should be seen.

Gillow & Co. The Gillow family originated in Lancashire; Robert Gillow went into partnership with his son Richard in 1757 to make furniture, and in 1760 opened a London warehouse at 176 Oxford Street; the firm supplied furniture made to some of Chippendale's designs; Gillow's adopted the Paris *ébénistes* and *menuisiers'* custom of stamping their furniture with the makers' name after about 1790, and several records have survived.

Goddard, John (1723/24-85). Leading cabinet-maker in Rhode Island, probably the originator of the block-front and shell-carved furniture of the mid 18th century. Two sons carried on his business.

Graham, George (1673-1751). Clockmaker who invented a form of compensated pendulum using a jar of mercury. He also developed the 'dead-beat' escapement in 1715, which reduced 'recoil' on the escapement, and in 1725 the cylinder escapement for watches.

Guarneri family. Italian family of instrument makers working in Cremona. Andrea Guarneri (1626-98) was apprenticed to **Nicolo Amati** 1640-46, then left, but returned *c*. 1650. He introduced a smaller-size cello, easier to manage than current Amati versions, and his skills were of the highest order. His son Pietro Giovanni (1655-1720) settled in Mantua and also made violins, but because he was also court musician to the duke of Mantua, only a small number were produced; they are noted for full, rich quality. His brother Giuseppe Giovanni (1660-1739) stayed with his father in Cremona, inheriting the firm in 1698. Giuseppe made fine cellos, but some of his violins are among the best ever made; his son, also Giuseppe (1698-1744), is widely regarded as one of the two supreme violin makers of all time, the other being **Stradivari.** Giuseppe Guarneri started in business on his own *c.* 1722 and made many superb instruments, reaching his peak in the mid 1730s.

Hardland, Thomas (d. 1807). American clockmaker, often called the ablest clockmaker from Connecticut in the late 18th century; many of his workmen went on to become gifted makers in their own right, the best known being **Eli Terry.**

Harrison, John (1693-1776). Famous for winning a prize for making an accurate chronometer, particularly useful for navigation purposes; he also invented the 'grid-iron' pendulum, which was made of rods of different metals to compensate for expansion and contraction. He was a carpenter by trade.

Heming, Thomas (fl. 1745-82). Major Welsh-born silversmith, making very fine wares; he was patronized by George III, who granted him a royal warrant.

Hepplewhite, George (d. 1786). Author of the successful book *The Cabinet-maker and Upholsterer's Guide* which his widow Alice published three years after his death; his designs are associated with furniture at Carlton House, though no bills exist for any work for the Prince of Wales. Hepplewhite produced Adam-style furniture, though how much if any was actually made by him we do not know, and no piece of any kind can be attributed to

him; he had no reputation in his lifetime. One of the principal designs associated with him is the shield-back pattern chair. He had premises in Redcross Street, Cripplegate, in London.

Hope, Thomas (*c.* 1770-1831). Furniture designer who published a number of works on interior design in the early 1800s. His designs are pure classical in style, and often uncomfortable and formal; contemporary interest in ancient Egypt, generated by Napoleon and his occupation of that country at the end of the 18th century, led Hope to produce, among other ideas, designs consisting of a mix of Egyptian and Greek motifs.

Jacob, Georges (1739-1814). French *menuisier* (joiner), probably the greatest of the 18th century, born in Burgundy; worked for the royal family and made numerous chairs, sofas, beds, day-beds and so forth; introduced oval and round backs with lightly carved frames for armchairs, developed upholstered sofas, and was the originator of the Louis XVI chair. He was the first *menuisier* to use mahogany for chairs in France, and may have invented the sabre leg; he was also capable of the finest skill as an *ébéniste* (cabinet-maker), as attested by repairs he carried out on several earlier articles of cabinet furniture.

Joubert, Gilles (1689-1775). French cabinet-maker about whom little is known; was principal cabinet-maker royal (*ébéniste du roi*) from 1751 to 1774, but must have been a cabinet-maker royal for much longer; his style was essentially Louis XV – indeed, he was the greatest exponent of the style. Only a few existing pieces are known to have been made by him, including a commode now in the Getty Museum and a pair of corner cupboards (*encoignures*) in the Wallace Collection, London. Joubert is regarded as having inspired a whole generation of royal cabinet-makers.

Kaendler, Johann Joachim
(1706-75). Chief modeller at the
Meissen porcelain factory. A sculptor
by training, he joined Meissen in
1731 and was made chief modeller
two years later, holding the job for
about forty years. Kaendler was a
dominating influence on porcelain
not only at Meissen (his animal,
especially bird, figures are among the
most beautiful works of art ever
executed in porcelain) nor indeed
only in Germany, but also in
England, and he produced so much
work that many articles served as
models for English porcelain makers
to copy for years to come.

Kandler, Charles (fl. 1725-50). An
outstanding and innovative
silversmith, German born. He
employed famous artists, including
the sculptor Rysbrack, to make
models for him to copy in silver.

Kent, William (1686-1748). Architect
by profession, who worked with the
Earl of Burlington for a time. Kent
designed furniture to match the
massive Palladian style of early 18th-
century interiors; side tables and
chairs were heavy, often with
excessive gilding; chair legs often
had lion's-paw feet. Examples may
be seen at Wilton House, Nr
Salisbury and at Chatsworth in
Derbyshire.

Knibb, Joseph (1650-1711) and **John**
(1650-1710). The brothers Knibb, of
London and Oxford, were noted for
their very fine bracket and longcase
clocks. Joseph introduced 'Roman'
striking, using different toned bells
to denote Roman numerals, and the
skeleton dial in which the chapter
ring was pierced between the
numerals.

Langlois, Peter (Pierre) (d. 1805).
Furniture-maker who formed a link
between the Rococo and the Neo-
classical styles. He came from Paris
to London in 1759 and set up in
Tottenham Court Road. Much of
his work is mistaken for French

Louis XV furniture, but it has a
distinctive style peculiar to himself as
an emigrant to Britain; he made
commodes, for example, with
appreciably more bulging (*bombeé*)
than those of the Paris craftsmen. He
was a fine executor of marquety.

Leleu, Jean Francois (1729-1807).
French cabinet-maker, born in Paris.
Worked under **Oeben** and developed
a distinctively simple and austere
style, though he also produced
pieces in more typical Rococo mode;
in the Louis XVI period made many
fine articles, including pieces with
porcelain decoration. Leleu had
hoped to succeed Oeben when the
latter died in 1763, but Mme. Oeben
gave the job to **Riesener** instead;
the two men were often at
loggerheads, and it is recorded that
he was prosecuted for assaulting
Riesener. He made much furniture
for Mme. du Barry and for Marie
Antoinette.

Lepaute, Jean André (1720-87).
Worked in Paris and was
clockmaker to the king. In 1752
made a clock with one wheel
showing hours, minutes and
seconds, and striking hours and
quarters; designed a pin-wheel
escapement which is still used, and a
pendulum clock with sixty swings
for the escapement of each tooth.
There are examples of his clocks in
the Wallace Collection, London.

Le Roy family. French clockmakers.
The most famous were Julien
(1686-1759) and Pierre (1717-85);
Julien was clockmaker to the king
from 1739, and was responsible for
raising the standard of French
clockmaking. His inventions include
a compensated pendulum and a
horizontal arrangement of
movement in turret clocks. Famous
for his turret clocks, he also made
repeating watches. Pierre, his son, is
regarded as the most eminent
horologist in France of his time; he
was a pioneer of chronometers, used
temperature compensation in the

balance wheel, and wrote learned papers, including some on marine timekeeping.

Lieutaud, Honoré (fl. *c*. 1750-80). Marseilles clock and watchmaker. There is a fine ebony and ormolu clock by him in the Wallace Collection, London.

Linnel, William (d. 1763) and **John** (*c*. 1737-96). William Linnell was a fine furniture-maker, supplied articles to Sir Richard Hoare over the years 1739-52. William and John both provided japanned items for the Chinese bedroom at Badminton, the home of the Dukes of Beaufort in Gloucestershire. John Linnell designed furniture in Oriental, Rococo and Neo-classical styles.

Marot, Daniel (1662-after 1702). Huguenot furniture-maker who reached Britain as a refugee in 1694 after a spell in Holland where he was employed by the chief *stadtholder* of the Netherlands, William of Orange (also William III of England). He worked at Hampton Court, and produced a book of designs in 1702 which show a mix of French and Dutch influence. Marot made a significant impact on furniture design, especially in popularizing the cabriole leg.

Mercator, Gerhardus (Gerhard Kremer) (1512-94). Flemish cartographer, geographer and mathematician; founded a school of geography at Louvain in 1534; published his first map in 1537 (of the Holy Land). Published a map of the world in two hemispheres in 1538 and a terrestrial globe in 1541; in 1554 he published a six-sheet map of Europe, and in 1585 started work on his great *Atlas*, which was completed by others. The projection now known as Mercator's projection was first used in his map of 1568.

Minton, Thomas (1766-1836). English potter. Established a pottery at Stoke-on-Trent in 1789, and began to make very high-quality bone china for table and ornamental purposes, continuing for about thirty years. Minton also produced a series of pattern books that probably had the same sort of impact on ceramics that the 'directories' of Chippendale and Hepplewhite had on furniture.

Morris, William (1834-96). Famous for his wallpapers and textile designs, as well as his poetry, prose, political (socialist) campaigning and his charitable works. He did not design much in the way of furniture, but his firm Morris, Marshall, Faulkner & Co produced distinctive furniture in both simple and elaborate styles. Morris was interested in promoting a return to the true craftsmanship of the medieval Gothic period, and this resulted in a major influence upon late-19th-century furniture, particularly in the use of oak, carving and so forth.

Mudge, Thomas (1715-94). Clock and watchmaker who invented lever escapement in 1757, which he used in a watch for Queen Charlotte. Originally apprenticed to **Graham,** he started his own business in Fleet Street, London, in 1751. He was particularly interested in maritime timepieces, and was also the first to use gemstones for pallets in watches.

Neale, John (1740-1814). English potter, a specialist in earthenware. He produced excellent figures in bright enamel colours. He worked at Hanley from about 1778, and was in partnership with Robert Wilson from 1786. A speciality was imitating Wedgwood styles.

Norden, John (1548-1625). English mapmaker, born in Somerset. He became a lawyer, but in about 1580 started to make a survey of the English counties. His county maps were the first to show roads and give a scale; he was employed making surveys of Crown lands.

Oeben, Jean Francois (*c.* 1720-63). German-born cabinet-maker, 'mechanic' and designer. Worked under C J Boulle (A-C Boulle's son) from 1751 to 1754, after several years experience elsewhere; in 1754 became a cabinet-maker royal (*ébéniste du roi*); over the next nine years established himself as the leading cabinet-maker of the reign of Louis XV after Cressent and Gaudreaux, and acquired a unique reputation for intricately designed pieces fitted with complex locking devices. Was commissioned by Mme. de Pompadour, worked at the Louvre, the Gobelins and the Arsenal, and introduced many new decorative techniques, including a means of disguising the fixing screws and nails of bronze mounts. Greatly developed marquetry skills, moving from geometric designs and contrasting grains to pictorial motifs, flowers, naturalistic subjects, trophies and so on; pioneered the change from the Rococo to the more classical Louis XVI – the period called the Transitional (1760-70), which he did not live to see through. His most celebrated piece was the famous *Bureau du Roi* (p. 28), begun in 1760 and completed by **Riesener** in 1769. Oeben was a poor manager of money and died bankrupt, but was nonetheless perhaps the finest of all the 18th-century cabinet-makers.

Ogilby, John (1600-76). Scottish map-maker, who went to London to teach dancing! Was impoverished during the Civil War, but afterwards was patronized by the Court, and then appointed to map London in its destroyed state after the Great Fire of 1666. This enabled him to set up a flourishing map-printing business, where he produced his famous strip road maps (which in some cases actually showed the roads being measured by a waywiser).

Ortelius (Abraham Ortel) (1527-98). Flemish map-maker, born at Antwerp; produced the *Theatrum Orbis Terrarum*, the world's first great atlas.

Phyfe, Duncan (1768-1854). Arguably the greatest of all the cabinet-makers working in America from the time of Independence to the mid 19th century; born in Scotland, emigrated as apprentice in Albany, New York, and after 1790 set up his own business in New York City, making Sheraton-style and Directoire-style articles, but stamped with his own particular genius. His furniture is elegant, well proportioned, and often incorporates cameo and lyre motifs as well as delicate reeding and fluting; made sofas, sideboards, pier tables, among other articles. Examples can be seen in the Museum of the City of New York, the Metropolitan Museum, and the Taft Museum at Cincinnati in Ohio. Said to have had about a hundred craftsmen working for him during his most busy and prosperous periods.

Quare, Daniel (1649-1724). Eminent clock- and watchmaker, invented the repeating mechanism for watches in about 1680, and made some excellent longcase clocks of one year duration (there is one at Hampton Court).

Ramsay, David (1580-1654). Scottish clockmaker who worked at Dundee and also in France, and moved to London in 1610. He was made Clockmaker Royal in 1613, and First Master of the Clockmakers' Company in 1632. Some of his creations are in the Victoria and Albert Museum in London.

Ravenscroft, George (1618-81). English glassmaker; in his earlier years a shipowner; became interested in glassmaking in the 1660s, and set up a glasshouse in London and another in Henley on Thames in 1673. Here he carried out research into better production methods for the Glass-Sellers Company, using ground silica from local flint stones and mixing it with potash. The first pieces, though very clear, acquired myriads of small cracks, called 'crisselling'; he solved this by reducing the potash and introducing lead oxide, which served also to produce an even more brilliant glass. Contemporaries called his glass 'flint-glass', and he made much for the Glass-Sellers.

Revere, Paul (1735-1818). American silversmith, sometimes described as the American **De Lamerie**. Son of a Huguenot emigrant, Apollos Rivoire, a goldsmith in Boston, he was apprenticed as goldsmith and silversmith, and also learned the art of engraving. He became caught up in the struggle for American Independence from Great Britain, and was actually involved in the affair of the Boston Tea Party, 1773, which sparked off the war. In 1775, Revere rode through the night from Boston to Lexington to warn the Colonists that the British army was marching against them, a ride that was later commemorated in a poem by Longfellow. Revere designed the first official seal of the Colonists, and also printed money. His very fine silverware, usually marked with his name inside a square, is in great demand among rich collectors.

Riesener, Jean Henri (1734-1806). German-born cabinet-maker, without doubt the greatest *ébéniste* of the Louis XVI period. Born at Essen; entered **Oeben**'s workshop in the late 1750s; on Oeben's death headed the business under the latter's widow whom he married in 1768. He became principal cabinet-maker royal (*ébéniste du roi*) in 1774. He held the post for ten years, but his alarmingly inflationary prices for his work, though admittedly for the best pieces of his generation, led the court to look elsewhere for a chief, though Marie Antoinette continued to commission extravagantly expensive works from him. Riesener's ideas manifestly inspired

the other main *ébénistes* of the Louis XVI period from about 1775 to the Revolution (1789). He was a very versatile designer and craftsman, specializing in elaborate marquetry; yet he was also quite capable of producing more sober and restrained decoration. Ironically, during the Revolution, one or two of his pieces were auctioned off by revolutionary fund raisers and they fetched but a fraction of their original cost to the royal family!

Robin, Robert (1742-1809). Paris clockmaster to Louis XV and Louis XVI, also the Republic in its early years. He made both watches and clocks, and wrote several papers on horological subjects. Examples of his work are at the Louvre, Paris and the Grand Trianon at Versailles.

Roentgen, David (1743-1807). German cabinet-maker and entrepreneur, born near Frankfurt, worked in his father's workshop at Neuwied. Visited Paris in 1774 and was given commissions by Marie Antionette soon afterwards, to the chagrin of the Paris craftsmen. In 1779 he set up a base in Paris, but still ran the Neuwied business, and also traded from Berlin and Vienna, travelling great distances round Europe; he even made and sold articles to Catherine the Great of Russia. He was one of the few really successful entrepreneurs, though his business was badly affected by the Revolution.

Rose, John (d. 1841). English potter; founded the Coalport factory on the Severn in Shropshire in 1795, and four years later bought the Caughley factory on the other side of the river. He made a considerable quantity of the finest bone china over the years, and in 1822 he obtained the moulds and stocks of **Billingsley**'s Nantgarw works. Rose invented a leadless glaze, which was hard and transparent; he was awarded a Gold Medal of the Royal Society of Arts.

Seddon, Thomas (1727-1801). Founder of an important family firm of cabinet-makers in the 1760s, with workshops in Aldersgate Street; produced excellent-quality furniture, much of it in satinwood. Some extant examples bear the maker's label.

Shearer, George. Furniture-maker of whom little is known. He is credited with the majority of drawings for *The Cabinet-Maker's London Book of Prices*, published in 1788, and an important classical-style sideboard of his (at Osterley) appeared in this book.

Sheraton, Thomas (1751-1806). Drawing master and designer, who may also have been employed as a cabinet-maker at some stage in his early career, but no pieces by him have been identified. He is known principally for his writings, notably *The Cabinet-Maker and Upholsterer's Drawing Book* published in four parts (1791-94); he also wrote religious tracts, and earned a reputation for being disputatious. The illustrations in his drawing book indicate that satinwood was a vogue wood for pieces; he also advocated the use of tropical woods for articles in the main apartments of a house. His influence was significant in his time, but he has been credited with a vast quantity of designs and ideas for which there is no evidence that he in fact was responsible.

Sherratt, Obadiah (1790s-1840s). A Burslem potter specializing in rustic groups, which he made well. Many of his wares were supported on flat or table bases, with short bracket feet; sometimes the name of the subject (occasionally misspelt) was stamped under the glaze at the front.

Shudi, Burkhardt (Berkat) (1702-73). Swiss-born harpsichord maker; emigrated to London as joiner in 1718 and moved to Great Pulteney St in 1742, by which time he had had several years experience making harpsichords. In 1769 he invented the Venetian swell mechanism (by which volume could be controlled by moveable louvres); his clients included Haydn. Mozart is said to have tried out one of his instruments when on his visit to London in 1765 (aged six). One of Shudi's workers was Zumpe, another was **John Broadwood.**

Speed, John (1552-1629). English cartographer, born in Cheshire. For a time he worked as a tailor in London, and then began to publish county maps at the start of the 17th century; these were filled with all sorts of extra information, such as relevant heraldry of great county names, scenes of famous battles, and the first town plans. He produced in all fifty-four maps of England and Wales.

Spode, Josiah (1733-97). Inventor of bone china. First apprenticed to **Whieldon,** then set up a pottery at Stoke on Trent, which was continued after him by his son Josiah Spode II (1754-1827) and then by his grandson Josiah Spode III (d. 1829). Spode made earthenware and porcelain before inventing bone china in 1793-4. His son developed bone china, and took on William Copeland as sales manager.

Sprimont, Nicholas (1716-71). English potter, born at Liége. He was apprenticed in his youth to his silversmith uncle; then came to England as a silversmith and joined the Chelsea porcelain works in 1745, learning the business. He specialized in porcelain figures, with emphasis on large flowers. In 1758 he became owner of the Chelsea works, and obtained commissions from the Duke of Cumberland, son of George II. In 1769 Sprimont sold the factory to another person who in turn sold it to **Duesbury.**

Stiegel, William Henry (1729-85). Emigrant German glassmaker working in America, born in Cologne, and emigrated in 1750. In the early 1760s he visited his homeland and invited German glass craftsmen to join him in America; in 1763, they set up a factory at Manheim in Pennsylvania where for eleven years they produced much lead glassware, especially tumblers in German shapes. Stiegel made much ware himself, but it is hard to find today. The firm, which also made coloured and moulded glass articles with fine ribbed networking patterns and fluting, went bankrupt in 1774.

Stradivari, Antonio (1644-1737); Italian instrument maker at Cremona; probably rightly regarded as the greatest violin maker of all time: 'the tonal excellence, design, beauty and accuracy of his instruments have never been surpassed'. Stradivari was apprenticed to **Nicolo Amati**; from about 1680 he began to make violins and cellos on his own, and when Amati died in 1684, he remained the leading craftsman in Italy. The period from about 1700 to 1720 is often regarded as the 'golden years', but he was still making instruments at the age of ninety-two. In his long career he made many hundreds of violins and cellos, and about 650 have survived, many of which are owned and used by the world's leading violinists and cellists.

Terry, Eli (1772-1852). Connecticut clockmaker who introduced mass-production of clocks into the USA, developing nine types, one of which is now known as the Terry clock. This mantel clock had a wooden movement, scroll-arched top and small round pillars at the sides. At one time he was in partnership with **Seth Thomas**.

Thiout, Antoine (1692-1767). Paris clockmaker, to the Duke of Orléans and to the Queen Dowager of Spain; he devised a turret clock escapement with escape wheel at right angles to the pallets.

Thomas, Seth (1774-1859). Bought up the **Terry** clock patent and worked in Plymouth, Connecticut; was originally a casemaker.

Tompion, Thomas (1639-1713). Often called the 'father of English watchmaking', he established English horology as supreme for nearly a century. Admitted to the Clockmakers Company in 1671, he made some of the earliest balance-spring watches. He is famous also for his clocks, especially very fine long-case types, and he also made year clocks. He eventually joined **George Graham** as partner in 1711. He is buried in Westminster Abbey.

Turner, John (1738-87). Worked as potter at Stoke on Trent, then set up business at Lane End in 1762, a firm continued by his sons. Turner was a very high-quality potter, whose products were often comparable with Wedgwood's best; he made creamware, jasperware and basalts.

Vile & Cobb. Outstanding firm of cabinet-makers established in St Martin's Lane in about 1750; in the 1760s William Vile worked for the royal family (some pieces at Windsor, including a lovely Rococo bookcase for Queen Charlotte, wife of George III); John Cobb succeeded as head of the firm when Vile retired in 1765. The work of both men was in many respects as good as anything to emerge from British cabinet-making in the 18th century, and they are at last being accorded their rightful place in furniture history.

Walton, John (1780s-1830s). Potter working in Staffordshire, who specialized in sentimental figures with a background of bocage. He used vivid colours. His lions are much sought after at present.

Wedgwood, Josiah (1730-95). Born at Burslem, son and grandson of potters; apprenticed to **Whieldon**

then became his partner from 1754-59. In 1768 he went into partnership with Thomas Bentley and opened the famous Etruria factory near Burslem. The partnership lasted until 1780, and he and Bentley made basalts and jasperware, mainly ornaments rather than domestic ware, and his special Egyptian black unglazed ware. In 1790 he took his sons into partnership, but they never made porcelain, although his son Josiah Wedgwood II (1769-1843), made bone china. Wedgwood employed several well-known artists and craftsmen, among them George Stubbs, John Flaxman, James Tassie and William Hackwood. It was said of him that 'he converted a rude and inconsiderable manufactory into an elegant art and an important part of national commerce.'

Weisweiler, Adam (*c*. 1750-after 1810). German-born cabinet-maker who was taught by **Roentgen**; made many articles for the royal family, especially for Marie Antoinette, including a cabinet (the *Cabinet du Roi*), for Louis XVI at Versailles in about 1780, which was sold at Sotheby's in July 1983 for a record £1 million. He was noted for straight, clean lines in the best Louis XVI Neo-classical style, with fine bronze mounts and mouldings, and he specialized in japanning and Sèvres porcelain decoration; used plain woods like mahogany and ebony.

Whieldon, Thomas (1719-95). One of the greatest potters in British ceramic history, who had a long-lived influence on all English pottery. He set up a pottery at Fenton in 1740, taking **Josiah Wedgwood** into partnership, and worked until about 1780. He was High Sheriff of Staffordshire in 1786, and made a huge fortune out of his superb quality wares. The site of his pottery at Fenton has been excavated at various times, and many different stonewares and earthenwares found.

Willard, Simon (1753-1848). Often regarded as America's foremost clockmaker, the most important of three brothers, famous in Massachusetts. In 1800 he patented an eight-day weight-driven banjo clock with slender waist and circular top; he also made fine longcase clocks which were frequently copied during his lifetime.

Wistar, Caspar (*c*. 1695-1752). Emigrant Dutch glassmaker who arrived in America in about 1717, and set up a glass-house near Salem in New Jersey, where he employed exclusively Dutch emigrant craftsmen. The firm made window glass, bottles, and much high-quality domestic ware, in clear and in coloured styles; his son continued the business to about 1775. The firm probably introduced the style known as South Jersey, noted for thin threading round the neck, pieces of which are in demand but hard to find.

PORCELAIN AND POTTERY MARKS

Porcelain

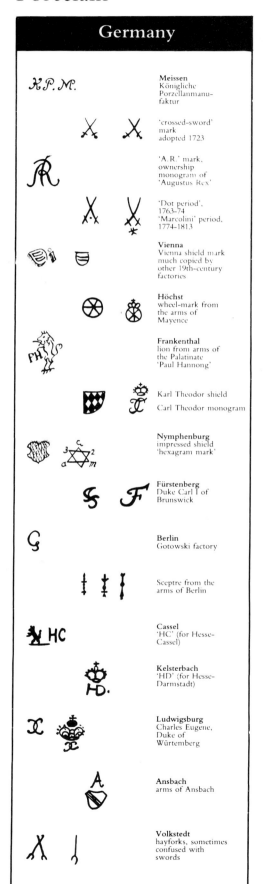

Germany

Meissen
Königliche Porzellanmanufaktur

'crossed-sword' mark adopted 1723

'A.R.' mark, ownership monogram of 'Augustus Rex'

'Dot period', 1763–74
'Marcolini' period, 1774–1813

Vienna
Vienna shield mark much copied by other 19th-century factories

Höchst
wheel-mark from the arms of Mayence

Frankenthal
lion from arms of the Palatinate 'Paul Hannong'

Karl Theodor shield

Carl Theodor monogram

Nymphenburg
impressed shield 'hexagram mark'

Fürstenberg
Duke Carl I of Brunswick

Berlin
Gotowski factory

Sceptre from the arms of Berlin

Cassel
'HC' (for Hesse-Cassel)

Kelsterbach
'HD' (for Hesse-Darmstadt)

Ludwigsburg
Charles Eugene, Duke of Würtemberg

Ansbach
arms of Ansbach

Volkstedt
hayforks, sometimes confused with swords

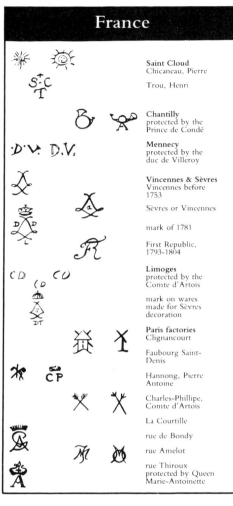

France

Saint Cloud
Chicaneau, Pierre

Trou, Henri

Chantilly
protected by the Prince de Condé

Mennecy
protected by the duc de Villeroy

Vincennes & Sèvres
Vincennes before 1753

Sèvres or Vincennes

mark of 1781

First Republic, 1793–1804

Limoges
protected by the Comte d'Artois

mark on wares made for Sèvres decoration

Paris factories
Clignancourt

Faubourg Saint-Denis

Hannong, Pierre Antoine

Charles-Phillipe, Comte d'Artois

La Courtille

rue de Bondy

rue Amelot

rue Thiroux protected by Queen Marie-Antoinette

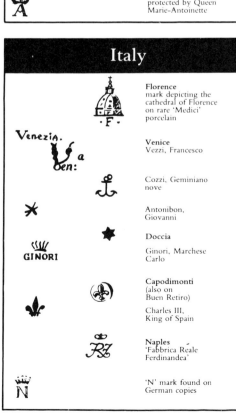

Italy

Florence
mark depicting the cathedral of Florence on rare 'Medici' porcelain

Venice
Vezzi, Francesco

Cozzi, Geminiano nove

Antonibon, Giovanni

Doccia
Ginori, Marchese Carlo

Capodimonti
(also on Buen Retiro)

Charles III, King of Spain

Naples
'Fabbrica Reale Ferdinandea'

'N' mark found on German copies

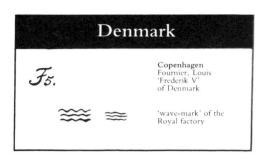

Denmark

Copenhagen
Fournier, Louis 'Frederik V' of Denmark

'wave-mark' of the Royal factory

Sweden

Marieberg

Berthevin, Pierre 1766–
Sten, Henrik, 1769–

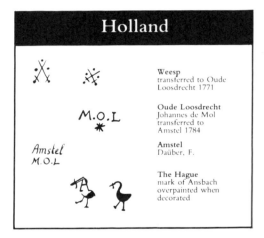

Holland

Weesp
transferred to Oude Loosdrecht 1771

Oude Loosdrecht
Johannes de Mol transferred to Amstel 1784

Amstel
Daüber, F.

The Hague
mark of Ansbach overpainted when decorated

Switzerland

Nyon
Jakob Dortu

Zürich
1763–1792

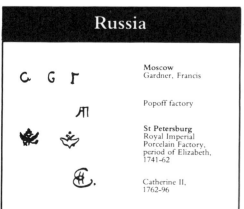

Russia

Moscow
Gardner, Francis

Popoff factory

St Petersburg
Royal Imperial Porcelain Factory, period of Elizabeth, 1741–62

Catherine II, 1762–96

Tin-Glazed Earthenware

Netherlands (Delftware)

	Drie Klokken (The Three Bells)
	De Roos (The Rose)
	De Paauw (The Peacock)
	De Grieksche A (The Greek 'A') Samuel van Eenhoorn Adriaenus Koeks
	't Jonge Moriaenshooft (The Young Moor's Head) Rochus Hoppesteyn Lieve van Dalen
	De Starre (The Star) Albertus Kiehl
	De Klaeuw (The Claw)
	Het Bijltje (The Axe)
	De Lampetkan (The Ewer)

France (Faience)

	Moustiers Olerys, Joseph Laugier, Jean-Baptiste
	Fouque, Joseph Pelloquin, Jean-François
	Ferrat, Jean-Baptiste
	Féraud, Jean-Gaspard
	Marseilles Leroy, Louis
	Fauchier, Joseph
	Veuve Perrin
	Savy, Honoré
	Robert, Joseph-Gaspard
	Bonnefoy, Antoine
	Strasbourg Hannong, Paul Hannong, Joseph
	Niderviller Beyerlé, Baron Jean-Louis de Custine, Comte de

English Porcelain and Pottery

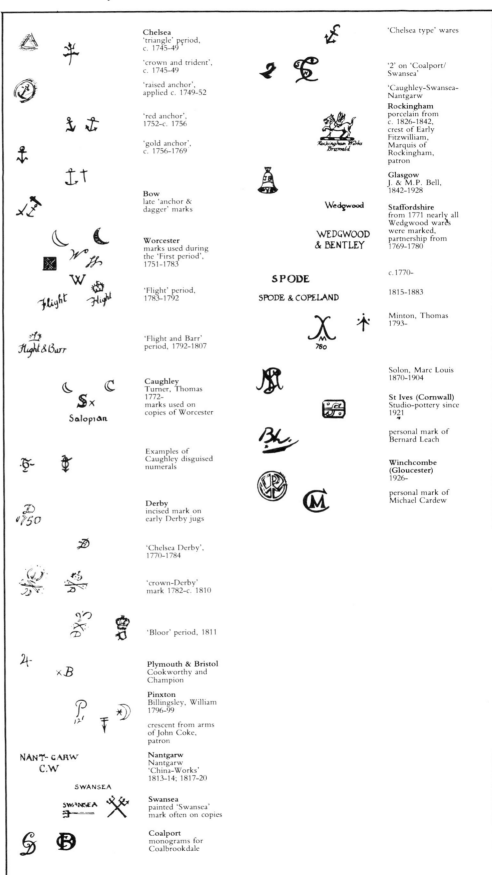

Chelsea
'triangle' period, c. 1745–49

'crown and trident', c. 1745–49

'raised anchor', applied c. 1749–52

'red anchor', 1752–c. 1756

'gold anchor', c. 1756–1769

Bow
late 'anchor & dagger' marks

Worcester
marks used during the 'First period', 1751–1783

'Flight' period, 1783–1792

'Flight and Barr' period, 1792–1807

Caughley
Turner, Thomas 1772–
marks used on copies of Worcester

Examples of Caughley disguised numerals

Derby
incised mark on early Derby jugs

'Chelsea Derby', 1770–1784

'crown-Derby' mark 1782–c. 1810

'Bloor' period, 1811

Plymouth & Bristol
Cookworthy and Champion

Pinxton
Billingsley, William 1796–99

crescent from arms of John Coke, patron

Nantgarw
Nantgarw 'China-Works' 1813–14; 1817–20

Swansea
painted 'Swansea' mark often on copies

Coalport
monograms for Coalbrookdale

'Chelsea type' wares

'2' on 'Coalport/ Swansea'

'Caughley-Swansea-Nantgarw

Rockingham
porcelain from c. 1826–1842, crest of Early Fitzwilliam, Marquis of Rockingham, patron

Glasgow
J. & M.P. Bell, 1842–1928

Staffordshire
from 1771 nearly all Wedgwood wares were marked, partnership from 1769–1780

c. 1770–

1815–1883

Minton, Thomas 1793–

Solon, Marc Louis 1870–1904

St Ives (Cornwall)
Studio-pottery since 1921

personal mark of Bernard Leach

Winchcombe (Gloucester) 1926–

personal mark of Michael Cardew

Index